MANAGING
DIABETES
FOR WOMEN

*The Only Canadian Woman's Guide
to Type 2 Diabetes*

M. SARA ROSENTHAL

Macmillan Canada
Toronto

Canadian Cataloguing in Publication Data

Rosenthal, M. Sara
    Managing diabetes for women

Includes index.
ISBN 0–7715–7627–7

1. Non-insulin-dependent diabetes—Popular works.   2. Women—Diseases.
I. Title.

RC662.18 R67 1999   616.4'62'0082   C99–930474–7

This book is available at special discounts for bulk purchases by your group or organization for sales promotions, premiums, fundraising and seminars. For details, contact: Macmillan Canada, Special Sales Department, 29 Birch Avenue, Toronto, ON M4V 1E2. Tel: 416-963-8830.

Cover and inside design: David Vereschagin
Composition: IBEX Graphic Communications Inc.
Author photograph: David Leyes

Macmillan Canada
CDG Books Canada Inc.
Toronto, Ontario, Canada

1 2 3 4 5 TRI 03 02 01 00 99

Printed in Canada

For Andrea

Other books by M. Sara Rosenthal

Managing Your Diabetes: The Only Complete Guide
to Type 2 Diabetes for Canadians (1998)

The Thyroid Sourcebook (3rd edition, 1998)

The Gyneocological Sourcebook (3rd edition, 1999)

The Pregnancy Sourcebook (2nd edition, 1997)

The Fertility Sourcebook (2nd edition, 1998)

The Breastfeeding Sourcebook (2nd edition, 1998)

The Breast Sourcebook (2nd edition, 1999)

The Gastrointestinal Sourcebook (1997; 1998)

IMPORTANT NOTICE

The purpose of this book is to educate. It is sold with the understanding that the author and Macmillan Canada shall have neither liability nor responsibility for any injury caused or alleged to be caused directly or indirectly by the information contained in this book. While every effort has been made to ensure its accuracy, the book's contents should not be construed as medical advice. Each person's health needs are unique. To obtain recommendations appropriate to your particular situation, please consult a qualified health care provider.

ACKNOWLEDGEMENTS

I wish to thank the following people for their commitment, hard work and guidance on *Managing Your Diabetes*, which helped to frame so much of the content of *Managing Diabetes for Women*:

Brenda Cook, RD, University of Alberta Hospitals; Tasha Hamilton, BaSc, RD, Diabetes Educator-Dietitian, Tri-Hospital Diabetes Education Centre, Toronto; Stuart Harris, MD, MPH, CCFP, ABPM, Assistant Professor, Departments of Family Medicine and Epidemiology and Biostatistics, University of Western Ontario, and former Medical Director, University of Toronto Sioux Lookout Program; Anne Kenshole, MB, BS, FRCPC, FACP, Medical Director of TRIDEC, Professor of Medicine, University of Toronto; Anne Levin, BScPT, MCPA, Physiotherapist and Certified Hydrotherapist, Baycrest Centre for Geriatric Care, Coordinator, Arthritis Education and Exercise Program, and Lecturer, Physical Therapy, Faculty of Medicine, University of Toronto; Barbara Mcintosh, RN, BScN., CDE, Nurse Coordinator, Adult Diabetes Education Program, Grand River Hospital, Kitchener, Ontario; James McSherry, MV, ChB, FCFP, FRCGP, FAAFP, FABMP, Medical Director, Victoria Family Medical Centre, Chief of Family Medicine, the London Health Sciences Centre; Robert Panchyson, BScN, RN, Nurse Clinician, Diabetes Educator, Hamilton Civic Hospitals, Hamilton General Division; Diana Phayre, Clinical Nurse Specialist, Diabetes Education Centre, The Doctor's Hospital; Robert Silver, MD, FRCPC, Endocrinologist, Division of Endocrinology and Metabolism, The Toronto Hospital.

Special thanks to Gary May, MD, FRCPC, Clinical Assistant Professor of Medicine, Department of Medicine, Division of Gastroenterology, University of Calgary, who provided some of the groundwork for this text through his role as medical adviser on a past work.

Gillian Arsenault, MD, CCFP, IBCLC, FRCP, Simon Fraser Health Unit, served as a past adviser on two works, and has never stopped advising and sending me valuable information. Irving Rootman, PhD, Director,

Centre for Health Promotion, University of Toronto, put me in touch with several experts, and always encourages my interest in primary prevention and health promotion issues.

I also wish to thank the following people for advising me on past women's health books, which has helped to frame so much of the material in this book: Suzanne Pratt, MD, FACOG; Susan R. George, MD, FRCP(C), FACP; Michelle Long, MD; and Masood A. Khatamee, MD, FACOG, Executive Director, the Fertility Research Foundation, New York City.

To all of the women interviewed for this book, your stories, struggles, and important suggestions regarding content for *Managing Diabetes for Women* are very much appreciated.

In the moral support department—my husband, Gary S. Karp, and all the relatives and friends who cheered me on—my sincere gratitude.

FOREWORD

Diabetes and the Family Doctor

Managing Diabetes for Women is a timely book indeed. Demographic trends tell us that the number of Canadians with Type 2 diabetes is going to increase dramatically over the next decade as the baby boomers move into middle age and beyond.

Type 2 diabetes is a particular problem for women as it tends to onset at a time, after menopause, when women are at a rapidly increasing risk for coronary heart disease even in the absence of diabetes. Fortunately, there have been important developments in our understanding of coronary heart disease, how its risk in women may be modified by hormone replacement therapy, and in the management of Type 2 diabetes generally. It is now clear that the serious complications of diabetes are potentially avoidable or at least treatable in a way that was impossible only a short time ago.

The gradual reductions in government funding for medical education that have occurred in the past decade have important implications for the way in which medical care is going to be provided in the future —there will be fewer medical specialists and their role will change from care provider to consultant.

Surveys tell us that 95 percent of Canadians consult their family physicians as their preferred point of entry into the health care system. Additionally, about 20 percent of Canadians with Type 1 diabetes and 80 percent with Type 2 receive their medical care from their family physicians at present; those figures are likely to increase as the scope of specialist practice changes. Family physicians, working as important members of a diabetes care team that includes nurses, diabetes educators, pharmacists, chiropodists and other health professionals, have already begun to prepare themselves for greater responsibilities in the care of patients with diabetes and other diseases.

With scientific advances, and likely changes in how medical care is going to be organized, has come the realization that diabetic care begins with the diabetic patient. The well-informed woman with diabetes is her own biggest asset in dealing with a disease that has potentially serious consequences. It is surely no secret that doctors can't look after patients who don't—or won't—look after themselves.

The next biggest asset is a well-informed and interested family physician who is not only knowledgeable about diabetes but who is proactive in organizing medical care by scheduling routine examinations, performing screening procedures for complications, and notifying diabetic patients when annual influenza immunizations are due.

Sara Rosenthal is to be commended for writing this book. I sincerely hope that it will help Canadians with diabetes increase their knowledge, become interested in developing new skills, and come to a fresh awareness of what they can do to help themselves. I also hope that new knowledge and attitudes will stimulate development of an effective partnership between women with diabetes and their family physicians. The effective patient–doctor relationship, founded on mutual respect and trust, requires patients to assume responsibility for all of the things they can and should do for themselves, and it requires doctors to be interested, well-informed, skilled clinicians—and good communicators. Are we all ready for that? I believe we are.

Dr. James McSherry, MD, ChB, FCFP, FRCGP, FRCP Glasg., FABMP,
Professor of Family Medicine, University of Western Ontario,
Chief of Family Medicine, London Health Sciences Centre

CONTENTS

Chapter 1

WHAT IS TYPE 2 DIABETES AND WHY SHOULD I WORRY ABOUT IT?

You've just come home from your doctor's office. You can't remember anything the physician said other than those three horrible words: "You have diabetes." You are besieged by questions: What does this mean? How will your life change? You've never been any good at diets, meal plans or exercising. And since you can't stand the sight of blood, how can you be expected to prick your finger every day to monitor your blood sugar? (The frequency of testing varies.)

Whether you're a woman who has just been diagnosed, or have been living with it for years, Type 2 diabetes is a difficult disease to understand. Part of the problem is that there are so many names for this one disease, and so many other types of diabetes, which also have more than one name, it's easy to lose track of what kind of diabetes you have. So I'm going to begin this chapter by clearing up all points of confusion regarding names, labels and definitions. Clearing up this confusion is the first step in managing Type 2 diabetes.

What's in a Name?

It was long known that there was a "milder" diabetes and a more severe form, but diabetes wasn't officially labelled Type 1 and Type 2 until 1979. Type 2 diabetes means that your pancreas is functioning. You are making plenty of insulin. In fact, you are probably making too much insulin, a condition called hyperinsulinemia ("too much insulin"). Insulin is a hormone made by your beta cells, the insulin-producing cells within the islets of Langerhans—small islands of cells afloat in your pancreas. The pancreas is a bird beak–shaped gland situated behind the stomach.

Insulin is a major player in our bodies. One of its most important functions is to regulate the body's blood sugar levels. It does this by acting as a sort of courier, "knocking" on your cells' door, and announcing: "Sugar's here; come and get it!" Your cells then open the door to let sugar in from your bloodstream. That sugar is absolutely vital to your health, and provides you with the energy you need to function.

But what happens if the cells don't answer the door? Two things. First, the sugar in your bloodstream will accumulate, having nowhere to go. It's the kind of situation that develops when your newspapers pile up outside the door when you're away. Second, your pancreas will keep sending out more couriers to try to get your cells to open that door and take in the "newspapers." The result of the cell's not complying is a pile of newspapers and a line-up of unsuccessful couriers by your door. When the cell doesn't answer the door, this is called insulin resistance; the cell is resisting insulin. Why this is happening is discussed later in the chapter. The end result, however, is diabetes, which means "high blood sugar." A synonym for diabetes is *hyperglycemia*, which also means "high blood sugar." If insulin resistance goes on for too long, the pancreas can become overworked and eventually may not make enough, or any, insulin. In effect, it's like a courier strike. And finally, the liver, being the good neighbour that it is, will lend a bowl or two of sugar to the sugar-deprived cell. (See further on.) However, this can exacerbate existing high blood sugar.

Type 1 diabetes

Type 1 diabetes, an autoimmune disease, is a completely different disease from Type 2 diabetes, a genetic disease. In Type 1, the immune system attacks the beta cells in the pancreas, causing them to be impaired or defective. The result is that no insulin is produced by the pancreas at all. That means no couriers are sent to knock at the cell's door. In this case, the result is a pile of newspapers without the line-up of couriers.

Type 1 diabetes is usually diagnosed before age 30, often in childhood. For this reason, Type 1 diabetes was once known as juvenile diabetes, or juvenile-onset diabetes. Because people with Type 1 diabetes depend on insulin injections to live, it was also called insulin-dependent diabetes mellitus (IDDM). The word *mellitis* comes from the Greek meaning "sweet," a leftover term from the days when diabetes was diagnosed by "urine tasters"; the urine becomes sweet when blood sugar is dangerously high, something that doesn't usually occur in Type 2. Only 10 percent of all people with diabetes have Type 1 diabetes.

Type 2—The Topic of This Book

Type 2 diabetes accounts for 90 percent of all people with diabetes. Since Type 2 diabetes doesn't usually develop until after age 45, it was once known as mature-onset diabetes or adult-onset diabetes. In rare cases when Type 2 develops before age 30, it is called mature-onset diabetes in the young (MODY). Since Type 2 diabetes is a disease of insulin resistance, rather than no insulin, it often can be managed through diet and exercise, without insulin injections. For this reason, Type 2 diabetes was also known as non-insulin-dependent diabetes mellitus (NIDDM).

Here's where it gets really confusing! When you are told that you have non-insulin-dependent diabetes, it's logical to conclude that you will never need to have an insulin injection. But this just isn't so. In fact, about one-third of all people with Type 2 diabetes will eventually need to begin insulin therapy, for reasons I explain on page 21. Does this mean you now have insulin-dependent diabetes, or Type 1? After all, if you need insulin, aren't you now insulin-dependent, which, by definition, means Type 1? This is a logical conclusion, but it's wrong. As stated above, Type 2 diabetes is a genetic disease; Type 1 diabetes is an autoimmune disease. Type 2 diabetes cannot "turn into" Type 1 diabetes any more than an apple can turn into a banana. So what do you call it when someone with Type 2 diabetes requires insulin? Try insulin-requiring Type 2 diabetes.

Something else you need to understand about Type 2 diabetes is that the high blood sugar that results from insulin resistance can lead to a number of other diseases, including cardiovascular disease (heart disease and stroke) and peripheral vascular disease (PVD), which means that the blood doesn't flow properly to other parts of your body. This can create a number of problems, discussed in chapter 8. Many women who suffer a heart attack or stroke have Type 2 diabetes.

Screening studies show that Type 2 diabetes is prevalent all over the world, particularly in countries that are becoming westernized. What's so disturbing is that Type 2 diabetes is increasing in the developed world at an annual rate of about 6 percent, while the number of people with Type 2 diabetes doubles every 15 years. Roughly 6 percent of all Caucasian adults have Type 2 diabetes, but the disease affects African–North Americans at a rate of 12 to 15 percent, Hispanics at a rate of 20 percent, and aboriginal North Americans at a rate exceeding 30 percent. In some aboriginal communities, up to 70 percent of adults have Type 2 diabetes.

"Full-Blown" Type 2

Many women with Type 2 diabetes won't find out they have it until they have "full-blown Type 2," meaning that the disease has progressed to the point where they are experiencing complications, or what I refer to as "Type 2-defining illnesses." This situation is analogous to the "HIV-positive" status versus "full-blown AIDS" scenario. In other words, you should be worried about Type 2 diabetes because of what the disease most often leads to: cardiovascular disease and peripheral vascular disease. People with Type 2 diabetes are four times more likely to develop heart disease and five times more likely to suffer a stroke than people without Type 2 diabetes.

Who's at Risk?

If you consume a diet higher in fat than carbohydrates, and low in fibre, you increase your risk for Type 2 diabetes if you are genetically predisposed to the disease. If you weigh at least 20 percent more than you should for your height and age (the definition of "obese"), are sedentary and over the age of 45, you are considered at high risk for Type 2 diabetes. Your risk further increases if you are:

- of aboriginal descent (this is true for aboriginal peoples all over the world, from Australia to North America; in Canada, First Nations people are at highest risk; in the United States, the Pima Indians are at highest risk);
- of African or Hispanic descent;
- have a family history of Type 2 diabetes;
- are obese (73 percent of all women with diabetes are obese, discussed in more detail in chapter 2);
- are pregnant (one in twenty women will develop gestational diabetes (see chapter 3) by their third trimester; this number increases with age, while gestational diabetes can predispose you to Type 2 diabetes later in life). See chapter 3 for a comprehensive discussion.

There are several co-factors that contribute to your risk profile, which can change your risk from higher to lower. The purpose of this section is to give you a clear idea of where you fit into this risk puzzle.

That way, you'll be more aware of early warning signs of the disease, which will make it easier for you to obtain an accurate diagnosis.

Risk Factors You Can Change

Type 2 diabetes more than meets the requirements of an epidemic. In 1985, the World Health Organization (WHO) estimated that roughly 30 million people globally had Type 2 diabetes. By 1993, that number jumped to 98.9 million, and it's estimated that 250 million people worldwide will have Type 2 diabetes by 2020.

As mentioned earlier, one in four Canadians over the age of 45 will be diagnosed with diabetes by 2004. Unless more people modify their risk factors, that number is likely to increase by 2020.

Thirty-two percent of people with diabetes have at least three of the risk factors that can double their risk of developing Type 2 diabetes, while 89 percent of people with the disease have at least one modifiable risk factor. That means you can lower your risk of developing diabetes by changing your lifestyle or diet.

Calculating your risk of getting a particular disease is very tricky business. To simplify matters, I've divided this "risk section" into two: modifiable risk factors—risk factors you can change; and risk markers—risk factors you cannot change, such as your age or genes. It's also crucial to understand that risk estimates are only guesses that are not based on you, personally, but on people like you, who share your physical characteristics or lifestyle patterns. It's like betting on a horse. You look at the age of the horse, its vigour and shape, its breeding, its training, and where the race is being run. Then you come up with odds. If you own the horse, you can't change its colour or breeding, but you can change its training, diet, jockey, and ultimately, where it's being raced, when and how often. Chance, of course, plays a role in horse racing; you can't control acts of God. But you can decide whether you're going to tempt fate by racing your horse during a thunderstorm.

Obesity

For women, the most important modifiable risk factor is obesity. The topic of obesity and women is complex, and is not limited to simple biology, "fat genes" or dieting. It involves many sociological and psychological issues, which are explored in detail in chapter 2. Unfortunately, obesity can lead to many of the health problems discussed in this section.

High Cholesterol

Cholesterol is a whitish, waxy fat made in vast quantities by the liver. That's why liver or other organ meats are high in cholesterol. Cholesterol is needed to make hormones as well as cell membranes. If you have high cholesterol, the excess cholesterol in your blood can lead to narrowed arteries, which can lead to a heart attack. Saturated fat is often a culprit when it comes to high cholesterol. The highest levels of cholesterol, however, are due to a genetic defect in the liver. Since people with diabetes are four times more likely to develop heart disease and five times more likely to suffer a stroke, lowering your cholesterol, especially if you're already at risk for Type 2 diabetes, is a very good idea.

Insulin's role in "fat control"

Insulin not only keeps blood sugar in check, it also keeps the levels of "good" cholesterol (HDL—high-density lipoproteins), "bad" cholesterol (LDL—low-density lipoproteins) and triglycerides in check. When you're not making enough insulin or your body isn't using insulin efficiently, your LDL levels and your triglycerides rise, but more important, your HDL levels fall, which can lead to heart disease. When diabetes is in control, cholesterol levels will return to normal, which will cut your risk of heart disease, as well as stroke.

Checking your cholesterol

Cholesterol levels are checked through a simple blood test. You can also ask your pharmacist about the availability of home cholesterol tests. The magic number is 200 milligrams per decilitre (200 mg/dl) or lower. At this level, you can have your cholesterol levels checked every five years.

If your blood cholesterol is between 200 and 239 mg/dl, as long as you don't smoke, are not obese, have normal blood pressure, are a premenopausal female and do not have a family history of heart disease—you're fine. Chances are, however, you do not meet all these criteria. In this case, discuss with your doctor how often you need to have your cholesterol levels checked.

A high cholesterol reading should always be followed up with an HDL-LDL analysis. If your LDL level is below 130 mg/dl, you're fine, but if it is between 130 and 160 mg/dl, you are considered a "borderline" case of high cholesterol. Once your LDL levels reach 160, you should definitely be on a treatment plan to lower your cholesterol.

Hypertension (a.k.a. High Blood Pressure)

About 12 percent of Canadian adults suffer from hypertension, or high blood pressure. What is blood pressure? The blood flows from the heart into the arteries (blood vessels), pressing against the artery walls. The simplest way to explain this concept is to use the analogy of a liquid-soap dispenser. When you want soap, you need to pump it out by pressing down on the little dispenser pump, the "heart" of the dispenser. The liquid soap is the "blood" and the little tube through which the soap flows is the "artery." The pressure that's exerted on the wall of the tube is therefore the "blood pressure."

When the tube is hollow and clean, you needn't pump very hard to extract the soap; it comes out easily. But when the tubing in the dispenser gets narrower as a result of old, hardened, gunky liquid soap blocking the tube, you have to pump much harder to get any soap, while the force the soap exerts against the tube is increased.

Likewise, the narrowing of the arteries, created by higher blood pressure, forces your heart to work harder to pump the blood. If this goes on too long, your heart muscle enlarges and becomes weaker, which can lead to a heart attack. Higher pressure can also weaken the walls of your blood vessels, which can cause a stroke.

The term hypertension refers to the tension or force exerted on your artery walls. (Hyper means "too much," as in "too much tension.") Blood pressure is measured in two readings: X over Y. The X is the systolic pressure, which is the pressure that occurs during the heart's contraction. The Y is the diastolic pressure, which is the pressure that occurs when the heart rests between contractions. In "liquid soap" terms, the systolic pressure occurs when you press the dispenser pump down; the diastolic pressure occurs when you release your hand from the pump and allow it to rise back to its "resting" position.

Normal blood pressure readings are 120 over 80 (120/80). Readings of 140/90 or higher are generally considered borderline, although for some people this is still considered a normal reading. For the general population, 140/90 is "lecture time," when your doctor will begin to counsel you about dietary and lifestyle habits. By 160/100, many people are prescribed a hypertensive drug, which is designed to lower blood pressure.

Let's examine some of the causes of hypertension. The same factors that put you at risk for Type 2 diabetes, such as obesity, can also put you at risk for hypertension. Hypertension is also exacerbated by tobacco and alcohol consumption, and too much sodium or salt in the diet. (It has been shown that people of African descent tend to be more salt-sensitive.)

If high blood pressure runs in the family, you're considered at greater risk of developing hypertension. High blood pressure can also be caused by kidney disorders (which may be initially caused by diabetes) or pregnancy (known as pregnancy-induced hypertension). Medications are also common culprits. Estrogen-containing medications (such as oral contraceptives), non-steroidal anti-inflammatory drugs (NSAIDS), such as ibuprofen, nasal decongestants, cold remedies, appetite suppressants, certain antidepressants and other drugs can all increase blood pressure. Be sure to check with your pharmacist.

How to lower your blood pressure without drugs

- Change your diet and begin exercising.
- Limit your alcohol consumption to no more than 2 oz of liquor or 8 oz of wine or 24 oz of beer per day, and lower still, for "liver health."
- Limit your salt intake to about $1\frac{1}{2}$ teaspoons per day. Cut out all foods high in sodium, such as canned soups, pickles, soy sauce and so on. Some canned soups contain 1,000 mg of sodium, for example. That's a lot!
- Increase your intake of calcium or dairy products and potassium (contained in such fruits as bananas). Some still-unproven studies suggest that people with hypertension are calcium- and potassium-deficient.
- Lower your stress levels. Studies show that by lowering your stress levels, your blood pressure decreases.

Sedentary Lifestyle

What's the definition of sedentary? Not moving! If you have a desk job or spend most of your time at a computer, in your car or watching television (even if it is PBS or CNN), you are a sedentary person. If you do roughly 20 minutes of exercise less than once a week, you're relatively sedentary. You need to incorporate some sort of movement into your daily schedule in order to be considered active. That movement can be anything: aerobic exercise, brisk walks around the block or walking your dog. If you lead a sedentary lifestyle and are obese, you are at significant risk of developing Type 2 diabetes in your forties, if you are genetically predisposed. If you are not obese, as a woman, your risk is certainly lowered, but you are then predisposed to a number of other problems. (see chapter 5 for a detailed discussion of exercise and Type 2 diabetes)

Smoking

Smoking and diabetes is a toxic combination. You already know that smoking leads to heart attacks. What you might not know is that if you have Type 2 diabetes, and do not smoke, you are already four times more likely to have a heart attack than a person without diabetes. If you smoke, *and* have Type 2 diabetes, you have an even greater risk of having a heart attack than non-smokers without diabetes.

Smoking and obesity

Smoking and obesity often coexist. Frequently, women begin to smoke in their teens as a way to lose weight. A 1997 study done by the Department of Psychology and Preventive Medicine at the University of Memphis in Tennessee, shows that this approach doesn't work. Smoking teens are just as likely to become obese over time as their non-smoking counterparts. Ironically, it was found that the more a person weighed, the more cigarettes the individual smoked. In fact, the heavier the person, the more cigarettes the individual smoked. In the long run, smokers often wound up weighing more than non-smokers because they substituted food for nicotine when they quit or attempted to quit.

Sleep deprivation or sleep disorders

Some studies link obesity, and hence, Type 2 diabetes, to lack of sleep, snoring, loss of REM sleep and a range of other sleep disorders. When you don't sleep well or get enough sleep—particularly REM sleep (rapid eye movement, which occurs in deep sleep)—you will be irritable and drowsy during the day. That means you'll eat more and will likely crave fast-energy foods high in sugar or starch. By visiting a sleep disorders clinic or, in some cases, by attending a time management seminar, you should be able to get your ZZZs.

Vitamin deficiency

Blood samples from people with diabetes show a tendency toward "oxidative stress," meaning that people with diabetes tend to be antioxidant-deficient. Antioxidants are vitamins found in coloured (i.e., non-green) fruits and vegetables, discussed in more detail in chapter 6.

Many people make the mistake of cutting out nutrients along with the fat in their diets. Experts recommend that to meet all vitamin needs through food alone, you need 1,200 calories per day if you're female and 1,500 calories per day if you're male. (Unless you need more or less vitamins due to a medical condition). Studies reveal that when diets fall to 1,000 calories, vitamin intake dropped to approximately 60 percent of their recommended levels. This is where vitamin supplements, meal replacement drinks or health bars come in. They're designed to give you your daily requirement of vitamins and minerals. If you're on a low-fat diet, make sure that you're not cutting out all protein, calcium or carbohydrates. You do need some of these!

Studies also show that approximately 25 percent of North Americans skip breakfast, while an additional 38 percent skip lunch. Eating breakfast will help you to lower your fat intake because this reduces that impulsive snacking in the late afternoon and actually improves the body's nutrient absorption.

Age can also interfere with vitamin intake. Research shows that seniors (over 65) tend to be deficient in vitamins A, C, D, protein and calcium. Yet these nutrients can boost the immune system and improve bone density, cardiovascular health and a thousand other things.

Risk Factors You Can't Change

By modifying any of the modifiable risk factors above, you can help to offset your risk of developing Type 2 diabetes if you have any of the risk markers described in this section. While you can't change your genetic makeup, medical history or age, you can significantly reduce the odds of these factors predisposing you to Type 2 diabetes.

Age

The risk of developing Type 2 diabetes increases with age. At no other time in history have we seen so many people over age 45—the so-called baby boom generation. This may, in part, account for the increase in the occurrence of Type 2 diabetes, as well as other age-related diseases. However, the lifestyle and dietary habits you practise before age 45 count—either against you or for you. So, by changing your diet and becoming more active before age 45, you may not necessarily be able to jettison your genetic fate, but you may certainly be able to delay it. Moreover, in the event that you develop Type 2 diabetes, a healthy diet and active lifestyle will go a long way in controlling the disease.

It's crucial to keep in mind that studies regarding diet, lifestyle and Type 2 diabetes are still unclear, although experts certainly agree that there is a strong relationship between genetic markers for diabetes and environmental factors, such as activity levels, weight and diet.

Menopause

When women reach menopause, estrogen loss can lead to some well-documented problems, such as osteoporosis (estrogen helps to maintain calcium levels) and heart disease (estrogen raises HDL levels, or "good" cholesterol, which protects premenopausal women from heart disease). Menopause also carries special concerns for women with Type 2 diabetes. As a result, I devote chapter 4 to a discussion of Type 2 diabetes and the menopausal woman.

Genes

Type 2 diabetes is a genetic disease, which means you are hard-wired for Type 2 diabetes at birth. Fortunately, we do understand some of the outside factors that can trip the Type 2 switch. Body shape, diet and activity levels are strong switch-trippers. On the other hand, if you don't have any Type 2 diabetes genes (in other words, you're not "wired" for this disease), these outside factors cannot, by themselves, cause you to develop Type 2 diabetes. For instance, there are plenty of obese and sedentary people who do not have Type 2 diabetes, nor will they develop the disease in the future.

When underdeveloped populations become urbanized and adopt a Western lifestyle, there is an explosion in Type 2 diabetes. However, the genes must be present in order to "allow" for the disease in the first place. This is more proof that there is a genetic-environmental combo platter at work when it comes to this disease. The question is, what aspect of westernization triggers Type 2 diabetes in these regions? "Western" means many things, including a higher-fat diet and less physical activity, as well as access to medical care, which means populations are living longer.

And what role does earlier screening and better detection of Type 2 diabetes play in the global increase of the disease? As one doctor put it, "When you don't look for it, you don't find it." More and more evidence points to the fact that Type 2 diabetes has been around for a long time.

What are the odds?

Type 2 diabetes is caused by multiple factors. The odds of developing the disease have to do with some genes interacting with some environmental factors. Obesity, excess calories, deficient calorie expenditure and aging can all lead to a resistance to insulin. If you remove the environmental risks, however, you can probably modify the risk of contracting Type 2 diabetes.

Who are you?

Aboriginal cultures develop Type 2 diabetes at far higher rates than other Canadians. On some reserves, Type 2 diabetes is present in 70 percent of the adult population.

Approximately 15 percent of African–North American adults have Type 2 diabetes, while about 20 percent of all North American Hispanics have Type 2 diabetes.

The "thrifty gene" is thought to be responsible for the higher rates of Type 2 diabetes in the aboriginal and African–North American populations. This means that the more recently your culture has lived indigenously or nomadically (that is, living off the land you came from and eating seasonally), the more efficient your metabolism is. Unfortunately, it is also more sensitive to nutrient excess. If you're an aboriginal North American, only about 100 years have passed since your ancestors lived indigenously. This is an exceedingly short amount of time to ask thousands of years of hunter-gatherer genes to adjust to a Western diet. If you're African–North American, your ancestors haven't lived here any longer than about 400 years; prior to that, they were living a tribal, nomadic lifestyle. Again, 400 years is not a long time.

As for Hispanic populations or other immigrant populations, many come from families who have spent generations in poverty. Their metabolisms adjusted to long periods of famine, and are often overloaded by Western foods. The other problem is poverty in North America. Aboriginal, African and Hispanic populations tend to have much lower incomes, and are therefore eating lower-quality food, which, when introduced to the "thrifty gene," can trigger Type 2 diabetes.

What about Easterners?

Type 2 diabetes seems to occur in South-East Asian populations at Western rates even when the diet is Eastern. East Indians, in particular, have very high rates of heart disease. In fact, India has the largest Type 2 population in the world. Urbanization is cited as a major factor.

Multiracial North Americans

Your risk of developing Type 2 diabetes depends on your mix of genes and your current and past lifestyle and diet. If you are part aboriginal and part European, for example, you will probably need to be more conscientious about your diet than if you were part Asian and part European. Studying your family history of Type 2 diabetes is the best way to assess the "damage" and make the necessary changes in your own diet and lifestyle to repair it.

Other medical conditions

There are certain diseases such as Prader-Willi, Down's syndrome, Turner's syndrome, Cushing's disease or acromegaly (large face, long arms and hands) that can lead to diabetes in the long term. In this case, diabetes is a presenting feature of the disorder. Many diseases run together and this is another example of that.

Impaired Glucose Tolerance (IGT)

Prior to September 1998, many people with Type 2 diabetes were told they had *impaired glucose tolerance* (IGT), which was more widely known as "borderline diabetes." For the record, there is no such thing as borderline diabetes. But in light of new guidelines announced in 1998, many people once diagnosed with IGT, will now be diagnosed with diabetes.

IGT was what many doctors referred to as the "gray zone" between normal blood sugar levels and "full-blown diabetes." Normal fasting blood sugar levels (what they are before you've eaten) are between 3 to 5 millimoles per liter—mmol/L).

In the past, three fasting blood glucose levels between 5 mmol and 7.8 mmol meant that you had IGT. A fasting blood glucose level over 7.8 mol or a random (any time of day) blood glucose level greater than 11.1 mmol meant that you had diabetes.

But that's all changed. Today, anyone with a fasting blood sugar level higher than 7.0 mmol is considered to be in the diabetic range, and is officially diagnosed with Type 2 diabetes. A new term, *impaired fasting glucose* (IFG), has also been introduced, which refers to blood glucose levels between 6.1 mmol and 6.9 mmol. The term IGT is now used only when describing people who have a blood glucose level between 7.8 and 11.1 mmol *two hours after an oral glucose tolerance test*. Take a look at Table 1.1 for more details. It's also possible to have abnormally low blood glucose levels, which is called *hypoglycemia* (discussed in detail further on).

Pancreatitis

Diabetes can be caused by a condition known as pancreatitis—inflammation of the pancreas. This occurs when the pancreas's digestive enzymes turn on you and attack your own pancreas, which can cause the gland to bleed, as well as serious tissue damage, infection and cysts. (Other organs, such as the heart, lungs and kidneys could be affected in severe cases.) Pancreatitis is most often chronic, as opposed to acute (sudden), caused by years of alcohol abuse. In fact, 90 percent of all chronic pancreatitis affects men between 30 and 40 years of age. In rare cases, chronic pancreatitis is inherited, but experts are not sure why. People with chronic pancreatitis tend to have three main symptoms: pain, weight loss (due to poor food absorption and digestion), as well as diabetes (the type depends on how much damage was done to your islet or insulin-producing cells).

The first step in treatment is to stop drinking alcohol. You will then need to be managed like any other diabetes patient: blood glucose monitoring, meal planning and, possibly, insulin injections.

"Side-effect Diabetes"

"Side-effect diabetes" is a term I've coined to describe what's known as "secondary diabetes." This condition occurs when your diabetes is a side effect of a particular drug or surgical procedure.

A number of prescription medications, including steroids or Dilantin, can raise your blood sugar levels, which would affect the outcome of a blood sugar test, for example. Prior to having your blood sugar checked, make sure you tell your doctor about all the medications you're taking. (For more about medications, see chapter 7.)

If you've had your pancreas removed (pancreatectomy), diabetes will definitely develop. It may also develop if you've experienced the following:

- severe injury to your pancreas;
- severe pancreatitis (see above);
- liver disease;
- iron overload;
- brain damage.

When Your Doctor Says "You Have Diabetes"

If you have been diagnosed with diabetes, the good news is that you are living at a time when self-managing your diabetes has never been easier. There are not only brand-new treatment options available, but also dozens of upgraded products to make your diabetes a lot easier to monitor. The bad news is that only you can manage your diabetes. This is one of those diseases that can't be managed by only your doctor. You have to take charge, while your doctor supervises from afar. For this reason, being diagnosed with diabetes may feel like being pushed out of an airplane without a parachute. Think of this section of the book as basic training. It will tell you what you need to know in order to plan for a safe landing.

Signs and Symptoms

By now you should have a pretty good idea of your risk profile for Type 2 diabetes. But knowing the signs of Type 2 diabetes is crucial. If you have any of the symptoms listed below, request to be screened for Type 2 diabetes.

- Weight gain. When you're not using your insulin properly, you may suffer from excess insulin, which can increase your appetite. This is a classic Type 2 symptom.

- Blurred vision or any change in sight (often there is a feeling that your prescription eyewear is "weak").
- Drowsiness or extreme fatigue at times when you shouldn't be drowsy or tired.
- Frequent infections that are slow to heal. (Women should be on the alert for recurring vaginal yeast infections or vaginitis, which means vaginal inflammation, characterized by itching and/or foul-smelling discharge.)
- Tingling or numbness in the hands and feet.
- Gum disease. High blood sugar affects the blood vessels in your mouth, causing inflamed gums; the sugar content can get into your saliva, causing cavities in your teeth.

Diabetes experts also point out that the following may be signs of Type 2 diabetes:
- Irregular periods, such as changes in cycle length or flow (this could be a sign of menopause as well, discussed in chapter 4);
- Depression, which could be a symptom of either low or high blood sugar;
- Headaches (from hypoglycemia);
- Insomnia and/or nightmares (from hypoglycemia);
- Spots on the shin (known as necrobiosis diabeticorum);
- Decaying toenails;
- Muscle pains or aches after exercise (high blood sugar can cause lactic acid to build up, which can cause pain that prevents you from continuing exercise).

You may also have diabetes if your doctor has diagnosed you with the following:
- High cholesterol;
- High blood pressure;
- Anemia;
- Cataracts;
- Salivary-gland stones.

What Kind of Diabetes Do I Have?

As explained earlier, there are several types of diabetes, and even several names for the one disease we now call Type 2 diabetes, the most common type of diabetes. You now know that Type 2 diabetes is a genetic disease that is triggered by environmental factors such as obesity or a sedentary lifestyle. Lean, fit, healthy people who are genetically predisposed to Type 2 diabetes can still develop the disease, but they may also prevent contracting it by modifying one or more environmental factors, discussed earlier. Type 2 diabetes is sometimes referred to as a disease of insulin resistance, which can be confusing because it can sound like a different disease, but in fact is simply a description of the physiology of Type 2 diabetes.

Type 1 diabetes is not likely your diagnosis. If it is, put down this book right now and find another book on Type 1 diabetes. While some of the issues I discuss in this book will be relevant, Type 1 diabetes, once known as insulin-dependent diabetes (IDDM), is a completely different disease than Type 2 diabetes—the focus of this book.

There are two other kinds of diabetes, too. Diabetes can be a side effect of something else, such as pancreatic surgery (see above). Diabetes can also develop during pregnancy, known as gestational diabetes mellitis (GDM), which occurs between the 24th and 28th week of pregnancy. (See chapter 3.)

The meaning of "insulin resistance"

It wasn't until the 1960s that researchers discovered that most people with Type 2 diabetes suffered from a resistance to insulin, not necessarily a lack of insulin. In fact, Type 2 diabetes is usually a disease of insulin resistance rather than "no insulin." The disease causes your body to overproduce insulin. Too much insulin has led to a decrease in insulin-receptor sites, small "keyholes" on the surface of insulin-producing cells, into which insulin (the "key") fits. Sometimes there are simply not enough receptor sites; other times, something is wrong with the connection or link between the key and keyhole.

At the beginning of this chapter, I explain the relationship between insulin and glucose, comparing insulin to a courier knocking on the cell's door with a message to "let sugar in." Again, insulin resistance occurs when there is no answer at the door. The insulin is there; the cell isn't responding to it. The result is diabetes—too much sugar in the blood. This causes all the classic symptoms of diabetes (see page 18) which may have led your doctor to diagnose diabetes or screen you for the disease.

Some experts believe that insulin resistance actually causes obesity, which is why obesity is such a risk factor. When the body uses insulin properly, it not only lowers blood sugar but assists in the distribution of fat and protein. Therefore, when your body doesn't use insulin properly, obesity can be the by-product. (see chapter 2 for a detailed discussion of women, obesity and diabetes.)

By the time you're diagnosed with Type 2 diabetes, it may be that you have inadequate or unreliable insulin secretion from your pancreatic beta cells.

Although Type 2 diabetes is usually a disease of insulin resistance, it is sometimes caused by a liver gone awry, a scenario in which the liver actually takes it upon itself to make glucose, increasing your levels of blood sugar. This is often the case in alcoholics.

Having Type 2 diabetes doesn't mean that you have only high blood sugar. This condition can cause other problems such as hypertension (high blood pressure), high cholesterol and insulin resistance in your muscles and liver. So even if you manage to get your blood sugar levels under control, you still may need to be treated for these other conditions, which can be greatly alleviated through diet and exercise. However, you don't have to have any symptoms to be diagnosed with Type 2 diabetes.

When you require insulin

Insulin resistance, characterized by the body's inability to use insulin, sometimes leads to a condition in which the pancreas stops making insulin altogether. The cells' resistance to insulin causes the pancreas to work harder, causing too much insulin in the system (a.k.a. hyper-insulinemia) until it's just plumb tuckered out, as the saying goes. Your pancreas is making the insulin and knocking on the door, but the cells aren't answering. Your pancreas will eventually say, "Okay, fine! I'll shut down production since you obviously aren't using what I'm making."

This isn't always the reason that you need insulin. Often the problem is that your body becomes increasingly more resistant to the insulin your pancreas is producing. This situation is sometimes exacerbated by medications or the disease over time. Controlling your blood sugar becomes harder and harder, until ultimately, you need to inject insulin. (For more about insulin, see chapter 7.)

Type 2 can also become an insulin-requiring disease if you go for long periods with high blood sugar levels. In this case, sugar toxicity occurs, in which the sugar poisons the cells of the body, including the insulin-producing cells in the pancreas, destroying them forever. The result is no insulin; hence, insulin-requiring Type 2 diabetes. This is not the same thing as insulin-dependent diabetes, or Type 1 diabetes, which is a completely different autoimmune disease.

If you have been told that you need insulin, and you are over age 45, or you were told you had impaired glucose tolerance (see page 16) and now need insulin, this is what probably happened to you.

Remember, there is no such thing as "borderline diabetes" or a "touch of diabetes." You either have diabetes or you don't. Again, the guidelines for diagnosing diabetes are changing, and what was once clinically known as impaired glucose tolerance (IGT) may soon be called, simply, diabetes.

Managing Type 2 Diabetes

Your goal in managing Type 2 diabetes is to control your blood sugar levels and weight through diet and exercise, and to prevent long-term complications of your disease. One of the most important Type 1 diabetes research projects ever undertaken is the Diabetes Control and Complications Trial (DCCT). This trial proved beyond a doubt that when people with Type 1 diabetes kept their blood sugar levels as normal as possible, as often as possible, they could dramatically reduce the odds of developing small blood-vessel diseases related to diabetes, such as kidney disease, eye problems and nerve disease, all discussed in chapter 8.

More recently, the results of a landmark British study, The United Kingdom Prospective Diabetes Study (UKPDS) showed that frequent blood sugar testing also helped reduce eye, kidney and nerve damage. See chapter 8 for more details.

Nevertheless, since Type 2 diabetes is associated more with cardiovascular complications, and the UKPDS did not show a direct link between frequent blood sugar testing and lowering heart attacks and strokes, two management philosophies have emerged regarding frequent self-testing of blood sugar and Type 2 diabetes.

Many physicians feel that frequent self-testing of blood sugar in Type 2 diabetes could complicate Type 2 diabetes management. In other words, it interferes with more crucial goals, such as getting your diet under control and incorporating exercise into your routine. Other physicians feel that the more involved you become in managing your blood sugar, the better off you'll be in the long run, and therefore, they support frequent self-testing of blood sugar in their Type 2 patients. The Canadian Diabetes Association has long recommended that people with Type 2 diabetes self-test their blood sugar. In fact, in a newly diagnosed person with Type 2 diabetes frequent daily testing will show *individual patterns* of glucose rises and dips. This information may help your health care team tailor your meal plans, exercise routines and medication regimens. And if you do have to take insulin in the future, you will need to get into the habit of testing your own blood sugar anyway. (Of course, by getting your diet under control, you can avoid requiring insulin.)

Regardless of your doctor's approach to self-testing blood sugar, the DCCT and UKPDS have caused an explosion in easy-to-use home blood sugar monitors, which could potentially eliminate that weekly trip to the doctor. Many people with Type 2 diabetes who would go to the doctor's for a blood sugar test once a week, or sometimes once a month, can now check their own blood sugar at home. And there's certainly no harm in testing your sugar frequently if you want to.

What about my weight?

Statistics suggest that about 80 percent of people with Type 2 diabetes weigh 20 percent more than their ideal weight, the technical definition of obese. If you begin a meal-planning program—which means eating the right combination and amount of food—with a diabetes educator and dietitian, as well as incorporate exercise into your routine, you'll lose weight. Weight loss can greatly improve your body's ability to use insulin. There is no need to start a crash diet or panic about your weight, however. Meal planning is managing your diabetes; weight loss will be a fringe benefit. As you lose weight, your blood sugar levels will drop, which may affect any diabetes medication you're on. For example, if you're taking pills that stimulate your body to make insulin, weight loss without adjusting your dosage may result in hypoglycemia (low blood sugar) discussed on page 30. Weight loss will also decrease the odds of developing complications from diabetes, such as heart disease. However, losing weight through meal planning is not as easy as it sounds, nor is exercising. (See chapter 2 for a discussion of women and weight issues, and chapter 5 for information on exercise.)

Essentially, the point of meal planning and exercise is to eliminate your diabetes symptoms and to remain as symptom-free as possible. Exercise makes insulin much more available to your cells, while your muscles use sugar as fuel.

High blood sugar (hyperglycemia)

If you can't seem to keep your blood sugar levels below 8 mmol/L, you are probably a candidate for an anti-diabetic pill or an oral hypoglycemic pill (see chapter 7). Early signs of high blood sugar are extreme thirst, dry and flushed skin, mood swings or unusual fatigue. Many people notice no symptoms at all.

Common reasons for a change in blood sugar levels revolve around the following:

- overeating or eating more than usual;
- a change in exercise routine;
- missing a medication dose or an insulin shot (if you're taking insulin);
- an out-of-the-ordinary event (illness, stress, upset, excitement);
- a sudden mood change (extreme fright, anger or sadness);
- pregnancy (see chapter 3).

In response to unusual strains or stress, your body taps into its stored glucose supplies for extra energy. This will raise your blood sugar level as more glucose than usual is released into your system. Whether you're fighting off a flu or fighting with your mother, digesting all that food you ate at that all-you-can-eat buffet or running away from a black bear, your body will try to give you the extra boost of energy you need to get through your immediate stress.

Blood sugar levels also naturally rise when you're ill. In the event of a cold, fever, flu or injury, you'll need to adjust your routine to accommodate high blood sugar levels, especially if you're experiencing vomiting or diarrhea. In some cases, you may need to go on insulin temporarily. When you're ill and you have Type 2 diabetes, it's crucial to see your doctor.

One thing you don't need to worry about, however, is forming ketones (a.k.a. ketone bodies), poisonous chemicals the body manufactures in desperation, to use as a source of energy when no glucose is available for energy. In people with Type 1 diabetes, high ketones along with high blood sugar cause diabetic ketoacidosis (DKA), which is an emergency situation. Signs of DKA include frequent urination (polyuria), excessive thirst (polydipsia), excessive hunger (polyphagia) and a fruity smell to the breath. People with Type 2 diabetes do not form ketones, because the cells never think they are "starving" since insulin still comes to knock at the door, and the liver continues to make glucose.

Monitoring Your Performance

If you want to test your own blood sugar, discuss with your health care practitioner how frequently to test yourself. Use Table 1.1 as a general guideline for testing times. As mentioned earlier, while there is still no conclusive proof that frequent blood sugar testing is helpful for people with Type 2 diabetes testing at home will certainly eliminate some of your trips to the doctor or lab. And that's less stress for you. The equipment you need for self-testing blood sugar is a good glucose monitor. There are several on the market; your doctor, pharmacist or diabetes educator can recommend the right brand for you. When you get your glucose monitor, experts suggest you compare your results to one regular laboratory test, to make sure you've purchased a reliable and accurate machine.

A brief history of blood sugar testing

Twenty years ago, the only way you could self-test for blood sugar level was by testing your urine for sugar, which meant that you had reached your renal threshold (kidney limit), where sugar spilled into your urine. The limitations of urine testing are that one can only test for really high blood sugar levels, over 11 mmol/L. Urine testing is useless for checking low blood sugar. Far more accurate home blood sugar testing became available with the development of glucose meters in 1982.

The first models measured glucose levels in whole blood, while laboratories were still measuring glucose levels in blood plasma. The difference is technical and not important to you personally. What you need to know, however, is that the readings vary. This meant that doctors needed to add about 12 percent to the glucose meter's recordings in order to get an accurate picture. This is changing. Today, most glucose meters measure glucose levels in plasma. What this means for you is that if you're a self-testing veteran, your next glucose meter may suddenly be giving you readings that are 12 percent higher than your last meter. This doesn't mean that you are losing control of your disease; rather, it means that your meter is measuring glucose levels in your plasma instead of whole blood. As a rule, before you purchase a new glucose meter, make sure you ask the pharmacist: "Is this a whole blood test or a plasma test?"

Choosing and using your glucose meter

As in the computer industry, glucose meter manufacturers tend to come out with technological upgrades every year. In fact, you can now purchase systems that download the time, date and blood sugar values for the last 125 glucose tests right onto your personal computer. This information can help you gauge whether your diet and exercise routine is working, or whether you need to adjust your medications or insulin. Of course, new upgrades cost money, but if you can't afford the "Pentium," a reliable "486" is fine. All glucose monitors will provide the following:

- a battery-powered, pocket-sized device;
- an LED screen (that is, a calculator-like screen);
- accurate results in 30 to 60 seconds;
- the date and time of your test result;
- a recall memory of at least your last 10 readings;
- at least a one-year warranty;
- the opportunity to upgrade;
- a 1-800 customer service hotline;
- mailings and giveaways every so often; and
- a few free lancets ("finger-pricker thingies") with your purchase; you may have to separately purchase what's known as a lancing device, a sort of Pez dispenser for your lancets. (Eventually, you'll run out of lancets and have to buy those, too.)

No matter which glucose meter you choose, these instructions can serve as a guideline:

- Wash your hands with an antibacterial soap.
- Pierce your finger on the side rather than top, and obtain a "hanging" drop of blood (some newer devices "suck out" your blood for you).

- Smear or blot your drop of blood onto a plastic strip that looks like a strip of tape without the sticky side. (Whether you smear or wipe depends on your glucose meter.)
- Turn on your glucose meter and place the strip into the machine.
- The results will show up on the calculator-like screen.
- Record these results in a logbook. Hint: A good result before meals ranges from 4 to 7 mmol/L; a good result after meals ranges from 5 to 10 mmol/L.

Factors that can taint your results

Most people are not testing their blood sugar under squeaky-clean laboratory conditions. The following outside factors may interfere with your meter's performance.

Other medications you're taking

Studies show that some meters can be inaccurate if you're taking acetaminophen, salicylate, ascorbic acid, dopamine or levodopa. As a rule, if you're taking any medications, check with your doctor, pharmacist and glucose meter manufacturer (call their 1-800 number) about whether the medications you're taking can affect the meter's accuracy. (For more information about medications, see chapter 7.)

Humidity

The worst place to keep your meter and strips is in the bathroom where humidity can ruin your strips, unless they're individually wrapped in foil. Keep your strips in a sealed container away from extreme temperatures. Use your "video" rules; don't store your meter and strips, for example, in a hot glove compartment. Don't keep them in the freezer, either.

Bright light

Ever tried to use a calculator or portable computer in bright sunlight? It's not possible because the light interferes with the screen. Some meters are photometric, which means they are affected by bright light. If you plan to test in sunlight, get a biosenser meter that is unaffected by bright light (there are several).

Touching the test strip

Many glucose meters come with test strips that cannot be touched with your fingers or a second drop of blood. If you're all thumbs, purchase a meter that is unaffected by touch and/or allows a second drop of blood.

Wet hands

Before you test, thoroughly dry your hands. Water can dilute your blood sample.

Motion

It's always best to test yourself when you're standing still. Testing on planes, trains, automobiles, buses and subways may affect your results, depending on the brand of glucose meter.

Dirt, lint and blood

Particles of dirt, lint and old blood can sometimes affect the accuracy of a meter, depending on the brand. Make sure you clean the meter regularly (follow the manufacturer's cleaning directions) to remove build-up. Make sure you change your batteries, too! There are meters on the market that do not require cleaning and are unaffected by dirt, but they may cost a little more.

Glycosylated hemoglobin

The most detailed blood sugar test cannot be done at home yet. This is a blood test that checks for glycosylated hemoglobin (glucose attached to the protein in your red blood cells), known as glycohemoglobin or HbA_{1c} levels. This test can tell you how well your blood sugar has been controlled over a period of two to three months by showing what percentage of it is too high. I compare this test to cars with special gas tank meters that can tell you what percentage of your last quarter tank is left before you need to refuel. That information is far more telling than just "F," "1/2," "1/4" and "E." It's recommended that you get an HbA_{1c} test every three months. This test is discussed in more detail in chapter 7.

Managing Low Blood Sugar

When you're diagnosed with Type 2 diabetes, whether your treatment revolves around lifestyle modification, oral hypoglycemic or insulin therapy, you may experience an episode of low blood sugar. This is clinically known as hypoglycemia. Hypoglycemia can come on suddenly, particularly overnight. If left untreated, hypoglycemia can also result in coma, brain damage and death. Hypoglycemia is considered the official cause of death in about 5 percent of the Type 1 population. In the past, hypoglycemia was a more common problem among people with Type 1 diabetes, but since 40 to 50 percent of all people with Type 2 diabetes will eventually graduate to insulin therapy, the incidence of hypoglycemia has increased by 300 percent in this group. Moreover, hypoglycemia is a common side effect of oral hypoglycemic pills, the medication the majority of people with Type 2 take when they are first diagnosed.

Any blood sugar reading below 3.8 mmol/L is considered too low. A hypoglycemic episode is characterized by two stages: the warning stage and what I call the actual hypoglycemic episode. The warning stage occurs when your blood sugar levels begin to drop, and can occur as early as a blood sugar reading of 6 mmol/L, in people with typically higher than normal blood sugar levels. When your blood sugar drops to the actual 3 mmol/L range, you are officially hypoglycemic.

During the warning stage, your body responds by piping adrenaline into your bloodstream. This causes symptoms such as trembling, irritability, hunger and weakness, some of which mimic drunkenness. The irritability can simulate the rantings of someone who is drunk, while the weakness and shakiness can lead to the lack of coordination seen in someone who is drunk. For this reason, it's crucial that you carry a card or wear a bracelet that identifies you as diabetic. (See Your Diabetes ID Card, page 38) Your liver will also release any glucose it has stored for you; but if it doesn't have enough glucose to get you back to normal, there won't be enough glucose for your brain to function normally and you will feel confused, irritable or aggressive.

Once your blood sugar is 3 mmol/L and falling, you'll notice a more rapid heartbeat, trembling and sweating. As the levels become lower, your pupils will begin to dilate and you will begin to lose consciousness, and could perhaps experience a seizure. No one with diabetes is immune to hypoglycemia; it can occur in someone with long-standing diabetes as much as in someone who is newly diagnosed. The important thing is to be alert to the warning signs, be prepared and try to avoid future episodes.

Who's at risk?

Since hypoglycemia can be the result of too high an insulin dose, it is often called insulin shock (or insulin reaction). This is a misleading term, however, because it implies that only people who take insulin can become hypoglycemic. For the record, all people with Type 1 or Type 2 diabetes can become hypoglycemic. If you are taking more than one insulin injection a day, you are at greater risk of developing hypoglycemia. Hypoglycemia can be triggered just as easily by:

- delaying or missing a meal or snack (see chapter 6);
- drinking alcohol;
- exercising too long or strong (without compensating with extra food) (see chapter 5);
- taking too high a dose of an oral hypoglycemic agent (this can happen if you lose weight but are not put on a lower dose of your pill).

If you're taking pills

Oral hypoglycemic agents (OHAs) can certainly cause hypoglycemia or low blood sugar. See chapter 7 for a detailed discussion on the side effects of OHAs, as well as on medications in general.

Recognizing the symptoms

If you can begin to recognize the warning signs of hypoglycemia, you may be able to stabilize your blood sugar before you lose consciousness. Watch out for the adrenaline symptoms: initially you will be hungry and headachy, then sweaty, nervous and dizzy. Those who live with or spend a lot of time with you should learn to notice sudden mood changes (usually extreme irritability, "drunklike aggression" and confusion) as a warning that you are "low." Whether you notice your own mood changes or not, you, too, will feel "suddenly" unwell. By simply asking yourself, "Why is this happening?" you should be able to remember that it's a warning that your blood sugar is low, and reach for your snack pack (see page 34). Not everyone experiences the same warning symptoms, but here are some signs to watch for:

- pounding, racing heart;
- breathing fast;
- skin turning white;
- sweating (cold sweat in big drops);
- trembling, tremors or shaking;
- goose bumps or pale, cool skin;
- extreme hunger pangs;
- light-headedness (feeling dizzy or that the room is spinning);
- nervousness, extreme irritability or a sudden mood change;
- confusion;
- feeling weak or faint;
- headache;
- vision changes (seeing double or blurred vision);

Some people will experience no symptoms at all. If you've had a hypoglycemic episode without any warning symptoms, it's important for you to eat regularly and to test your blood sugar. If you're experiencing frequent hypoglycemic episodes, diabetes educators recommend that by keeping your sugar above normal, you can prevent low blood sugar. In some cases of long-standing diabetes and repeated hypoglycemic episodes, experts note that the warning symptoms may not always occur. It's believed that in some people, the body eventually loses its ability to detect hypoglycemia and send adrenaline. Furthermore, if you've switched from an animal to human insulin, warning symptoms may not be as pronounced.

Treating low blood sugar

If you start to feel symptoms of hypoglycemia, stop what you're doing (especially if it's active) and consume some sugar. Next, test your blood sugar. If your blood sugar is below 3.5 mmol/L, ingest some glucose. Regular food will usually do the trick. Real fruit juice is better when your blood sugar is low. The best way to get your levels back up to normal is to ingest simple sugar; that is, sugar that gets into your bloodstream fast. Half a cup of any fruit juice or ⅓ of a can of a sugary soft drink is a good source of simple sugar. Artificially sweetened soft drinks are useless. It must contain real sugar. If you don't have fruit juice or soft drinks handy, here are some other sources high in simple sugar:

- 2 to 3 tablets of commercial dextrose, sold in pharmacies. If you're taking acarbose (see chapter 7) or combining it with an oral hypoglycemic agent or insulin (see chapter 8), the only sugar you can have is dextrose (Dextrosol or Monoject), due to the rate of absorption
- 3 to 5 hard candies (that's equal to about 6 Life Savers)
- 2 teaspoons of white or brown sugar (or 2 sugar cubes)
- 1 tablespoon of honey

Once you've ingested enough simple sugar, your hypoglycemic symptoms should disappear within 10 to 15 minutes. Test your blood sugar 10 minutes after consuming your sugar to see if your blood sugar levels are coming back up. If your symptoms don't go away, have more simple sugars until they do.

If you've had a close call to the point where you experienced those adrenaline symptoms, be sure to eat a snack or meal as soon as possible. If your next meal or snack is more than an hour away, eat half a sandwich or some cheese and crackers, which will ensure that your blood sugar levels don't fall again. Then, check your blood sugar levels after you eat to make sure your levels are where they should be. Try to investigate the cause of your episode by asking yourself whether your routine has varied in any way (missed or delayed meals, etc.)

Glucagon

Most people will be able to treat their low blood sugar without becoming unconscious. On rare occasions, however, it can happen. If that's the case, it's too late for juice, soft drinks and any other kind of sugar. That's where something known as a Glucagon Kit comes in. Ask your doctor or pharmacist about purchasing such a kit, which comes with complete instructions.

Recipes for prevention

The recipe for preventing hypoglycemia or low blood sugar is the same one for preventing high blood sugar: frequent blood sugar monitoring if your doctor feels it's necessary, following your meal plan (chapter 6), following an exercise plan (chapter 5) and taking your medication as prescribed (chapter 7). Any changes in your routine, diet, exercise habits or medication dosages should be followed up by a period of very close blood sugar monitoring until your routine is more established.

Frequent episodes of hypoglycemia may also be a sign that your body is changing: you may be losing weight, thanks to those lifestyle changes you've made, and the dosage of pills that were prescribed to you when you weighed 190 may be too strong now that you're down to 145. Or, you may be taking too high an insulin dose.

Anybody with Type 1 or 2 diabetes should have a snack pack with them for emergencies or for unplanned physical activity. The pack should contain:

- juice (2 to 3 boxes or cans);
- sweet soft drinks—sweetened with real sugar, not sugar substitutes (2 cans);

- a bag of hard candies;
- some protein and carbohydrates (packaged cheese/crackers);
- granola bars (great for after exercise); and
- a card that says "I have diabetes." (See Table 1.2).

When you're diagnosed with Type 2 diabetes, changing your lifestyle is the optimum therapy. That means meal planning and exercising. If you can do that, you probably won't need any medication, and your body may begin to use its own insulin efficiently again. But less than 10 percent of people with Type 2 diabetes are prepared to make the necessary lifestyle changes to keep their diabetes under control. Why? First, the older people get, the harder it is for them to change their eating habits. Second, many people may not be able to incorporate exercise or physical activity into their routine. Third, and perhaps most crucial, there are powerful social and psychological issues that affect women when it comes to food and weight. In fact, many writers present "fat as a feminist issue," not a biological one. All of these complex issues are explored in the next chapter.

TABLE 1. 1
Prior to September 1998, what constituted diabetes, impaired glucose tolerance (IGT) or normal blood sugar?

	NORMAL	IGT	DIABETES
Fasting	<7.8	<7.8	>7.8
2 hours after meals	<7.8	7.8–<11.1	≥11.1

Today, new guidelines stipulate the following:

	NORMAL	IFG*	DIABETES
Fasting	6.1	>6.1 & <7.0	>7.0

	NORMAL	IGT**	DIABETES
2 hours after an oral glucose tolerance test . . .	7.8	>7.8–<11.1	>11.1

*IFG stands for impaired fasting glucose.

**IGT stands for impaired glucose tolerance, referring to test results 2 hours after an oral glucose tolerance test.

Note: the symbol > means "greater than": the symbol < "less than"

When to Test Your Blood Sugar

In the days when diabetes patients went to their doctors' offices for blood sugar testing, they were usually tested first thing in the morning before eating (called a fasting blood sugar level) or immediately after eating (known as a postprandial or postmeal blood sugar level). It was believed that if either the fasting or postprandial levels were normal, the patient was stable. This is now known to be completely false. In fact, your blood sugar levels can bounce around all day long. Because your blood sugar is constantly changing, a blood sugar test in a doctor's office is pretty useless because it measures what your blood sugar is only for that nanosecond. In other words, what your blood sugar is at 2:15 p.m. is not what it might be at 3:05 p.m.

It makes the most sense to test yourself before each meal, so you know what your levels are before you eat anything, as well as about two hours after meals. Immediately after eating, everybody's blood sugar is high, so this is not the ideal time to test anybody. In a person without diabetes, blood sugar levels will drop about two hours after eating, in response to the natural insulin the body makes. Similarly, test yourself two hours after eating to make sure that you are able to "mimic" a normal blood sugar pattern, too. Ideally, this translates into at least four blood tests daily: When you wake up; after breakfast/ before lunch (i.e., two hours after breakfast); after lunch/before dinner (i.e., two hours after lunch); after dinner/or at bedtime (i.e., two hours after dinner);

The most revealing information about your blood sugar control is in the answers to the following questions:

1. What is your blood sugar level as soon as you wake up? (It should be at its lowest point.)
2. What is your blood sugar level two hours after a meal? (It should be much lower two hours after eating than one hour after eating.)
3. What is your blood sugar level when you feel ill? (You need to avoid dipping too low or high since your routine is changing.)

Variations on the theme

- Test yourself four times a day (times indicated above), two to three times a week, and then test yourself two times a day (before breakfast and before bedtime) for the remainder of the week.
- Test yourself twice a day, three to four days a week, in a rotating pattern (before breakfast and dinner one day; before lunch and bedtime the next).
- Test yourself once a day every day, but rotate your pattern (day 1 before breakfast; day 2 after dinner; day 3 before bedtime).

Test yourself four times a day (times indicated above), two days a month.

TABLE 1. 2

Your Diabetes ID Card

If you don't carry the following information on you already, photocopy this section and put it in an obvious place in your wallet or on your person.

I have diabetes. If I am unconscious or if my behaviour appears unusual, it may be related to my diabetes or my treatment. I am not drunk. If I can swallow, give me sugar in the form of fruit juice, a sweet soft drink, candies or table sugar. Phone my doctor or the hospital listed below. Or phone 911 if I am unconscious.

Name: _____

Address: _____

_____

Phone Number: _____

Chief Contact: _____ Relation: _____

My doctor's name is _____

My doctor can be reached at (phone number): _____

after hours: _____

My hospital: _____ Phone number: _____

My blood type is: ☐ A ☐ B ☐ AB ☐ O ☐ Rh+ ☐ Rh–

I wear: ☐ lens implants ☐ dentures ☐ contact lenses

☐ an artificial joint ☐ a pacemaker

I'm allergic to: _____

My Health Card/Insurance Number is: _____

My Group Insurance Number is: _____

Source: Adapted from *Health Record For People With Diabetes*, 1996, McNeil Consumer Products Company.

Chapter 2

WOMEN, WEIGHT AND

TYPE 2 DIABETES

At least 80 percent of women with Type 2 diabetes weigh 20 percent more than they should for their height and age—the technical definition of "obese." Many obese women say that they've "dieted themselves up" to their present weight. When these women visit their doctors, diabetes educators or dietitians, they will be given meal plans, lists of what and what not to eat, diabetes "codes" from the Canadian or American Diabetes Associations, and so on. However, the solution to a weight problem is more complex than simply eating less "fattening" foods. The key to losing weight for many women is to examine *why* they became overweight to begin with.

Obesity is the strongest risk factor for developing Type 2 diabetes. The longer you've been obese, the more you are at risk. Amazingly, diabetes experts have noted that when their patients lose only five pounds, the body begins to use insulin more effectively. But the sentence "eat sensibly and exercise" just doesn't hold any weight for most women battling their's.

Why do we eat so much in North America and where did the modern diet come from? After all, you didn't create the modern Western diet; you were born into it. In fact, the root word of "diet" comes from the Greek *diatta*, meaning "way of life." Since controlling your diet and weight are the tools to managing Type 2 diabetes, let's start with understanding how diet and lifestyle became linked to Type 2 diabetes to begin with.

The Good Times Disease

Type 2 diabetes is referred to as the Good Times Disease partly because of the work of Dr. Bouchardat, a French physician in the 1870s, who noticed that his diabetic patients seemed to do rather well in war. When their food was rationed, the sugar in Dr. Bouchardat's diabetic patients' urine disappeared. It was at this point that a connection between food quantity and diabetes was made. This observation paved the way for special low-carbohydrate diets as a treatment for diabetes, but it seemed to be effective only in eliminating sugar from the urine in "milder" diabetes, which was what Type 2 diabetes was called before the disease was better understood.

Economies and Scales

Bouchardat's observations were observed throughout Europe a few decades later. Many European countries experienced a significant drop, not only in "mild" diabetes, but in a number of obesity-related diseases during the First and Second World Wars, when meat, dairy food and eggs became scarce in large populations. Wartime rations forced people to survive on brown bread, oats and barley meal and home-grown produce.

Had it not been for the Depression, we may indeed have seen an increase in Type 2 diabetes much earlier than we did in North America. The seeds of sedentary life were already planted in the 1920s, as consumer comforts, mainly the automobile and radio, led to more driving, less walking and more non-active recreation. The Depression interrupted what was supposed to be prosperous times for everyone. It also intercepted obesity and all diseases related to obesity, as most industrialized nations barely ate enough to survive.

The Depression years, which ended in Canada when Britain declared war on Germany in 1939, combined with six long years of war, led to an unprecedented yearning for consumer goods such as cars, refrigerators, stoves, radios and washing machines. As the boys marched home, they were welcomed with open arms into civilian bliss. By 1948, university enrolment had doubled in a decade, leading to an explosion in desk jobs and a commuter economy. The return of the veterans led to an unprecedented baby boom, driving the candy, sweets and junk-food markets for decades to come. Moreover, a sudden influx of money from Victory Bond investments and veterans' re-establishment grants coincided with the first payments of government pensions and family allowances. Never before had North Americans had so much money.

Manufacturers and packaged-goods companies were looking for better ways to compete and sell their products. The answer to their prayers arrived in the late 1940s with the cathode ray tube: television. Television became the appliance most responsible for dietary decline and sedentary lifestyle as it turned into a babysitter that could mesmerize the baby boom generation for hours.

The Diet of Leisure

Naturally, after the war, people wanted to celebrate. They gave parties. They drank wine. They smoked. They went to restaurants. More than ever before, the North American diet began to include more high-fat items, refined carbohydrates, sugar, alcohol and chemical additives. As women began to manage large families, easy-fix meals in boxes and cans were being manufactured in abundance and sold on television to millions.

The demand for the "diet of leisure" radically changed agriculture, too. Today, 80 percent of our grain harvest goes to feed livestock. The rest of our arable land is used for other cash crops such as tomatoes, sugar, coffee and bananas. Indeed, cash crops helped to create the modern Western diet: an obscene amount of meat, eggs, dairy products, sugar and refined flour.

Since 1940, chemical additives and preservatives in food have risen by 995 percent. In 1959, the Flavour and Extract Manufacturers Association of the United States (FEMA) established a panel of experts to determine the safety status of food flavourings to deal with the overwhelming number of chemicals that companies wanted to add to foods.

One of the most popular food additives is monosodium glutamate (MSG), the sodium salt of glutamic acid, an amino acid that occurs naturally in protein-containing foods such as meat, fish, milk and many vegetables. MSG is a flavour enhancer that researchers believe contributes a "fifth taste" to savoury foods such as meats, stews, tomatoes and cheese. The substance was originally extracted from seaweed and other plant sources to function in foods the same way as other spices or extracts. Today, MSG is made from starch, corn sugar or molasses from sugar cane or sugar beets. MSG is produced by a fermentation process similar to that used for making products such as beer, vinegar and yogurt. Although MSG is labelled Generally Recommended As Safe (GRAS) by the United States Food and Drug Administration (FDA), questions about the safety of ingesting MSG have been raised because food sensitivities to it have been reported. This fact notwithstanding, the main problem with MSG is that it arouses our appetites even more. Widespread in our food supply, MSG makes food taste better; and the better food tastes, the more we eat.

Hydrolyzed proteins are also used as flavour enhancers. These are made by using enzymes to chemically digest proteins from soy meal, wheat gluten, corn gluten, edible strains of yeast or other food sources. This process, known as hydrolysis, breaks down proteins into their component amino acids. Today, our foods contain several hundred additive substances like these, including sugar, baking soda and vitamins (see chapter 6).

Of course, one of the key functions of food additives is to preserve foods for transport. The problem is, once we begin to eat foods that are not indigenous to our country, they lose many of their nutrient properties. Refrigerators make it possible to eat tropical foods in Canada and Texas-raised beef in Japan. As a result, few industrialized countries eat "indigenously" anymore.

Minimum wage, maximum fat

The legacy of the Western diet of leisure is that it has become cheaper to eat out of a box or can than off the land. In the developed Western world, where there's minimum wage, there is also maximum fat. At one time, fat was a sign of prosperity and wealth. Today, wealth is defined by thinness and fitness. Ironically, low-fat foods, diet programs and fitness clubs attract the segment of our population least affected by obesity. In fact, eating disorders tend to plague women who live in higher income brackets.

In 1997, the Coalition for Excess Weight Risk Education, a Washington-based organization comprising the American Diabetes Association, the American Association of Diabetes Educators, the American Society for Clinical Nutrition, the North American Association for the Study of Obesity and four pharmaceutical manufacturers issued statistics on obesity in the United States. This data can be used to interpret obesity patterns throughout the Western world. Based on a 33-city survey, the National Weight Report found that cities with high unemployment rates and low per-capita income tended to have higher rates of obesity. Areas with high annual precipitation rates and a high number of food stores also contributed to obesity. (More rainy or snowy days leads to more snacking in front of the television set!). The study also revealed:

- Restaurant-rich New Orleans had the highest obesity rate in the United States, where 37.5 percent of its adult residents were

obese; Denver, known for its outdoor living, had the lowest rate
of obesity, where only 22.1 percent of its residents were obese.

- Eating meals away from home and equating high-fat, fried food to
a sense of "family" was most commonly reported among obese
adults. (This suggests that a commuter society increases fast-food
eating, while stress and a lack of emotional support leads people
to eat for comfort rather than hunger.)

- Ethnic food (despite the fact that much of it can be lower in fat)
tempted Cleveland, Ohio, residents (31.5 percent of Cleveland's
adults are obese), while many people blamed their obesity on the
cold climate, which made them crave meat, biscuits and French
fries to help them fuel up.

- People in hot climates, such as Phoenix, Arizona, where 24.3 percent of the adult population is obese, reported that they gained
weight when the weather got too hot for outdoor exercise. (This is
a case for eating seasonably. Heavy foods in hot climates are unnecessary.)

Other statistics reveal that 35 percent of North American men and
27 percent of North American women are obese. Unfortunately,
obesity, physical inactivity and dietary-fat intake are factors we have
to look at when trying to understand why 6 percent of Canadian
adults (the number is much higher in aboriginal populations)
between ages 18 and 74 currently have diabetes; and why 12 percent
of Canadian adults, who were once diagnosed with impaired glucose
tolerance (IGT), will soon be told they have diabetes under the new
guidelines (as of September 1998). (See chapter 1.)

Chronic Dieting

The road to obesity is paved with chronic dieting. It is estimated that
at least 50 percent of all North American women are dieting at any
given time, while one-third of North American dieters initiate a diet
at least once a month. Dieting in your teens and twenties can

predispose you to obesity in your thirties, forties and beyond. This occurs because most people "crash and burn" instead of eating sensibly. In other words, they're chronic dieters.

The crash-and-burn approach to diet is what we do when we want to lose a specific number of pounds for a particular occasion or outfit. The pattern is to starve for a few days then eat what we normally do. Or, we eat only certain foods (like celery and grapefruit) for a number of days then eat normally after we've lost the weight. Most of these diets do not incorporate exercise, which means that we burn up some of our muscle as well as fat. Then, when we eat normally, we gain only fat. And over the years, that fat simply grows fatter. The bottom line is that when there is more fat on your body than muscle, you cannot burn calories as efficiently. It is the muscle that makes it possible to burn calories. Diet it away, and you diet away your ability to burn fat.

If starvation is involved in our trying to lose weight, our bodies become more efficient at getting fat. Starvation triggers an intelligence in the metabolism; our body suddenly thinks we're living in a war zone and goes into "super-efficient nomadic mode," not realizing that we're living in North America. So, when we return to our normal caloric intake, or even a lower-than-normal caloric intake after we've starved ourselves we gain more weight. Our bodies say: "Oh look—food! Better store that as fat for the next famine." Some researchers believe that starvation diets slow down metabolic rates far below normal so that weight gain becomes more rapid after each starvation episode.

This cycle of crash or starvation dieting is known as the yo-yo diet syndrome, the subject of thousands of magazine articles throughout the last 20 years. Breaking the pattern sounds easy: combine exercise with a sensible diet. But it's not that easy if you've led a sedentary life most of your adult years. Ninety-five percent of the people who go on a diet gain back the weight they lost, as well as extra weight, within two years. The failure often lies in psychological and behavioural factors. We have to understand why we need to eat before we can eat less. The best way to break the yo-yo diet pattern is to educate children early about food habits and appropriate body weight. Experts say that unless you are significantly overweight to begin with or have a medical condition, don't diet. Just eat well.

But if you're going to diet . . .

A recent study suggests that prepackaged balanced meals can help you stick to a meal plan more easily if you do indeed need to lose weight. Therefore, plan your meals in advance with a nutritionist and try to prefreeze or refrigerate them. This will help curb impulse eating. If you're contemplating a diet, you should also consider the following:

- Determine a reasonable weight for yourself, given your genetic makeup, family history, age and culture. A smaller weight loss in some people can produce dramatic effects.
- Aim to lose weight at a slower rate. Too much too fast will probably lead to gaining it all back.
- Incorporate exercise into your routine, particularly activities that build muscle mass.
- Eat your vitamins. Make sure you're meeting the Canadian Recommended Nutrient Intakes (RNIs). Many of the popular North American diets of the 1980s, for example, were nutritionally inadequate (the Beverly Hills Diet contained zero percent of the U.S. recommendation for vitamin B_{12}).

Eating Disorders

Imagine three steps: chronic dieting is the bottom step; eating disorders are the middle step; obesity is the top step. Many women become obese after dieting on and off for several years. Other women develop eating disorders after chronic dieting, and then become obese later in life.

For two percent of the female population in North America, starving and purging are considered a normal way to control weight. Only a small portion of women are obese because of truly hereditary factors. Most women who think they are overweight are, in fact, at an ideal weight for their height and body size. In Western society, the fear of obesity is so crippling that 60 percent of young girls develop distorted body images between grades one and six, believing that they are "fat"; 70 percent of all women begin dieting between the ages of 14 and 21. A U.S. study of high-school girls found that 53 percent were unhappy with their bodies by age 13; by age 18, 78 percent were dissatisfied. The most disturbing fact, revealed in the 1991 critically acclaimed Canadian documentary *The Famine Within*, is that when given a choice, most women would rather be dead than fat! Eating disorders are so widespread that abnormal patterns of eating are increasingly accepted in the general population. It is a shocking fact that there are parents who actually starve their young daughters to keep them thin.

The two most common eating disorders involve starvation: anorexia nervosa ("loss of appetite due to mental disorder"), and bingeing followed by purging, known as bulimia nervosa ("hunger like an ox due to mental disorder"). Women will purge after a bingeing episode by inducing vomiting, abusing laxatives, diuretics and thyroid hormone. The most horrifying examples occur in women with Type 1 diabetes who sometimes deliberately withhold their insulin to control their weight.

Perhaps the most accepted weight control behaviour is overexercising. Today, rigorous, strenuous exercise is used as a method of "purging," and has become one of the tenets of socially accepted feminine behaviour in the 1990s. A skeleton with biceps is the current ideal.

Why are we doing this?
Eating disorders are diseases of control that primarily affect women, although the incidence of eating disorders in men has increased in recent years. Bulimics and anorexics are usually overachievers in other aspects of their lives, and view excess weight as an announcement to the world that they are "out of control." This view becomes more distorted as time goes on, until the act of eating food in public (in bulimia) or at all (in anorexia) is equivalent to a loss of control.

In anorexia, the person's emotional and sensual desires are perceived through food. These unmet desires are so great that the anorexic fears that once she eats she'll never stop, since her appetite will know no natural boundaries; the fear of food drives the disease.

Most of us find it easier to relate to the bulimic than the anorexic; bulimics express their loss of control through bingeing in the same way that someone else may yell at his or her children. Bulimics then purge to regain their control. There is a feeling of comfort for bulimics in both the binge and the purge. Bulimics are sometimes referred to as "failed anorexics" because they'd starve if they could. Anorexics, however, are masters of control. They never break. I once asked a recovering anorexic the dumb question, "But didn't you get hungry?" Her response was that the hunger pangs made her feel powerful. The more intense the hunger, the more powerful she felt; the power actually gave her a "high."

The role of runways
Most women have a desired weight goal set at roughly ten pounds under their ideal weight; many women who think they are overweight are either at an ideal weight or ten pounds underweight. Supermodels like Kate Moss, who are seriously underweight, but whose weight is considered ideal by some, don't help much. Indeed, the epidemic of eating disorders is fuelled by the fashion industry, which imposes impossible standards of beauty on the average woman. Normal body fat for a healthy woman is 22 to 25 percent; most models and actresses have roughly 10 percent body fat. In order to achieve model-thinness, many women resort to the unhealthy habits discussed above.

To help establish what is a reasonable weight for you, experts suggest you ask yourself four questions:

1. What is the lowest weight you have maintained as an adult for at least one year?
2. What is the largest size of clothing you feel you can "look good" in and how much do you need to weigh to wear that size?

3. Think of someone your age and height who you know (versus a model or actress) who appears to be a "normal" weight. What does that person actually weigh?
4. What weight can you live with?

The message is this: accepting a normal body weight in your twenties and thirties can prevent obesity in your forties and fifties.

The impact of "low-fat" products

Since the late 1970s, North Americans have been deluged with low-fat products. In 1990, the United States government launched Healthy People 2000, a campaign to urge manufacturers to double their output of low-fat products by the year 2000. Since 1990, more than a thousand new fat-free or low-fat products have been introduced into North American supermarkets annually.

Current guidelines tell us that we should consume less than 30 percent of calories from fat, while no more than one-third of fat calories should come from saturated fat (see chapter 9). According to U.S. estimates, the average person gets between 34 to 37 percent of calories from fat and roughly 12 percent of all calories from saturated fat. Data shows that in terms of "absolute fat," the intake has increased from 81 grams per day in 1980 to 83 grams per day in the 1990s. Total calorie intake has also increased from 1,989 per day in 1980 to 2,153 calories per day. In fact, the only reason that data shows a drop in the percentage of calories from fat is because of the huge increase in calories per day. The result is that we weigh more today than in 1980, despite the fact that roughly 10,000 more low-fat foods are available to us now than in 1980.

Most of these low-fat products, however, actually encourage us to eat more. For example, if a bag of regular chips has 9 grams of fat per serving (1 serving usually equals about 5 chips or one handful), you will be more likely stick to that one handful. However, if you find a low-fat brand of chips that boasts "50 percent less fat" per serving, you're more likely to eat the whole bag (feeling good about eating "low-fat" chips), which can easily triple your fat intake.

Low-fat or fat-free foods trick our bodies with ingredients that mimic the functions of fat in foods. This is often achieved by using modified fats that are only partially metabolized, if at all. While some foods reduce the fat by removing the fat (skim milk, lean cuts of meat), most low-fat foods require a variety of "fat copycats" to preserve the taste and texture of the food. Water, for example, is often combined with carbohydrates and protein to mimic a particular texture or taste, as is the case with a variety of baked goods or cake mixes. In general, though, the low-fat "copycats" are carbohydrate-based, protein-based or fat-based.

Carbohydrate-based ingredients are starches and gums that are often used as thickening agents to create the texture of fat. You'll find these in abundance in low-fat salad dressings, sauces, gravies, frozen desserts and baked goods. Compared to natural fats, which are at about 9 calories per gram, carbohydrate-based ingredients run anywhere from zero to 4 calories per gram.

Protein-based low-fat ingredients are created by "doing things" to the proteins that make them behave differently. For example, by taking proteins such as whey or egg white, and heating or blending them at high speeds, you can create the look and feel of "creamy." Soy and corn proteins are often used in these cases. You'll find these ingredients in low-fat cheese, butter, mayonnaise, salad dressings, frozen dairy desserts, sour cream and baked goods. They run between 1 to 4 calories per gram.

Low-fat foods that use fat-based ingredients tailor the fat in some way so that we do not absorb or metabolize it fully. These ingredients are found in chocolate, chocolate coatings, margarine, spreads, sour cream and cheese. You can also use these ingredients as low-fat substitutes for frying foods (you do this when you fry eggs in margarine, for example). Olestra, the new fat substitute approved by the United States Food and Drug Administration (FDA), is an example of a fat substitute that is not absorbed by our bodies, providing no calories (see chapter 9). Caprenin and salatrim are examples of partially absorbed fats (they contain more long-chain fatty acids), and are the more traditional fat-based low-fat ingredients. These are roughly 5 calories per gram.

There's no question that low-fat foods are designed to give you more freedom of choice with your diet, supposedly allowing you to cut your fat without compromising your taste buds. Studies show that taste outperforms "nutrition" in your brain. Yet, many experts believe that low-fat products create more of a barrier to weight loss in the long term. Researchers at the University of Toronto suggest that these products essentially allow us to increase our calories even though we are reducing our overall fat intake. For example, in one study, women who consumed a low-fat breakfast food ate more during the day than women who consumed a higher-fat food at breakfast.

The good news about low-fat or fat-free products is that they are, in fact, lower in fat, and are created to substitute for the "bad foods" you know you shouldn't have but cannot live without. The boring phrase "everything in moderation" applies to low-fat products, too. Balancing these products with "good stuff" is the key. A low-fat treat should still be treated like its high-fat original. In other words, don't have double the amount because it's low-fat. Instead, have the same amount as you would of the original.

Psychological Roles of Fat

An understanding of the role of food and fat in women's lives is crucial in dealing with weight control issues. Being fat and/or the overeating behaviour that causes us to be fat is frequently perceived to be a very public rebellion against the sometimes conflicting roles women are expected to play in this society. So it's important to explore what being fat means to you, personally, and the issues surrounding food addiction.

As women, we are the ones who usually purchase and prepare food for our families. At the same time, we are continuously deluged with impossible standards of beauty, fitness and thinness through media images. How do these conflicting roles affect us? For many women, the effect is a feeling of powerlessness. Manipulating body size to be bigger or smaller by eating or refusing food, we express an unconscious desire to achieve more control over our lives.

For the record, compulsive eating is more often a woman's problem, which tells us that it has much more to do with "being a woman" than we are generally told by doctors and dietitians. Psychotherapists who specialize in compulsive eating disorders stress that the only way to help women lose weight is to help them understand what conscious or unconscious needs are being met by the fat.

The Meaning of Your Fat

Therapists who work with women on weight loss issues observe that fat both isolates a woman on one hand, and makes her an object of failure on the other. Women, of course, know this, and sometimes use this for psychological advantage. In other words, to the woman, the fat can "protect" her from being successful in two specific areas: sexual and financial. Many women who are striving for financial or career-related success find that a thin body size immediately interferes with that goal. When they are thin, they fear being perceived on sexual terms by male colleagues, or have been so perceived in the past. They may even fear their own sexual desires, or fear being rejected as a sexual object. When they are fat, however, they feel liberated from being perceived as a sexual or "decorative" object and enjoy the financial rewards of their success nonetheless, or simply enjoy being perceived as productive or competent. By being overweight, women can also help to keep their families together by removing themselves from "the market"—avoiding affairs with other men.

On the flip side, many women who have never had success in their lives—sexual or financial—use their weight as a way to remain isolated. This allows them to say to themselves: "If I were thin, I'd be successful." The fatness becomes the reason for failed attempts at personal success, which shields many women from facing their own inner demons and fears, keeping them from achieving the successes they really want.

When fat means "mother"

For many women, especially women who have gained their weight after childbirth, fat has nothing to do with sexuality or personal/ financial success. It has to do with their relationship with their mother, and their own feelings of nurturing and being a mother. After all, it is a mother's breasts that initially nurtures us, and is through our mothers that we learn about food and food behaviours. Our mothers are also the source of love, comfort and emotional support. Even if we do not get this from our own mothers, we still associate "mothering" with these emotions. Therapists have observed that body size and eating gets tangled up in mother-daughter relationships, and can have varied meanings for the overweight woman. In other words, what your fat says to your mother can mean anything from: "I'm a big girl and can look after myself" to "I'm a mess and can't look after myself." Some daughters use fat to actually reject their mother's role, or to express anger at their mothers for inadequate nurturing.

In some cases, being overweight is an unconscious desire to incorporate your mother into your body because she's soothing and nurturing. It's a rather brilliant way of taking your mother with you wherever you go.

The Act of Getting Fat: Compulsive Eating

When we hear "eating disorder," we usually think about anorexia or bulimia. There are many women, however, who binge without purging. This is also known as binge eating disorder (a.k.a. compulsive overeating). In this case, the bingeing is still an announcement to the world that "I'm out of control." A woman who purges is hiding her lack of control. A person who binges and never purges is advertising her lack of control. The purger is passively asking for help; the binger who doesn't purge is aggressively asking for help. It's the same disease with a different result. The desire to get fat is often behind compulsive eating. This controversial idea is often rejected by the overeater who insists that fat is a consequence of eating food, not a goal. Many therapists who deal with overeating disagree; they believe that if a woman admits that she has an emotional interest in actually being large, she may be much closer to stopping her compulsion to eat.

Furthermore, many women who eat compulsively do not recognize that they are doing so. The following is a typical profile of a compulsive eater:

- Eating when you're not hungry;
- Feeling out of control when you're around food, either trying to resist it or gorging on it;
- Spending a lot of time thinking/worrying about food and your weight;
- Always feeling desperate to try another diet that promises results;
- Feelings of self-loathing and shame;
- Hating your own body;
- Being obsessed with what you can or will eat, or have eaten;
- Eating in secret or with "eating friends";
- Appearing in public to be a professional dieter who's in control;
- Buying cakes or pies as "gifts" and having them wrapped to hide the fact that they're for you;
- Having a "pristine" kitchen with only the "right" foods;
- Feeling either out of control with food (compulsive eating), or imprisoned by it (dieting);
- Feeling temporary relief by "not eating";
- Looking forward with pleasure and anticipation to the time when you can eat alone;
- Feeling unhappy because of your eating behaviour.

The Issue of Hunger

Most people eat when they're hungry. But if you're a compulsive eater, hunger cues have nothing to do with when you eat. You may eat for any of the following reasons:

- As a social event: this includes family meals or restaurant meals with friends. The point is that you plan food as the "social entertainment." Most of us do this, but often we do it when we're not even hungry.
- To satisfy "mouth hunger"—the need to have something in your mouth, even though you are not hungry.
- To prevent future hunger: "Better eat now because later I may not get a chance."
- As a reward for a bad day or bad experience; or as a reward for a good day or good experience.
- Because "It's the only pleasure I can count on!"
- To quell nerves.
- To combat boredom.
- Eating now because you're "going on a diet" tomorrow. (The eating is done out of a real fear that you will be deprived later.)
- Eating because food is your friend.

12 Steps to Change

Food addiction, like other addictions, can be treated successfully with a 12-step program.

The 12-step program was started in the 1930s by an alcoholic, who was able to overcome his addiction by essentially saying, "God, help me!" He found other alcoholics who were in a similar position, and through an organized, nonjudgemental support system, they overcame their addiction by realizing that "God" (a higher power, spirit, force, physical properties of the universe or intelligence) helps those who help themselves. In other words, you have to want the help. This is the premise of Alcoholics Anonymous—the most successful recovery program for addicts that exists.

TABLE 2.1
The 12 Steps of Overeaters Anonymous

Step One: I admit I am powerless over food and that my life has become unmanageable.

Step Two: I've come to believe that a Power greater than myself can restore me to sanity.

Step Three: I've made a decision to turn my will and my life over to the care of a Higher Power, as I understand it.

Step Four: I've made a searching and fearless moral inventory of myself.

Step Five: I've admitted to a Higher Power, to myself, and to another human being the exact nature of my wrongs.

Step Six: I'm entirely ready to have a Higher Power remove all these defects of character.

Step Seven: I've humbly asked a Higher Power to remove my shortcomings.

Step Eight: I've made a list of all persons I have harmed and have become willing to make amends to them all.

Step Nine: I've made direct amends to such people wherever possible, except when to do so would injure them or others.

Step Ten: I've continued to take personal inventory and when I was wrong, promptly admitted it.

Step Eleven: I've sought through prayer and meditation to improve my conscious contact with a Higher Power, as I understand it, praying only for knowledge of Its will for me and the power to carry that out.

Step Twelve: Having had a spiritual awakening as the result of these steps, I've tried to carry this message to compulsive overeaters and to practice these principles in all my affairs.

Source: Overeaters Anonymous, 1997.

People with other addictions have adopted the same program, using Alcoholics Anonymous and the "The 12 Steps and 12 Traditions," the founding literature for Alcoholics Anonymous. Overeaters Anonymous (OA) substitutes the phrase "compulsive overeater" for "alcoholic" and "food" for "alcohol." The theme of all 12-step programs is best expressed through the Serenity Prayer, which begins with the following line: "God grant me the serenity to accept the things I cannot change; change the things I can, and the wisdom to know the difference." In other words, you can't take back the food you ate yesterday or last year but you can control the food you eat today instead of feeling guilty about yesterday.

Every 12-step program includes the 12 Traditions, which, essentially, is a code of conduct. To join an OA program, you need only to take the first step. Abstinence and the next two steps is what most people are able to do in a 6- to 12-month period before moving on. In an OA program, "abstinence" means three meals daily, weighed and measured, with nothing in between except sugar-free or non-calorie beverages, and sugar-free gum. Your food is written down and called in. The program also advises you to get your doctor's approval before starting. Abstinence is continued through a continuous process of one-day-at-a-time and "sponsors"—people who call you to check in, and who you can call when the cravings hit. Sponsors are recovering overeaters who have been there and who can talk you through your cravings.

OA membership is predominantly female; if you are interested in joining OA and are male, you may feel more comfortable in an all-male group. Many women overeaters overeat because they have been harmed by men, and their anger is often directed at the one male in the room; this may not be a comfortable position if you're a male overeater. For this reason, OA is divided into all-female and all-male groups.

Biological Causes of Obesity

Eating too much high-fat or high-calorie food while remaining sedentary is certainly one biological cause of obesity. Furthermore, a woman's metabolism slows down by 25 percent after menopause, which means that unless she either decreases her caloric intake by 25 percent or increases her activity level by 25 percent, to compensate, she will probably gain weight. There are also other hormonal problems that contribute to obesity, such as an underactive thyroid gland (hypothyroidism), common in women over 50.

Since diet and lifestyle changes are so difficult, there is an interest in finding genetic causes for obesity. That would mean that obesity is beyond our control, something we've inherited, which would probably be comforting for many people. Now in the midst of the Human Genome Project, which seeks to map every gene in the human body, researchers are actively trying to find the "obesity gene" or "fat gene." Few scientists, however, believe that obesity is simply genetic. There are so many environmental and social factors that can trip the obesity switch, finding a specific gene for obesity is about as worthwhile as finding the anger gene or crime gene.

Some Theories

Some experts believe that insulin resistance causes obesity. It's believed that when the body produces too much insulin, we eat more to try to maintain a balance. This is why weight gain is often the first symptom of Type 2 diabetes. But then we have to ask what causes insulin resistance to begin with; and many researchers believe that it is triggered by obesity. So it becomes a "chicken or egg" puzzle.

There are also many theories surrounding the function of fat cells. Are some people genetically programmed to have more, or "fatter," fat cells than others? An interesting question, but no answers here yet.

What about the relationship between the brain and obesity? Some researchers propose that obesity is "all in the head" and has something to do with the hypothalamus (a part of the brain that controls messages to other parts of the body) somehow malfunctioning when it comes to sending the body the message "I'm full." It's believed that the hypothalamus may control "satiation messages."

To other researchers, the problem has to do with some sort of defect in the body that doesn't recognize hunger cues or satiation cues. The studies in this area, however, are not conclusive.

What about the fat hormone?

A study reported in a 1997 issue of *Nature Medicine* showed that people with low levels of the hormone leptin may be prone to weight gain. In this study, people who gained an average of 50 pounds over three years started out with lower leptin levels than people who maintained their weight over the same period. Therefore, this study may form the basis for treating obesity with leptin. Experts speculate that 10 percent of all obesity may be due to a leptin resistance. Leptin is made by fat cells and apparently sends messages to the brain about how much fat our bodies are carrying. Like other hormones, it's thought that leptin has a stimulating action that acts as a thermostat of sorts. In experiments with mice, adequate amounts of leptin somehow signalled the mouse to become more active and eat less, while too little leptin signalled the mouse to eat more while becoming less active.

Interestingly, Pima Indians who are prone to obesity and also at highest risk for Type 2 diabetes in the United States, were shown to have roughly one-third less leptin in blood analyses. Human studies of injecting leptin to treat obesity are in the works right now, but to date have not been shown to be effective.

Researchers are currently working on using leptin as a prevention drug for Type 2 diabetes. Not only does leptin block the formation of fat in body tissues, it appears to lower blood sugar levels, too. It's believed that leptin somehow improves the function of insulin-producing cells in the pancreas, which helps the body to use insulin more effectively. Since you won't find leptin on your drugstore shelves just yet, you're going to have to be your own fat hormone and do the difficult work of losing some weight.

Drug Treatment for Obesity

Drug treatment for obesity has an awfully shady history. Throughout the 1950s, 1960s and 1970s, women were prescribed thyroxine, which is thyroid hormone, to speed up their metabolisms. Unless a person has an underactive thyroid gland, or no thyroid gland (which may have been surgically removed), this is a very dangerous medication, which can cause heart failure. Request a thyroid function test before you accept this medication.

Amphetamines or "speed" were often widely peddled to women as well by doctors, but these drugs too are dangerous, and can put your health at risk.

Anti-obesity pills

The U.S. government recently approved an anti-obesity pill that blocks the absorption of almost one-third of the fat that people eat. One of the side effects of this new prescription drug, called orlistat (Xenical), causes diarrhea each time you eat fatty foods. To avoid the drug's side effects, simply avoid fat! The pill can also decrease the absorption of vitamin D and other important nutrients.

Not yet available in Canada, orlistat is the first drug to fight obesity through the intestine instead of the brain. Taken with each meal, it binds to certain pancreatic enzymes to block the digestion of 30 percent of the fat you ingest. How it affects the pancreas in the long term is not known. Combined with a sensible diet, people on orlistat lost more weight than those not on orlistat. This drug is not intended for people who need to lose a few pounds; it is designed for medically obese people (i.e., people who weigh 20 percent more than their ideal body weight for their height and age.) (Orlistat was also found to lower cholesterol, blood pressure and blood sugar levels.)

Another anti-obesity pill, called Redux, alters brain chemicals to trick the body into feeling full. A similar competitor, Sibutramine, is still in clinical trials.

One of the most controversial anti-obesity therapies was the use of Fenfluramine and Phentermine (Fen/Phen). Both drugs were approved for use individually more than 20 years ago, but since 1992, doctors tended to prescribe them together for long-term management of obesity. In 1996, U.S. doctors wrote a total of 18 million monthly prescriptions for Fen/Phen. And many of these prescriptions were issued to people who were not obese. This is known as "off-label" prescribing. In July 1997, the FDA, researchers at the Mayo Clinic and the Mayo Foundation made a joint announcement warning doctors that Fen/Phen can cause heart disease. Fen/Phen also wreaks havoc on serotonic levels. On September 15, 1997, "Fen" was taken off the market. In light of the safety concerns regarding anti-obesity drugs, diet and lifestyle modification are still considered the best pathways to wellness.

Smoking and obesity

Obviously no health care provider will prescribe nicotine as a weight loss drug, but many women will take up the habit anyway as a way to lose weight, or worse, revisit the habit long after they've quit.

Smoking satisfies "mouth hunger"—the need to have something in your mouth. It also causes withdrawal symptoms that can drive people to eat. If you are overweight, smoke and have Type 2 diabetes, something has got to give! Smoking restricts small blood vessels, which can put you at risk for a host of complications associated with Type 2 diabetes (see chapter 8). The best way around this problem is to ask your health care team for some information on credible smoking-cessation programs.

Chapter 3

FERTILITY, PREGNANCY

AND TYPE 2 DIABETES

This chapter is designed for two specific groups of women. The first group is already diagnosed with Type 2 diabetes, has delayed having children (probably for social reasons), but nevertheless is planning a pregnancy or is already pregnant. Many of the women in this group may also have been dealing with infertility, or may be undergoing fertility treatments. Many women in their mid- to late forties, for example, have more options regarding pregnancy as a result of egg donation. Therefore, the old thinking—"Women with Type 2 diabetes are too old to have babies and don't need this information"— is being radically revised. In fact, there has been an upsurge in what is called "postmenopausal pregnancy" as a direct result of new fertility treatments.

The second group of women will not have been diagnosed with Type 2 diabetes, but with gestational diabetes, which means "diabetes during pregnancy." Gestational diabetes is not the same disease as Type 2 diabetes, even though it usually behaves the same way. It is a condition during pregnancy in which your body is resistant to the insulin it makes, but which can often be managed through dietary changes and meal planning. And it often disappears after pregnancy. Gestational diabetes, however, is often a warning that unless lifestyle and dietary habits change between pregnancies or after childbirth, Type 2 diabetes may occur after all.

The Estrogen Connection

What exactly is estrogen responsible for in our bodies? In addition to protecting our bones and maintaining our reproductive organs, estrogen also helps to maintain appropriate levels of high density lipoprotein (HDL), which keeps our arteries clear of plaque, preventing them from clogging and causing heart attacks and strokes. By raising HDL, known as the "good" cholesterol, the "bad" cholesterol, the low density lipoproteins that cause fatty substances to collect in the arteries (causing arteriosclerosis) drop. Estrogen also helps protect us from rheumatoid arthritis. It's our ovaries, of course, that make estrogen, but other sources of estrogen come from the hormone androstenedione and testosterone, which are converted by our tissues into a form of estrogen called estrone, a weaker form of estrogen than the kind our ovaries produce. In obese women, it is estrone which they have in greater amounts. Although this may prevent any severe menopausal symptoms, estrone is not considered a potent enough form of estrogen to protect against osteoporosis or heart disease.

Does estrogen influence blood sugar levels and insulin requirements. The answer is yes. There is also evidence that estrogen-containing products can even trigger insulin resistance in women who have a family history or genetic predisposition to Type 2 diabetes. Estrogen usually raises blood sugar levels, which will interfere with medication or insulin doses. This is why estrogen-containing medications, such as oral contraceptives or hormone replacement therapy (HRT) after menopause, were once considered unacceptable for women with diabetes. It is also why diabetes is still labelled a contraindication (a condition that is not compatible with a given therapy or medication) for many estrogen-containing products. Recently, however, the guidelines for women with diabetes are being revised to reflect, in part, more knowledge about the health benefits of various therapies, as well as lower doses of estrogen in newer generations of medications.

There are some health benefits for women with diabetes who opt for hormonal contraception, or hormone replacement therapy. There are also health risks that need to be carefully assessed by each individual woman with Type 2 diabetes. Unfortunately, there is no sure-fire mathematical equation to calculate how severely your own blood sugar levels will be affected by the estrogen your ovaries make naturally, or by the external estrogen that may be prescribed to you in the form of birth control or hormone replacement therapy. Much of the risk has to do with how well controlled your blood sugar already is. Therefore, the message of this chapter is a simple one: you may find that you need to adjust your diabetes medication, insulin or blood sugar monitoring habits to accommodate the estrogen that is "in your life." That estrogen can be in your life from natural sources, such as your own ovaries (women find that they need to adjust their blood sugar monitoring habits or medication at certain time in their cycle), or from synthetic sources, in the form of pills, patches, and so on. If taking estrogen from external sources is too high a risk for you (something you must determine with your health care practitioner), there are alternative forms of birth control and postmenopausal therapy you can review with your health care provider.

Periods with diabetes

When estrogen levels are naturally high in the cycle, your body may be more resistant to its own insulin or to the insulin you inject. Most women find that their blood sugar levels will be high for about 3 to 5 days before, during or after their periods. Every woman is different, so the only way to manage your blood sugar levels at this time is to test your levels and chart them along with your cycle. Many experts advise that you check your blood sugar levels 2 to 4 times a day the week before, during, and after your cycle for 2 to 3 months. (See chapter 1 for details on blood sugar monitoring.) This will help you to establish an accurate chart, and find your own individual pattern.

PMS *and High Blood Sugar*

Most women will experience premenstrual symptoms 7 to 10 days before their periods. (You know the ones—feeling tender, bloaty and irritable) However, there is some evidence that high blood sugar can exacerbate these symptoms, meaning that instead of feeling blue or sad or moody you would feel *really* blue, sad or moody. This creates a vicious cycle (no pun intended) because these feelings of anxiety and moodiness can raise your blood sugar even more, making blood sugar control even more difficult. The only way to prevent severe premenstrual syndrome (PMS) is to keep your blood sugar as controlled as possible around this time in your cycle. Charting your cycles and keeping track of when your PMS strikes will help to pinpoint when in your cycle you need to monitor your blood sugar more frequently.

Many of you may be approaching menopause, and may be experiencing changes in your cycles as a result of your "station in life," rather than high blood sugar. What you may wish to do is ask your doctor to test your levels of FSH, to determine if they are high, which is an indication that you're approaching menopause. This will help sort out whether severe PMS is related to sugar or your age. In many cases, unfortunately, it is related to both.

Food cravings, PMS *and diabetes*

Food cravings are a classic symptom of PMS, but can be especially problematic for women trying to manage diabetes. These cravings are caused by an increase in progesterone at this time in your cycle, which affect all women equally, regardless of whether they have diabetes. Cravings, like all PMS symptoms, will diminish after meno-pause. Most often, these cravings point women in the direction of chocolate or sweet foods. The advice from many experts is to simply allow yourself the food you are craving, in a sugar-free or fat-free for-mat, such as fat-free chocolate pudding, or "lite" chocolate desserts. (See chapter 7.) If you deprive yourself of the food you're craving, you may wind up food bingeing, which can be far more destructive, and which can set off a pattern of bingeing and purging, or bingeing and guilt. (See chapter 2).

Bear in mind, however, that the food you eat during this craving period may alone be responsible for a rise in your blood sugar. Chart-ing the foods you eat during your cycle may also help to pinpoint when to anticipate a change in blood sugar levels. It's also important to note that many women have less energy as a result of PMS or because of the period itself. This can interfere with daily activities or an exercise routine, which will also affect blood sugar levels, causing them to rise.

Birth Control and Diabetes

There is a widely circulated myth that diabetes causes infertility, and that women with poorly controlled diabetes cannot get pregnant. This is completely false, which is why it's important to understand how various birth control options affect you if you have diabetes.

Getting Pregnant

You have Type 2 diabetes, but you still want to get pregnant. What do you need to do in order to have a healthy baby, while staying healthy yourself?

The first step is to plan ahead. Get yourself under tight control through diet and exercise, and frequent blood sugar monitoring. If you are taking oral medication for your diabetes, you must stop; these medications cannot be taken during pregnancy. You must either discuss with your health care professional managing your diabetes through diet and exercise alone, or go on insulin during your conception phase and pregnancy. If you have to go on temporary insulin, read chapter 7 for some "getting started" information and useful tables that explain what kinds of insulins are available. However, be forewarned: you must be able to handle taking insulin and going through a fairly radical change in your lifestyle habits, as well as being able to handle another huge lifestyle change—having a baby! Please have a frank discussion with your partner and doctor prior to making this decision.

Experts recommend that you should ideally plan your pregnancy three to six months in advance so that you can make sure that your glycosylated hemoglobin levels (known as HbA_{1c} levels (see chapters 1 and 7) are within normal ranges during this period. A normal level means that your diabetes is well managed, therefore the risk of birth defects is low. (This is a risk in the early stages of pregnancy if you have high blood sugar.) The following tests prior to getting pregnant are also recommended:

- eye exam (to rule out diabetes eye disease);
- blood pressure and urine test to check your kidney function;
- a gynaecological exam (this should include a pelvic exam, breast exam, Pap test and screening for vaginal infections or STDs);
- a general check-up to rule out heart disease or other circulatory problems.

Obesity

Regardless of your diabetes, obesity may be a sign that your pregnancy will become high risk. As explained earlier, the definition of "obese" means that you weigh at least 20 percent more than you should for your height and age. In the United States, roughly 32 million women (one-sixth of the population) fit this definition. And 40 percent of these women are young. As if you didn't have enough to worry about, there is some bad news: a recent study showed that women who are obese prior to conceiving are 60 percent more likely to have a Caesarean delivery than women of average weight. If you are obese with your first pregnancy, the news is even worse: you're 64 percent more likely to require a Caesarean section. And, the heavier you are, the more likely you are to have that C-section. (For more about Caesarean sections, see page 83).

This is not a conspiracy. It just so happens that when you're obese prior to the pregnancy, the odds of a number of complications during pregnancy increase, including gestational diabetes.

Experts strongly suggest that the only way to combat this problem is to help women achieve a normal weight prior to conceiving, which would lead to a marked decrease in C-section deliveries. In fact, the current first-time Caesarean delivery rate of 20 percent to 25 percent is blamed on the obesity issue. If all women were of normal weight for their ages and heights, experts speculate that the C-section rate in the United States would drop to roughly 12 percent for first-time Caesareans and 3 percent for repeat C-sections.

Having Sex

Getting pregnant means having sex (usually!). As a woman with diabetes, however, having sex can interfere with blood sugar levels since it is, after all, an activity. Therefore, many experts recommend that you treat sexual activity as any other activity and plan for it accordingly as a physical exercise of sorts. The risk of developing low blood sugar, or hypoglycemia, is actually not uncommon with sexual activity and diabetes. You may need to eat after sexual intercourse, or eat something beforehand to ward off low blood sugar.

There is also the opposite problem: no desire for sex. This can occur because of vaginal infections (see chapter 8), or because of changing hormones if you are approaching menopause. Studies that looked specifically at the effect of diabetes on women and sexuality found that loss of libido was often caused by the following: high blood sugar; vaginal infections, and resulting pain or itching during inter-course; the sheer fear of pain or itching during intercourse; and nerve damage, which affects blood flow to the female genitalia, and hence, can interfere with pleasure, sensation and orgasm.

Many women also report that they feel more unattractive as a result of their diabetes. They are concerned not only with their own performance, but also with their ability to please their partners. Fears of a "low blood sugar attack in the sack" are particularly common. The only way to deal with feelings of unattractiveness or fears is to be open with your partner. Discussing these issues with a sex therapist or counsellor may also be valuable.

Who Should Not Get Pregnant?

If your diabetes has affected your kidneys (see chapter 8), then pregnancy is not in your best interests. You will need to weigh your desire to procreate against the risks of dying from kidney failure. By controlling your diabetes during pregnancy, it is still possible to give birth to a healthy child even when you have kidney disease, but it is unlikely that you will live to see that child's fifth birthday. Since people with diabetic kidney disease do not do well on dialysis, unless you have a kidney transplant, pregnancy will put your life in danger. I recommend that any woman with diabetic kidney disease contem-plating pregnancy rent the film *Steel Magnolias*. It may give you a different perspective.

Infertility and Diabetes

And then, of course, there are those of you who want to get pregnant but cannot. This section may shed some light on a common problem affecting many women with Type 2 diabetes. It is a condition known as polycystic ovarian syndrome (PCO), which is also a classic female infertility problem in the general population.

What happens in PCO is that your body secretes far too much androgen, the male hormone, which counteracts your ovaries' ability to make enough progesterone necessary for a normal cycle. Here, your estrogen levels are fine, and in fact, your luteinizing hormone (LH) levels are higher than usual, working overtime to try to kickstart the cycle. But the androgen levels interfere with your FSH (follicle stimulating hormone), which you need to trigger progesterone. So your follicles never develop, and turn into small, pea-sized cysts on your ovaries. Your ovaries can then enlarge. Because your androgen levels are out of whack, you can develop hursutism—facial hair, hair on other parts of your body (this happens in 70 percent of the cases) or even a balding problem. Acne is another typical symptom because of an increase in androgen, as well as obesity (although women who have a normal weight or are thin can also have this syndrome.) Your periods will also be irregular, and as a result you might be at greater risk for developing endometrial hyperplasia, a condition in which your uterine lining thickens to the point of becoming precancerous. (If you have endometrial hyperplasia, you may be put on progesterone supplements to induce a period or you may require a D&C to get rid of the lining.) Because of your high levels of androgens, you may also be at an increased risk of cardiovascular disease. Diet can help reduce the onset of heart problems.

If PCO was caught earlier on in your menstrual history, you would have simply been put on a combination oral contraception to induce normal withdrawal bleeding, and pump your system with normal levels of estrogen and progesterone. Or, you would have been put on progestin, a synthetic progesterone supplement, and would have been instructed to take it about mid-cycle.

If you were treated earlier on with progestin, you won't experience problems with your cycle unless you go off it for some reason. However, women who were treated with oral contraceptives for irregular cycles at a very young age may not know why they suffered from irregular periods to begin with. When these women go off contraception to conceive, they'll be plagued by the same symptoms that warranted oral contraception initially.

Although it is uncommon, women who have had normal cycles for many years may develop PCO later in life. In this case, they develop irregular cycles (called secondary amenorrhea) out of the blue.

It's recently been discovered that insulin resistance and polycystic ovary syndrome go hand in hand. Women with insulin resistance are either at risk for, or have been diagnosed with, Type 2 diabetes. Women who are obese (many of whom are also insulin-resistant) can be predisposed to PCO because their fatty tissues produce estrogen, which can confuse the pituitary gland.

Lowering insulin in women with polycystic ovary syndrome seems to help restore menstrual cycles and lower male hormone levels. Oral hypoglycemic agents used to treat Type 2 diabetes are now being used to treat PCO, although these agents must be stopped once you become pregnant. Only about half the women diagnosed with PCO have insulin resistance, however. Before you're placed on an insulin-lowering drug, ask your doctor about how diet and exercise can help your body use insulin more efficiently.

In general, PCO is heriditary, and is more common among women of Mediterranean descent. Generally, a PCO woman will begin to experience menstrual irregularities within three to four years after her menarche (first period). About four percent of the general female population suffer from this, which accounts for half of all hormonal disorders affecting female fertility.

Why are estrogen levels normal in PCO women?

Normal estrogen levels come as a surprise to women with PCO. In normally fertile women, estrogen is made from the follicles. In this case, however, your body converts the androgens into estrogen. If you're obese, estrogen will also be stored in fat cells. This constant estrogen level really confuses the hypothalamus, which assumes that high estrogen levels are present because of a developing egg inside the follicle. The hypothalamus will then tell the pituitary to slow down the release of FSH. Without FSH, your follicles won't mature, won't burst, and hence, you won't ovulate.

Reversing PCO

To reverse infertility in women with PCO, doctors will use the fertility drug clomiphene citrate in tablet form. You'll start clomiphene citrate around day 5 of your cycle, and then go off the tablet at about day 10. If you've had long bouts of amenorrhea, before starting on clomiphene citrate, your period will first be induced via a progesterone supplement. An average dosage of clomiphene citrate in this case ranges between 25 to 50 milligrams. In some cases, an anti-estrogen drug called tomoxifen (also used as treatment in certain kinds of breast and gynaecological cancers) will be used along with clomiphene citrate. Roughly 70 to 90 percent of all PCO women on clomiphene will ovulate, but pregnancy rates really vary; 30 to 70 percent of PCO women on clomiphene will conceive.

If you're still not ovulating after taking clomiphene citrate, human chorionic gonadotropin (HCG) may be added to your hormonal "diet" during the luteal phase, or second phase of your cycle (roughly one week after your last dose of clomiphene citrate).

If this regimen fails, you'll graduate to a very potent fertility drug, human menopausal gonadotropin (HMG—Pergonal or Metrodin). This drug is pure FSH, made from the urine of menopausal women. (During menopause, FSH naturally soars in the body to compensate for tired ovaries.)

Prior to starting HMG, you'll need to have an hysterosalpingogram, which is a procedure that checks whether your fallopian tubes are clear. You may also need a pelvic ultrasound to rule out other structural abnormalities. PCO women don't do as well on HMG as they do on clomiphene citrate. While 70 to 80 percent will ovulate with HMG, only 20 to 40 percent will conceive. While taking HMG, you'll also need to be monitored through blood tests (to check estrogen levels) and ultrasound (to check follicle growth).

For more information on the side effects, costs and risks associated with fertility drugs and other fertility treatments, consult my book, *The Fertility Sourcebook*.

I do caution any woman with diabetes, however, to consult her diabetes specialist prior to going on any fertility drugs. Estrogen can raise blood sugar levels, and you need to know how these drugs will affect your blood sugar, not just your ovaries.

Other treatments for PCO

In many PCO women, weight loss is considered the "cure"—just as it often is for insulin resistance. However, when infertility is a concern, and your birthdays are coming fast and furious, weight loss may not be a realistic short-term treatment since it's a slow, time-consuming process. If you have PCO, and are being treated with fertility drugs, you may be able to reverse your fertility through natural weight loss for future pregnancies. Your diabetes educator or a dietitian can help you with meal planning, which will not only help you control your diabetes, but may help you get pregnant.

If the ovaries have large cysts on them, some fertility specialists may want to attempt cauterizing the ovary (in about 8 to 10 small spots) through laproscopic surgery. This procedure is still considered experimental, but roughly 62 percent of PCO women who have this surgery go on to conceive, and when the surgery is combined with fertility drug therapy, the pregnancy rates are as high as 80 percent.

In some PCO women, androgens are also produced in the adrenal glands. Under these circumstances, your doctor may want to put you on a corticosteroid to suppress the adrenal gland, thus lowering the production of androgens. This will help induce ovulation as well.

Bromocriptine, which suppresses prolactin, will be given to 15 to 20 percent of all PCO women. The high levels of estrogen associated with PCO commonly cause hyperprolactenemia, meaning "too much prolactin," which can interfere with fertility.

A *hairy situation*

Women who have had diabetes for long periods of time may notice hirsutism, or overgrowth of hair. Apparently, some studies show that prolonged use of insulin can trigger higher levels of testosterone, which can cause facial hair growth. This is also one of the unpleasant symptoms of PCO. Typically, this hair growth appears on the face, navel or breasts, and many women will want to treat this. An anti-androgen drug, which is available in pill or cream form, will take care of the problem. You'll need to discuss your exact dosage with your doctor, and specifically how this drug will affect your blood sugar. You'll begin to see hair growth slow down after about five months on the drug.

In the interim, electrolysis is the most effective treatment for hair growth on the face, navel or breasts. Make sure you go to a reputable clinic, and ask to meet past clients. Sloppy electrolysis can result in burning and other skin problems.

Other *causes of infertility*

There are many other causes of female-factor and male-factor infertility that are completely unrelated to blood sugar. Roughly 80 percent of all female-factor infertility is caused by tubal blockage. This could be due to pelvic inflammatory disease (PID)—a condition that erupts when bacterial infections (from a sexually transmitted disease or bacteria entering during pelvic surgery or previous childbirth) travel up the reproductive tract, causing tubal scarring and inflammation. Endometriosis is another cause of tubal blockage. For more information on other causes of infertility, refer to *The Fertility Sourcebook*.

Being Pregnant

If you're diagnosed with either Type 1 or Type 2 diabetes prior to becoming pregnant, you have what's known as pregestational diabetes (diabetes before pregnancy). If you develop diabetes *during* pregnancy, refer to the section on gestational diabetes on page 78.

So long as your blood glucose levels are normal throughout your pregnancy and you have normal blood pressure, you and your baby should be fine. Nevertheless, there are some concerns unique to women with Type 2 diabetes. For example, if you have Type 2 diabetes, statistics indicate that you're probably in worse shape than your Type 1 counterparts. First, you don't have the years of practice Type 1 women have at monitoring blood sugar levels. Second, if you were taking oral hypoglycemic agents prior to your pregnancy, you may not have learned to be as strict with your diet as you should be—something you cannot afford during pregnancy. But since these pills cannot be taken during pregnancy (they cause birth defects), your doctor will switch you to insulin before you conceive, which puts you in the difficult predicament of "learning" a whole new disease. The danger of taking oral hypoglycemic agents during pregnancy is that the drug crosses the placenta and gets into the baby's bloodstream, which can cause very low blood sugar in the fetus. Insulin, however, does not the cross the placenta, and is safe during pregnancy.

Unfortunately, unless you are an expert on your diabetes, you're in for a bumpy ride. In fact, the early weeks of pregnancy are so critical that if your blood sugar levels were not under control three to six months prior to your pregnancy, you should seriously ask your doctor whether they advise continuing the pregnancy.

It is during the first three months of pregnancy that the fetus develops its brain, nervous system and other body organs. It is also during this time that your blood sugar levels are most vulnerable as a result of vomiting, fatigue and hormonal changes.

Staying in Control

No matter what type of diabetes you have, every diabetes book will tell you that a healthy pregnancy depends on how well you manage your disease. If you can keep your blood sugar levels as close to normal as possible throughout your pregnancy, then, as most books will also tell you, your chances of having a healthy baby are as good as non-diabetic woman's. The only way to do this is to carefully plan out your meals, exercise and insulin requirements with your doctor, if in fact, you do require insulin during your pregnancy. And if you do, your insulin requirements will continue to increase as your pregnancy progresses. Keep in mind that the state of pregnancy means that your blood sugar levels are usually lower than they are for women who are not pregnant. Therefore, what's considered to be in the normal range for non-pregnant women will be different values than what is considered "normal" for pregnant women. Consult your doctor about what the normal range should be for you.

When you lose control

If you lose control of your blood sugar levels in the first eight weeks of pregnancy, your baby is at risk for birth defects. High blood sugar levels may interfere with the formation of your baby's organs, causing heart defects or spina bifida (open spine). Once your baby's organs are formed, the risk of birth defects from high blood sugar levels disappears, but new problems surface.

High blood sugar levels will cross the placenta and feed your baby too much glucose, causing your baby to grow too big for its gestational age. This condition is called *macrosomia*, defined as birth weight greater than 4000 grams, or greater than the 90th percentile babies. In addition, your baby is at risk for becoming lethargic and developing a malfunctioning metabolism in utero, which can lead to stillbirth. This problem is solved when you regain control of your blood sugar levels. Babies with macrosomia are usually not able to fit through the birth canal; they often sustain damage to their shoulders (the shoulders get stuck) during a vaginal birth. So, if your baby is too big, you will need a Caesarean section.

The extra glucose that gets into your baby also causes his or her pancreas to make extra insulin. Then, after birth, your baby's body needs time to adjust to normal glucose levels (since the placenta is gone), and this can cause the baby to suffer from hypoglycemia, or low blood glucose levels. These babies are also at higher risk for

---

Four Steps to Good Glucose

1. Use a home blood glucose monitor to test your blood sugar levels. Pregnancy can mask the symptoms of low blood glucose, so you cannot rely on how well you "feel." The goal is to get your blood glucose levels to copy those of a non-diabetic pregnant woman, which would be lower than in a non-diabetic, non-pregnant woman.
2. Ask your doctor when you should test your blood glucose levels. During pregnancy, it's common to test up to eight times per day, especially after eating.
3. Record your results in a journal you keep handy. Take the journal with you when you go out—especially to restaurants.
4. In a separate journal, keep track of when you're exercising and what you're eating.
5. Check with your doctor or diabetes educator before you make any changes to your diet/insulin plan. Midwives and doulas (who provide emotional and physical support during pregnancy) are not the appropriate practitioners to rely on for diabetes information.

---

breathing problems, and are at a higher risk for obesity later in life, as well as for developing Type 2 diabetes.

Your baby may also develop jaundice after birth, which is very common for all newborns but tends to happen more frequently in babies born to mothers with diabetes. Newborn jaundice is caused by a build-up of old, or "leftover," red blood cells that aren't clearing out of the body fast enough. Breastfeeding is the best cure for newborn jaundice.

Your Diabetes Prenatal Team

A healthy pregnancy depends on a good prenatal team who can help you stay in control of your condition. In the same way that you would handpick various skill sets for a baseball team, you must do the same for this team. Here are the specialists to look for (see also diabetes support list in chapter 7):

1. An endocrinologist or internist who specializes in diabetes—and diabetic pregnancies.
2. An obstetrician who specializes in high-risk pregnancies, particularly diabetic pregnancies.
3. A neonatologist, a specialist for newborns, or a pediatrician who is trained to manage babies of diabetic moms.
4. A nutritionist or registered dietitian who can help you plan a realistic diet/insulin plan during your pregnancy.
5. A diabetes educator who is available to answer questions throughout your pregnancy.
6. For additional support, a midwife or doula (although these are *not* diabetes specialists).

Gestational Diabetes

Gestational diabetes refers to diabetes that is first diagnosed during the 24th to 28th week of pregnancy. If you had diabetes prior to your pregnancy (Type 1 or Type 2), it is known as pregestational diabetes, which is a completely different story in that the risks to the fetus exist throughout pregnancy.

Technically, gestational diabetes means "high blood sugar (hyperglycemia) first recognized during pregnancy." Three to 12 percent of all pregnant women will develop gestational diabetes between weeks 24 and 28 of their pregnancies. The symptoms of gestational diabetes are extreme thirst, hunger or fatigue, but many women do not notice these symptoms.

What Is Gestational Diabetes Mellitis (GDM)?

During pregnancy, hormones made by the placenta can block the insulin the pancreas normally makes. This forces the pancreas to work harder and manufacture three times as much insulin as usual. In many cases, the pancreas isn't able to keep up and blood sugar levels rise. Gestational diabetes mellitus (GDM) is therefore a common pregnancy-related health problem, and is in the same league as other pregnancy-related conditions that develop during the second or third trimesters, such as high blood pressure.

Since pregnancy is also a time in your life when you're gaining weight, some experts believe that the weight gain contributes to insulin resistance, as the pancreas cannot keep up with the new weight, and hence new demand for insulin. This situation is akin to a small restaurant with only 10 tables suddenly being presented with triple the number of customers. It will be understaffed, and unable to accommodate the new demand for "tables."

GDM usually takes the form of Type 2 diabetes in that it can be managed through diet and blood sugar monitoring. However, recent research on California women with gestational diabetes showed that only a third were able to control their condition through diet and blood sugar monitoring. Therefore, insulin may be necessary if your GDM cannot be controlled. GDM will usually disappear once you deliver, but it recurs in future pregnancies two out of three times. In some cases, GDM is really the unveiling of Type 2 or even Type 1 diabetes during pregnancy. If you are genetically predisposed to Type 2 diabetes, you are more likely to develop Type 2 in the future after a bout of gestational diabetes.

Moreover, if you have GDM, you're more at risk for other pregnancy-related conditions, such as hypertension (high blood pressure), pre-eclampsia (water retention, high blood pressure and protein in urine) and polyhydramnios (too much amniotic fluid). And if you're carrying more than one fetus, your pregnancy is even more at risk. Therefore, it's wise to seek out an obstetrician if you have GDM. In very high-risk situations, a perinatologist (an obstetrician who specializes in high-risk pregnancies) may have to be consulted (see list of specialists, chapter 7, page 146).

Diagnosing Gestational Diabetes Mellitis (GDM)

GDM is diagnosed through a test known as glucose screening. Obviously, if you've already been diagnosed with Type 2 diabetes, you will not need to be screened for diabetes during pregnancy. Candidates for glucose screening are women who are worried about developing diabetes during pregnancy because they believe they have risk factors (see chapter 1), a family history of gestational diabetes or a personal history of gestational diabetes from a previous pregnancy.

There is a debate in the medical community over the issue of universal glucose screening during pregnancy. Many practitioners feel that all women should be given a glucose tolerance test between their 24th and 28th week of pregnancy, regardless of risk factors. (See chapter 1). U.S. studies show that by screening only women with risk factors, almost half of all gestational diabetes is missed.

Since blood sugar levels rise steadily throughout pregnancy, it's entirely possible to have normal blood sugar levels at week 24 and high levels at week 28, which is the reason that, according to many physicians, universal screening produces more problems than it catches. Many feel that the anxiety this test creates in women who have high blood sugar levels is an issue worth considering. And some doctors wonder if even selective screening— screening only those women with risk factors—reduces the problem of macrosomic babies (fat, glucose-gorged babies; see below).

Jelly beans vs cola

A new Jelly Bean Glucose Test is being made available to replace the cola-like beverage traditionally used, which causes nausea, vomiting, abdominal pain, bloating and profuse sweating. By eating 18 jelly beans and having blood glucose tested an hour later, gestational diabetes is just as accurately rooted out as it was with the old, horrid beverage. Furthermore, the jelly beans do not appear to cause any side effects other than a mild headache or nausea in a small percentage of women. If you are going to have your blood glucose tested, ask for the jelly beans!

Many women may be worried that a history of gestational diabetes means they will eventually develop Type 2 diabetes. If you developed (or will develop) gestational diabetes during pregnancy, consider yourself put on alert. Approximately 20 percent of all women with gestational diabetes develop Type 2 diabetes, presuming no other risk factors. If you are genetically predisposed to Type 2 diabetes, a history of gestational diabetes can raise your risk of eventually developing the disease. Gestational diabetes develops more often in women who are overweight prior to pregnancy, and women who are over 35 because gestational diabetes increases with maternal age.

Who should be screened?

The symptoms of gestational diabetes are extreme thirst, hunger or fatigue, all of which can be masked by the normal discomforts of pregnancy. Therefore, all women should be screened for GDM during weeks 24 to 28 of their pregnancy (see glucose screening section above). This is particularly crucial if:

- you are of aboriginal, African or Hispanic descent;
- your mother had GDM;
- you previously gave birth to a baby with a birth weight of more than 9 pounds;
- you've miscarried or had a stillbirth;
- you're over 35 years of age;
- you're overweight or obese (20 percent above your ideal weight);
- you have high blood pressure.

Risks to the Fetus

Fortunately, because gestational diabetes occurs well after the baby's body has been formed, birth defects are not a risk with GDM, although they are with pregestational diabetes. Gestational diabetes is only linked to heart defects when the condition is severe enough to necessitate insulin treatment in the last trimester.

The main risk to the fetus with GDM is that the high blood sugar levels cross the placenta and feed the fetus too much glucose, causing it to grow too fat and large for its gestational age. This condition is called macrosomia, which is technically defined by a birth weight greater than 4,000 grams.

Babies with macrosomia are usually not able to fit through the birth canal because their shoulders get stuck (known as shoulder dystocia). Therefore, most women with macrosomic babies will need to deliver by Caesarean section.

The extra glucose that gets into the baby can also cause its pancreas to work harder, which can cause hypoglycema after birth.

Treating GDM

The treatment for GDM is controlling blood sugar levels through diet, exercise, insulin, if necessary, and blood sugar monitoring. To do this, you must be under the care of a pregnancy practitioner (obstetrician, midwife, etc.), a diabetes specialist and a dietician (see list of specialists, chapter 7, page 146). Guidelines for nutrition and weight gain during a diabetic pregnancy depend on your current health, fetal size and your weight.

At least 80 percent of the time, gestational diabetes disappears after delivery. Unfortunately, it is destined to come back in subsequent pregnancies 80 to 90 percent of the time, unless you get yourself in good physical shape between pregnancies. Experts report that each subsequent bout of gestational diabetes is more severe than its predecessor.

Treating low blood sugar in pregnancy

Many women with gestational diabetes will find they have episodes of low blood sugar, which is not harmful to the fetus, but very unpleasant for the mother. The thinking is that it's better to risk low blood sugar (hypoglycemia) in pregnancy to avoid high blood sugar (hyperglycemia), which is damaging to the fetus. Treating low blood sugar is the same in pregnancy as any other time. (See chapter 1, page 33 for details.)

Special Delivery

About one in four babies is delivered by Caesarean section. A Caesarean section, or C-section, is a surgical procedure that is essentially "abdominal delivery." The procedure, as the name suggests, dates back to Julius Caesar, who, purportedly, was born in this manner. Whether Caesar truly was a Caesarean birth is hotly debated among historians, but what historians do know is that the abdominal delivery dates back to Ancient Rome. In fact, Roman law made it legal to perform a Caesarean section only if the mother died in the last four weeks of pregnancy. The procedure therefore originated only as a means to save the child. Using the procedure to save the mother was not even considered until the 19th century, under the influence of two prominent obstetricians, Dr. Max Sanger and Dr. Eduardo Porro.

Women who have diabetes during pregnancy (pregestational or gestational) are at a higher risk of requiring a Caesarean section than the general pregnant population. That's because they can be giving birth to very large (macrosomic) babies, who may not be able to fit through the birth canal (see page 76). Prior to your due date, ask your pregnancy health care provider about what situations would warrant a Caesarean section.

This is considered major pelvic surgery that usually involves either a spinal or epidural (a type of local anaesthetic). A vertical or horizontal incision is made just above your pubic-hair line. Then the surgeon (usually) cuts horizontally through the uterine muscle and eases the baby out. Sometimes, this second cut is vertical, known as the classic incision. It is this second cut, into the uterine muscle, that will allow a VBAC (Vaginal Birth After Caesarean) or not. With a horizontal cut, women have gone on to have normal second vaginal births; with the classic cut, the scar is less stable, and will mean that for you, "once a C-section, always a C-section" is a reality.

In some instances, you'll know in advance whether you need to have a Caesarean section. Your pelvis may be clearly too small or you may have irreparable scarring on your cervix from previous pelvic surgery that will prevent dilation. Or an emergency situation may be detected that requires the fetus to be taken out immediately.

Unnecessary Caesareans

Many unnecessary Caesarean sections are performed. Most second Caesareans are not necessary, for instance, if the uterine cut was horizontal. Another common practice is to perform a C-section when a woman fails to go into labour after being induced. Reasons for being induced usually have to do with progressing past the due date. In this case, if the fetus isn't in distress, you may want to wait, or get a second opinion regarding a C-section. In a U.S. study, situations in which a C-section was performed depended more on the doctor than on any other single factor; the rate of C-sections varied from 19 percent to 42 percent according to the individual doctor's preference. This is a huge discrepancy. What it boils down to is the doctor's definition of "emergency," which may arise in the event of any of the problems listed on page 85. No competent doctor will delay a C-section if it is determined that the labour is endangering the baby's or mother's health.

To avoid an unnecessary procedure, consult with your practitioner and midwife before the third trimester. Find out what situations truly warrant a C-section, and whether you're a VBAC (pronounced vee-back) candidate. If you're experiencing a difficult or high-risk pregnancy or will be having a multiple birth, you may be more likely to have a Caesarean section than a woman with a low-risk pregnancy.

A Dozen Good Reasons to Have a C-Section
1. When a vaginal delivery, even with intervention, is risky. (You may fall into this category if your baby is large.)
2. A prolonged labour (caused by failure to dilate, failure for the labour to progress, too large a head and several other reasons).
3. A failed induction attempt. (Labour induction sometimes fails, and when the baby is overdue, a Caesarean is the next alternative.)
4. When the baby is in a breech position.
5. Placental problems.
6. Fetal distress.
7. Health problems in the mother that prevent normal vaginal delivery.
8. A history of difficult deliveries or stillbirth.
9. When the baby is in a transverse lie (horizontal position).
10. When the mother has primary genital herpes or other sexually transmitted diseases, such as genital warts, chlamydia or gonorrhea, which are in danger of being passed on to the newborn via vaginal delivery.
11. When the mother is HIV positive.
12. A multiple birth.

After the Baby is Born

The question that may be at the top of your list after you give birth is whether your diabetes is "gone." This is only a valid question for women who have had gestational diabetes. In this case, the only way to tell is to have another glucose tolerance test when you get your first postpartum menstrual period (if you're breastfeeding), or alternatively, six weeks after childbirth. If the test results are normal, then your diabetes is, indeed, gone—but should not be forgotten. It's a warning to you that you better "shape up" between pregnancies, or forever after. Otherwise, future bouts of gestational diabetes or Type 2 diabetes in later years could come back to haunt you. Of course, there are some other issues that will surface for mothers who have (or had) diabetes.

If your test results show continuing high blood sugar, it's probably safe to assume that you have Type 2 diabetes that has just revealed itself during your pregnancy. In this case, your diabetes is a permanent health condition that was simply diagnosed during pregnancy, or even, perhaps, triggered by it.

Should You Breastfeed?

Yes.

Why Was I Told Not to Breastfeed?

Ill-informed practitioners may tell you that you can't breastfeed if you've had diabetes. This is completely false! If your diabetes is well controlled, and you've given birth to a healthy baby, breastfeeding is the normal way to feed your baby, and does not place your baby at risk to the numerous, undisputed and well-documented health problems associated with babies fed with artificial milk.

Several studies show that breastfed babies have lower incidences of both Type 1 diabetes and Type 2 diabetes later in life. Stick to your "pregnancy rules" and keep self-monitoring your blood sugar levels so that you can adjust your diet and exercise routine to your new levels of hormones. Estrogen levels affect blood sugar levels; when they rise, your blood sugar rises; when they drop—which is what happens during breastfeeding as a result of the hormone prolactin—blood sugar levels may drop, which could mean you may need to eat more while breastfeeding to keep your levels up. If you had gestational diabetes, this natural drop in blood sugar levels is nature's way of helping you bounce back to health faster if you breastfeed. If you need to take insulin to control high blood sugar after childbirth, your baby doesn't care! Insulin cannot be ingested, so even if it crosses into the breast milk, it will have zero effect on the baby. Remember, if insulin could be ingested, you wouldn't need to inject it in the first place.

If you have high blood sugar in the days or weeks following childbirth, your milk will be much sweeter than usual. This is not dangerous to the baby; the baby has a functioning pancreas that can produce the insulin needed to handle the sweetness. However, the baby could begin to put on too much weight as a result of ingesting the sweet milk. In some cases, the sweetness is a turn-off to the baby, who becomes unreceptive to the milk. This situation will cause problems with your milk supply, or cause painful engorgement, and can put you at risk for mastitis (inflammation in the breast, usually due to bacterial infection). In general, the main danger of high blood sugar during breastfeeding is to you; you'll want to control your diabetes so that you can be as healthy and fit as possible. This is the case for every woman with Type 2 diabetes—whether she has children or not, and whether she's breastfeeding or not.

Postpartum Blues and Diabetes

Many women will find the enormous lifestyle adjustment after childbirth tiring. They may feel fatigued, stressed, overwhelmed, and all the other normal feelings that accompany the event of giving birth. Unfortunately, some women may also suffer from postpartum depression, which is characterized by a loss of interest in formerly pleasurable activities, changes in appetite, sleep patterns (which happens anyway after childbirth), sadness and a host of other emotional and physical symptoms.

Just because you have diabetes does not mean that you can't develop another condition on top of it, such as postpartum depression. Keeping your blood sugar in check after childbirth will help to avoid a common problem of high or low blood sugar levels—and their associated mood swings—masking postpartum depression. Or vice versa. It's also recommended that you have your thyroid checked after childbirth to make sure that you are not also suffering from postpartum thyroid disease, which affects about 18 percent of the postpartum population, and can be misdiagnosed as postpartum depression, too.

For more information on postpartum depression, consult my book, *The Pregnancy Sourcebook*.

Diabetes affects women in unique ways at different stages of their lives. The next chapter is the one to read after your baby graduates. It discusses both the natural and surgical menopausal facts of life for women with diabetes, which include the myths of menopause, the symptoms of menopause, the osteoporosis issue and the variety of health problems that women with diabetes face as they age.

■ ■ ■

Some of this material previously appeared in *The Pregnancy Sourcebook*, 2nd ed (Lowell House, 1977) by the same author.

Chapter 4

THE MENOPAUSAL

WOMAN AND

TYPE 2 DIABETES

"Menopause" is a Greek term taken from the words *menos*, which means "month," and pause, which means "arrest"—the arrest of the menstrual cycle. It is a time in every woman's life when her ovaries are slowing down, running out of eggs and getting ready to retire. The process involves a complex shutting down of hormones that have nourished the menstrual cycle until this point. As a result, the normal hormonal fluctuations women are used to throughout their menstrual cycles become far more erratic, responsible for the infamous menopausal mood swings that have created much of the negative mythology surrounding menopause in our culture.

Natural menopause and menarche (the first menstrual period) have a lot in common: they are both gradual processes that women ease into. A woman doesn't suddenly wake up to find herself in menopause any more than a young girl wakes up to find herself in puberty. However, when menopause occurs surgically—the by-product of an oophorectomy (surgical removal of one or both ovaries), ovarian failure following a hysterectomy (the surgical removal of the uterus) or certain cancer therapies, such as chemotherapy or radiation—it can be an extremely jarring process. One out of every three women in North America will not make it to the age of 60 with her uterus intact. These women may indeed wake up one morning to find themselves in menopause, and as a result, will suffer far more noticeable and severe menopausal symptoms than their natural-menopause counterparts. It is because of surgical menopause that hormonal replacement therapy (HRT) and estrogen replacement therapy (ERT or "unopposed estrogen") have become such hotly debated issues in women's health. The loss of estrogen, in particular, leads to drastic changes in the body's chemistry that trigger a more aggressive aging process. Remember that your age, medical history and menopausal symptoms all need to be factored into the HRT or ERT decision, and weighed against the health risks your diabetes poses.

Women with Type 2 diabetes have a little more to be concerned about than women without Type 2 diabetes. Estrogen loss increases all women's risk of heart disease, which is the major cause of death for postmenopausal women. In postmenopausal women with diabetes, the risk of heart disease is two to three times higher than in the general female population. Furthermore, as estrogen and progesterone levels drop, women with diabetes can expect fluctuations in their blood sugar levels, and possibly more episodes of low blood sugar (see chapter 1). After menopause, women taking insulin may find that their insulin requirements have dropped by 20 percent.

Natural Menopause

When menopause occurs naturally, it tends to take place anywhere between the ages of 48 and 52, but it can occur as early as your late thirties, or as late as your mid-fifties. When menopause occurs before 45, it is technically considered "early menopause," but just as menarche is genetically predetermined, so is menopause. For an average woman with an unremarkable medical history, what she eats or does in terms of activity will not influence the timing of her menopause. However, women who have had chemotherapy, or who have been exposed to high levels of radiation (such as radiation therapy in their pelvic area for cancer treatment) may go into earlier menopause. In any event, the average age of menopause is 50 to 51.

Other causes that can trigger early menopause include mumps (in small groups of women, the infection causing mumps has been known to spread to the ovaries, prematurely shutting them down) and women with specific autoimmune diseases, such as lupus or rheumatoid arthritis (in some of these women, their bodies develop antibodies to their own ovaries and attack the ovaries).

The Stages of Natural Menopause

Socially, the word "menopause" refers to a process, not a precise moment in the life of your menstrual cycle. Medically, however, the word "menopause" does indeed refer to one precise moment: the date of your last menstrual period. However, the events preceding and following menopause amount to a huge change for women both physically and socially. Physically, this process is divided into four stages:

1. *Premenopause:* although some doctors may refer to a 32-year-old woman in her childbearing years as "premenopausal," this is not really an appropriate label. The term "premenopause" ideally refers to women on the cusp of menopause: their periods have just started to get irregular, but they do not yet experience any classic menopausal symptoms such as hot flashes or vaginal dryness. A woman in premenopause is usually in her mid to late forties. If your doctor tells you that you're premenopausal, you might want to ask how he or she is using this term.

2. *Perimenopause:* this term refers to women who are in the thick of menopause—their cycles are wildly erratic, they are experiencing hot flashes and vaginal dryness. This label is applicable for about four years, covering the first two years prior to the official last

menstrual period to the next two years following the last period. Women who are perimenopausal will be in the age groups discussed above, averaging to about 51.

3. *Menopause:* this term refers to your final menstrual period. You will not be able to pinpoint your final period until you've been completely free from periods for one year. Then you count back to the last period you charted, and that date is the date of your menopause. Important: after more than one year of no menstrual periods, any vaginal bleeding is now considered abnormal.

4. *Postmenopause:* this term refers to the last third of most women's lives, ranging from women who have been free of menstrual periods for at least four years to women celebrating their 100th birthday. In other words, once you're past menopause, you'll be referred to as postmenopausal for the rest of your life. Sometimes, the terms "postmenopausal" and "perimenopausal" are used interchangeably, but this is technically inaccurate.

Used in a social context, however, nobody really bothers to break down the term "menopause" as precisely. When you see the phrase "menopausal" in a magazine article, you are seeing what's become acceptable medical slang, referring to women who are premenopausal and perimenopausal—a time frame that includes the actual menopause. When you see the word "postmenopausal" in a magazine article, you are seeing another accepted medical slang, which includes women who are in perimenopause and "official" postmenopause.

"Diagnosing" premenopause or perimenopause
When you begin to notice the signs of menopause, either you'll suspect the approach of menopause on your own, or your doctor will put two and two together when you report your "bizarre" symptoms. There are two very simple tests that will accurately determine what's going on, and what stage of menopause you're in. Your FSH (follicle stimulating hormone) levels will dramatically rise as your ovaries begin to shut down; these levels are easily checked from one blood

test. In addition, your vaginal walls will thin, and the cells lining the vagina will not contain as much estrogen. Your doctor will simply do a Pap-like smear on your vaginal walls—simple and painless—and then analyze the smear to check for vaginal atrophy—the thinning and drying out of your vagina. You will need to keep track of your periods and chart them as they become irregular. Your menstrual pattern will be an additional clue to your doctor about whether you're pre- or perimenopausal.

Signs of Natural Menopause

In the past, a long list of hysterical symptoms have been attributed to the "change of life" but medically, there are really just three classic short-term symptoms of menopause: erratic periods, hot flashes and vaginal dryness. All three symptoms are caused by a decrease in estrogen. The emotional symptoms of menopause, such as irritability, mood swings, melancholy and so on, are actually caused by a rise in FSH. As the cycle changes and the ovaries' egg supply dwindles, FSH is secreted in very high amounts and reaches a lifetime peak—as much as 15 times higher; it's the body's way of trying to jump-start the ovarian engine. This is why the urine of menopausal women is used to produce human menopausal gonadotropin (HMG), the potent fertility drug that consists of pure FSH (see chapter 3).

Women make the understandable mistake of assuming that mood swings are caused by estrogen deficiency. During our childbearing years, our premenstrual symptoms are caused by peak levels of estrogen and progesterone; the symptoms are relieved when the flow starts, and the estrogen and progesterone levels drop. So it's not possible for low levels of estrogen to cause premenstrual symptoms during menopause. Ironically, the only other time in a woman's life when her FSH levels are as high as they are in menopause is during puberty. (This may be why the classic mother/daughter "hormone clash" tends to occur when a daughter is entering puberty, while the mother is entering menopause. At this stage, both mother and daughter are more "sex hormone matched" in terms of hormonal levels than at other times in their relationship.) In fact, the erratic up-and-down moods of puberty mirror the mood swings that can characterize menopause for the same reasons. However, decreased levels of estrogen can make you more vulnerable to stress, depression and anxiety because estrogen loss affects REM (rapid eye movement) sleep. When we're less rested, we're less able to cope with stresses that normally may not affect us.

Every woman entering menopause will experience a change in her menstrual cycle; however, not all women will experience hot flashes or even notice vaginal changes. This is particularly true if a woman is overweight. Estrogen is stored in fat cells, which is why overweight women also tend to be more at risk for estrogen-dependent cancers. What happens is that the fat cells convert fat into estrogen, creating a type of estrogen reserve that the body will use during menopause, which can reduce the severity of estrogen-loss symptoms.

Erratic menstrual periods

Every woman will begin to experience an irregular cycle before her last menstrual period. Cycles may become longer or shorter with long bouts of amenorrhea (absence of periods). There will also be flow changes, where periods may suddenly become light and scanty, or very heavy and crampy. The impact of suddenly irregular, "wild" cycles can be disturbing, however, because menstrual cycle changes may also signify other problems, discussed throughout previous chapters. That's why it's imperative to chart your periods and try to sort out your own pattern of "normal" irregular cycles. It's also crucial to bring your chart to your gynaecologist and either confirm your suspicions that you are indeed entering menopause, which can involve a few simple diagnostic procedures, such as checking your FSH levels via blood tests (high FSH levels are tell-tale signs that your estrogen levels are dropping and that you are entering menopause) or vaginal smears that analyze whether the vaginal walls are thinning out (also tell-tale signs that your estrogen levels are dropping.) If you're not entering menopause, you'll need to isolate the cause of your cycle changes.

Of course, since you can go into menopause earlier than you might have anticipated, irregular cycles may not always be on your list of suspected causes behind your sudden cycle changes. Is there any way you can predict more accurately when your own menopause might occur? Yes. Find out how old your mother was when she went into menopause. If she's no longer living, ask other women who were close to her, or ask your father. Although most women can expect to reach menopause in their fifties, women who go into earlier menopause will usually have a family history of earlier menopause. Menstrual periods will generally become erratic approximately two years before the final period. However, some women may experience a longer premenopausal process than others.

Hot flashes

Roughly 85 percent of all pre- and perimenopausal women experience what's known as "hot flashes." These episodes can begin when periods are either still regular, or have just started to become irregular. The hot flashes usually stop between one to two years after your final menstrual period. A hot flash can feel different for each woman. Some women experience a feeling of warmth in their face and upper body. Some experience hot flashes as a simultaneous sweating with chills. Some women feel anxious, tense, dizzy or nauseated just before the hot flash. Some feel tingling in their fingers or heart palpitations just before the hot flash occurs. Some women experience their hot flashes during the day; others experience them at night, and may wake up so wet from perspiration that they need to change their bedsheets and/or nightclothes.

While nobody really understands what causes a hot flash, researchers believe that it has to do with mixed signals from the hypothalamus, a part of the brain that controls both body temperature and sex hormones. Normally, when the body is too warm, the hypothalamus sends a chemical message to the heart to cool off the body by pumping more blood, causing the blood vessels under the skin to dilate, which makes you perspire. During menopause, however, it's believed that the hypothalamus gets confused and sends this "cooling off" signal at the wrong times. A hot flash is not the same as being overheated. Although the skin temperature often rises between 4° to 8° Fahrenheit, the internal body temperature drops, creating this odd sensation.

Why does the hypothalamus get so confused? Decreasing levels of estrogen. We know this because when synthetic estrogen is given to replace natural estrogen in the body, hot flashes disappear. Some researchers believe that a decrease in LH (luteinizing hormone) is also a key factor. A variety of other hormones that influence body temperature are being looked at as well.

Although hot flashes are harmless in terms of health risks, they are disquieting and stressful symptoms. Certain groups of women will experience more severe hot flashes than others:

- Women who are in surgical menopause;
- Women who are thin. When there's less fat on the body to store estrogen reserves, estrogen-loss symptoms are more severe;
- Women who don't sweat easily. An ability to sweat makes extreme temperatures easier to tolerate. Women who have trouble sweating frequently experience more severe hot flashes.

Just as you must chart your menstrual periods when your cycles become irregular, it's also important to chart your hot flashes. Keep track of when the flashes occur and how long they last, and number their intensity from 1 to 10. This will help you determine a pattern, and allow you to prepare for them in advance—which will reduce the stress involved in the flashes to begin with. It's also crucial to report your hot flashes to your doctor, just as you would any changes in your cycle. Symptoms of hot flashes can also indicate other health problems, such as circulatory problems, and so on.

What can I do about my hot flashes?

Short of taking ERT or HRT, the only thing you can do about your hot flashes is to lessen your discomfort by adjusting your lifestyle to cope with them. The more comfortable you are, the less intense your flashes will feel. Once you establish a pattern by charting the flashes, you can do a few things around the time of day your flashes occur. Some suggestions:

- Avoid synthetic clothing, such as polyester, because it traps perspiration.
- Use only 100 percent cotton bedding if you have night sweats.
- Avoid clothing with high necks and long sleeves.
- Dress in layers.
- Keep cold drinks handy.
- If you smoke, cut down or quit. Smoking constricts blood vessels and can intensify and prolong a flash. It also leads to severe complications from diabetes, discussed in chapter 8.
- Avoid "trigger" foods such as caffeine, alcohol, spicy foods, sugars, and avoid eating large meals. Substitute herbal teas for coffee or regular tea.
- Discuss with your doctor the benefits of taking vitamin E supplements. Evidence suggests that vitamin E is essential for proper circulation and the production of sex hormones.
- Exercise to improve your circulation (see chapter 5).
- Reduce your exposure to the sun; sunburn will aggravate your hot flashes because burnt skin cannot regulate heat as effectively. (See page 102 for a discussion of sun-related problems.)

Vaginal changes

Estrogen loss will also cause vaginal changes. Since it is the production of estrogen that causes the vagina to continuously stay moist and elastic through its natural secretions, the loss of estrogen will cause the vagina to become drier, thinner and less elastic. This may also cause the vagina to shrink slightly in terms of width and length. In addition, the reduction in vaginal secretions causes the vagina to be less acidic. This can put you at risk for more vaginal infections, particularly if you have high blood sugar. As a result of these vaginal changes, you'll notice a change in your sexual activity. Your vagina may take longer to become lubricated, or you may have to depend on lubricants to have comfortable intercourse.

Estrogen loss can affect other parts of your sex life as well. Your libido may actually increase because testosterone levels can rise when estrogen levels drop. (The general rule is that your levels of testosterone will either stay the same, or increase.) However, women who do experience an increase in sexual desire will also be frustrated that their vaginas are not accommodating their needs. First, there is the lubrication problem: more stimulation is required to lubricate the vagina naturally. Second, a decrease in estrogen means that less blood flows to the vagina and clitoris, which means that orgasm may be more difficult to achieve or may not last as long as it did in the past. Estrogen loss also affects the breasts. Normally, estrogen causes blood to flow into the breasts during arousal, which makes the nipples more erect, sensitive and responsive. Estrogen loss causes less blood to flow to the breasts, which makes them less sensitive. Finally, since the vagina shrinks as estrogen decreases, it doesn't expand as much during intercourse, which may make intercourse less comfortable, particularly since the vagina is less lubricated.

Menopause and Blood Sugar

As you approach menopause, you'll want to revisit your blood sugar monitoring habits because menopause often masks the symptoms of low or high blood sugar, and vice versa. For example, hot flashes (or sweating), moodiness and short-term memory loss are also associated with low blood sugar. Experts recommend that before you decide that "you're low" and bite into that chocolate bar, you may want to test your blood sugar first to see if your symptoms are caused by "sugar or hormones." Otherwise, ingesting more sugar than you need could cause high blood sugar unnecessarily.

That said, many women find that because their estrogen and progesterone levels are dropping, they are experiencing more frequent and severe episodes of low blood sugar as a result. As mentioned earlier, estrogen can trigger insulin resistance; the loss of estrogen will therefore have the opposite effect, causing insulin to be taken up more quickly by the body, which could result in low blood sugar. An easy way to remember how estrogen levels affect blood sugar is to note that when estrogen is up, so is blood sugar; when estrogen is down, so is blood sugar. Therefore, high estrogen levels = high blood sugar; low estrogen levels = low blood sugar.

The only way to cope with these fluctuations is to try to eliminate other causes for blood sugar fluctuations, such as stress, deviating from meal and exercise plans, and so on. If you're on oral hypoglycemic agents, you may need to adjust your dosages around menopause to compensate for less resistance to insulin as your hormone levels drop. (Although, if you go on hormone replacement therapy, you may need to readjust your dosages again.)

Women who have persistent high blood sugar levels may find normal menopausal symptoms, such as vaginal dryness, for example, exacerbated. By gaining more control over their blood sugar levels, those women may find their menopausal symptoms are less severe.

Mood swings

Mood swings can be an especially tricky symptom of both menopause and swinging blood sugar levels. Many women with diabetes struggle with severe mood swings, which can make controlling blood sugar more difficult. While anger and depression can be symptoms of low blood sugar, anxiety and irritability can be symptoms of high blood sugar. Factor in hormonal changes during menopause, and the moods can be severely affected. Unfortunately, depression and irritability can lead women to poor control of their diabetes. Frequent monitoring of your blood sugar levels and sticking to your meal plan can help to prevent drastic mood swings.

Surgical Menopause

Surgical menopause is the result of a bilateral oophorectomy—the removal of both ovaries before natural menopause. Surgical menopause can also be the result of ovarian failure following a hysterectomy or following cancer therapy, such as chemotherapy or radiation treatments. A bilateral oophorectomy is often done in conjunction with a hysterectomy, or sometimes as a single procedure, when ovarian cancer is suspected, for example. (See below for a discussion of what happens when you have just one ovary removed.)

Bilateral Oophorectomy Symptoms

If you've had your ovaries removed after menopause, you won't be in "surgical menopause." You won't feel any hormonal differences in your body. If you've had your ovaries removed before you've reached natural menopause, you'll wake up from your surgery in postmenopause.

Once the ovaries are removed, your body immediately stops producing estrogen and progesterone. Your FSH will skyrocket in an attempt to "make contact" with ovaries that no longer exist. Unlike women who go through menopause naturally, women wake up after a bilateral oophorectomy in immediate estrogen "withdrawal." It's that sudden: one day you have a normal menstrual cycle, the next, you have none whatsoever. This can cause you to become more depressed, and you'll also feel the physical symptoms of estrogen loss far more intensely than a woman in natural menopause. That means that your vagina will be extremely dry, your hot flashes will feel like sudden violent heat waves that will be very disturbing to your system and, of course, your menstrual periods will cease altogether, instead of tapering off naturally. The period that you had prior to your surgery will have been your last, so you won't even experience pre- or perimenopause; just postmenopause. That means that you'll need to begin estrogen replacement therapy (ERT) immediately following surgery to prevent these sudden symptoms of menopause. If you no longer have your uterus, you'll be on estrogen only, or unopposed estrogen. If you still have your uterus, you'll be placed on estrogen and progesterone hormone replacement therapy (HRT). Any short-term menopausal symptoms will be alleviated by HRT/ERT. Prior to your going on

HRT/ERT, your doctor will perform a vaginal smear and a blood test to detect your FSH levels, which will indicate how much estrogen you need. Dosages will vary from woman to woman, so don't compare notes with your friends and wonder why "she's taking only X amount" when you're taking Y amount.

If you've just had one ovary removed
If the blood supply leading to your ovary was not damaged during your surgery, you should still be able to produce enough estrogen for your body. If you begin to go into ovarian failure, the symptoms will depend on how fast the ovary is failing; you may experience symptoms more akin to natural menopause, or you may experience sudden symptoms, mirroring the surgical menopause experience.

Ovarian Failure Resulting From Cancer Therapy

Chemotherapy and radiation treatments that involve the pelvic area may throw your ovaries into menopause. You may experience a more gradual menopausal process, or you may be overwhelmed by sudden symptoms of menopause. This depends on what kind of therapy you've received, and the speed at which your ovaries are failing. Before you undergo your cancer treatment, discuss with your specialist how the treatments will affect your ovaries, and what menopausal symptoms you can expect.

Long-Term Effects of Estrogen Loss: Postmenopausal Symptoms

The long-term effects of estrogen loss have to do with the traditional symptoms of aging. One of the key reasons that women will choose HRT or ERT is to slow down or even reverse these symptoms. Yet it's important to keep in mind that the long-term effects of estrogen loss will not immediately set in after menopause; these changes are subtle, and happen over several years. Even women who experience severe menopausal symptoms will not wake up to find that they've suddenly aged overnight; these changes occur gradually whether you experience surgical or natural menopause.

Blood Sugar Levels

As stated above, decreasing levels of estrogen and progesterone in your bloodstream lead to decreased blood sugar levels as your body's responsiveness to insulin improves. As a result, you may need to adjust your diabetes medication or insulin regimen if you require insulin.

You may also need to adjust your meal and exercise plan, because menopause slows down your metabolism. That means that it will be easier to gain weight on fewer calories. The only way around this is to increase activity or decrease your calorie intake (see chapters 5 and 6.)

Skin Changes

As estrogen decreases, skin, like the vagina, tends to lose its elasticity; it too becomes thinner because it is no longer able to retain as much water. Sweat and oil glands also produce less moisture, which is what causes the skin to gradually dry, wrinkle and sag.

Good moisturizers and skincare will certainly help to keep your skin more elastic, but there is one known factor that aggravates and speeds up the skin's natural aging process, damaging the skin even more: the sun. If you cut down your sun exposure, you can dramatically reduce visible aging of your skin. Period. The bad news is that much of the sun's damage on our skin is cumulative, the result of many years of exposure. In fact, many researchers believe that when it comes to visible signs of aging, estrogen loss is only a small factor. For example, it's known that ultraviolet (UV) rays break down collagen and elastin fibres in the skin, which cause it to break down and sag. This is also what puts us at risk for skin cancer, the most notorious of which is melanoma, one of the most aggressive and malignant of all cancers.

Other sun-related problems traditionally linked to estrogen loss are what we call "liver spots"—light brown or tan splotches that develop on the face, neck and hands as we age. First, these spots have nothing to do with the liver; they are sun spots and are caused by sun exposure. In fact, they are sometimes the result of HRT, known in this case as hyperpigmentation.

Currently, dermatologists are recommending sunblocks with a minimum of SPF (Sun Protectant Factor) 15. In fact, sun damage is so widespread in our population that women will put on sunblock as regularly as a daily moisturizer.

Women who have high blood sugar levels may find that their skin is drier, more scaly, while vaginal dryness may be more severe. They may also notice that their nails are deteriorating more rapidly. Controlling blood sugar can reverse this.

The Osteoporosis Issue

Osteoporosis literally means "porous bones" and is perhaps the most feared condition among postmenopausal women. Unfortunately, osteoporosis is not always preventable, and is a classic symptom of aging. Normally, in the life of a healthy woman, by her late thirties and forties her bones become less dense. By the time she reaches her fifties, she may begin to experience bone loss in her teeth, and become more susceptible to wrist fractures. Gradually, the bones in her spine weaken, fracture and compress, causing upper-back curvature and loss of height, known as a "dowager's hump." Osteoporosis is more common in women because when her skeletal growth is completed, a woman typically has 15 percent lower bone mineral density and 30 percent less bone mass than a man of the same age. Studies show that women lose more trabecular bone (the inner, spongy part that makes up the internal support of the bone) at a higher rate than men.

There are three types of osteoporosis women are prone to: post-menopausal, senile, and secondary. Postmenopausal osteoporosis usually develops roughly 10 to 15 years after the onset of menopause. In this case, estrogen loss interferes with calcium absorption, and you begin to lose trabecular bone three times faster than the normal rate of trabecular bone loss. You will also begin to lose parts of your cortical bone (the outer shell of the bone), but not as quickly as the trabecular bone.

Senile osteoporosis affects men and women. Here, you lose cortical and trabecular bone because of a decrease in bone cell activity that results from aging. Hip fractures are seen most often with this kind of osteoporosis. The decreased bone cell activity affects your capacity to rebuild bone in the first place, but is also aggravated by low calcium intake.

Secondary osteoporosis means that there is an underlying condition that has caused bone loss. These conditions include: chronic renal disease; hypogonadism (an overstimulation of the sex glands, or gonads); hyperthyroidism (an overactive thyroid gland); some forms of cancer, and gastrectomy (removal of parts of the intestine that interfere with calcium absorption).

Right now, one and a half million Canadians are affected by osteoporosis; 1 in 4 are women over age 50.

Fractured statistics

At least 30 million North American women over the age of 45 are affected by osteoporosis, while more than 500,000 postmenopausal women in the United States alone will have an osteoporosis-related fracture each year. These fractures usually involve the spine, hip or wrists. In Canada, the number of hip fractures linked to osteoporosis will have increased by 73.7 percent between 1987 and 2006.

Fractures lead to death 12 to 20 percent of the time as a result of pneumonia. As the ribcage moves forward toward the pelvis, gastrointestinal and respiratory problems increase. Meanwhile, at least 23 percent of all fractures lead to permanent disability after one year. Osteoporosis-related fractures of the wrist, usually the result of a fall on the outstretched hand, are painful and can require a cast for four to six weeks.

Women with diabetes who are suffering from other complications (see chapter 8), such as nerve damage, poor vision or foot problems, are also more likely to fall and suffer a fracture

What causes bone loss anyway?

Our bones are always regenerating (known as "remodelling"). This process helps to maintain a constant level of calcium in the blood, essential for a healthy heart, blood circulation and blood clotting. About 99 percent of all the body's calcium is located in the bones and teeth; when blood calcium drops below a certain level, the body will take calcium from the bones to replenish it. By the time we reach our late thirties, our bones lose calcium faster than it can be replaced. The pace of bone calcium loss speeds up for "freshly postmeno-pausal" women, who are three to seven years beyond menopause. The pace then slows once again, but as we age, the body is less able to absorb calcium from food.

One of the most influential factors on bone loss is estrogen; it slows or even halts the loss of bone mass by improving our absorption of calcium from the intestinal tract, which allows us to maintain a higher level of calcium in the blood. And the higher the calcium levels in the blood, the less chance you have of losing calcium from your bones to replenish your calcium blood levels. In men, testosterone does the same thing for them when it comes to calcium absorption, but unlike women, men never reach a particular age when their testes stop producing testosterone. If they did, they would be as prone to osteoporosis as women.

Estrogen alone cannot prevent osteoporosis. There is a long list of other factors that affect bone loss. One of the most obvious factors is calcium in our diet. Calcium is regularly lost through urine, feces and dead skin. We need to continuously account for this loss in our diet. In fact, the less calcium we ingest, the more we force our body into taking it out of our bones. Exercise also greatly affects bone density; the more we exercise, the stronger we make our bones (see chapter 5). In fact, the bone mass we have in our late twenties and early thirties will affect our bone mass at menopause.

Finally, there are several physical conditions and external factors that help to weaken our bones, contributing to bone loss later in life. These include:

- heavy caffeine and alcohol intake—because they are diuretics, they cause you to lose more calcium in your urine;
- smoking—research shows that smokers tend to go into earlier menopause, while older smokers have 20 to 30 percent less bone mass than non-smokers;
- women in surgical menopause who are not on ERT—losing estrogen earlier than you would have if you'd experienced natural menopause increases your bone loss;
- antacids that contain aluminum and corticosteroids—they interfere with calcium absorption;
- diseases of the small intestine, liver, and pancreas—which prevent the body from absorbing adequate amounts of calcium from the intestine;
- lymphoma, leukemia and multiple myeloma (a type of tumour);
- chronic diarrhea from ulcerative colitis or Crohn's disease—this causes calcium loss through feces;
- surgical removal of part of the stomach or small intestine—this affects absorption;
- hypercalciuria, a condition where one loses too much calcium in the urine;
- early menopause (before age 45)—the earlier you stop producing estrogen, the more likely you are to lose calcium;
- lighter complexions—women with darker pigments have roughly 10 percent more bone mass than fairer women because they produce more calcitonin, the hormone that strengthens bones;
- low weight—women with less body fat store less estrogen, which makes the bones less dense to begin with, and more vulnerable to calcium loss;

- women with eating disorders (yo-yo dieting, starvation diets, binge/purge eaters)—when there isn't enough calcium in the bloodstream through our diet, the body will go to the bones to get what it needs. These women also have lower weight (see above);
- a family history of osteoporosis—studies show that women born to mothers with spinal fractures have lower bone mineral density in the spine, neck and mid body.
- high-protein diet—this contributes to a loss of calcium in urine;
- women who have never been pregnant—they haven't experienced the same bursts of estrogen in their bodies as women who have been pregnant;
- lactose intolerance—since so much calcium is in dairy foods, this allergy is a significant risk factor;
- teenage pregnancy—when a woman is pregnant in her teens, her bones are not yet fully developed and she can lose as much as 10 percent of her bone mass unless she has an adequate calcium intake of roughly 2,000 mg during the pregnancy and 2,200 while breastfeeding;
- scoliosis (abnormal lateral curvature of the spine).

Osteoporosis and diabetes

If you are overweight, as at least 80 percent of women with Type 2 diabetes are, you're less at risk for osteoporosis, but at greater risk of developing other health problems. If you have a history of chronic dieting, however, or eating disorders, your risk of osteoporosis increases because you may have deprived yourself of vital nutrients in the past, necessary for healthy bone density.

Regardless of your weight, however, high blood sugar levels can also increase your risk of osteoporosis, although high insulin levels—the nature of Type 2 diabetes—is conversely associated with a lower risk of osteoporosis.

Preventing osteoporosis

The best way to prevent osteoporosis is to ingest more calcium, and increase your bone mass. This boils down to eating right and exercising. It's not enough to just take calcium supplements or eat high-calcium foods; you need to cut down on foods that have diuretic qualities: caffeine and alcohol.

How much is "enough" calcium? According to the U.S.-based National Institutes of Health Consensus Panel on Osteoporosis, pre-menopausal women require approximately 1,000 mg of calcium a day; perimenopausal or postmenopausal women already on HRT or ERT require 1,000 mg.; and peri- and postmenopausal women not taking estrogen require roughly 1,500 mg a day. For women who have already been diagnosed with osteoporosis, the Panel recommends 2,500 mg of calcium a day.

Foods that are rich in calcium include all dairy products (an 8-oz glass of milk contains 300 mg calcium), fish, shellfish, oysters, shrimp, sardines, salmon, soybeans, tofu, broccoli, dark green vegetables (except spinach, which contains oxalic acid, a substance that prevents calcium absorption).

It's crucial to determine how much calcium you're getting in your diet before you start taking calcium supplements; too much calcium can cause kidney stones in people who are risk for them. In addition, not all supplements have been tested for absorbency. In his book *Calcium and Common Sense*, Dr. Robert Heaney suggests that you test absorbency by dropping your supplement into a glass of warm water, while stirring occasionally. If the supplement doesn't dissolve completely, chances are it won't be absorbed by your body efficiently. It's crucial to remember that a calcium supplement is, in fact, a supplement and should not replace a high-calcium diet. So the dosage of your supplement would only need to be the usual 400 to 600 mg a day, while your diet should account for the remainder of your 1,000 to 1,500 daily intake of calcium. (See chapter 10 to learn more about calcium.)

As for exercise, the best kind of activities are walking, running, biking, aerobic dance or cross-country skiing. These are considered good ways to put more stress on the bones, increasing their mass.

Carrying weights is also a good way to increase bone mass (see chapter 5).

The most accurate way to measure your risk of osteoporosis is through a bone densitometry (or DEXA), which measures bone mass and provides you with a "fracture risk estimate." This test involves low-dose X-rays and takes about 30 minutes. For more information about osteoporosis, contact the Osteoporosis Society of Canada at 1-800-463-6842.

Other Postmenopausal Concerns

As you age, there are several health problems that might plague you as a result of estrogen loss. Here is a brief overview:

Concerns about Heart Disease

Ladies, if you have Type 2 diabetes, you must educate yourselves about the signs and symptoms of heart disease. Heart disease kills more postmenopausal women than lung cancer or breast cancer because estrogen loss increases the risk of coronary artery disease. If you have Type 2 diabetes, your risk increases two to three times. Other risk factors, such as smoking, high blood pressure, high cholesterol, obesity and an inactive lifestyle will further increase your risk. In fact, the Nurses' Health Study, a study that looked at 120,000 middle-aged women, found that women who were obese had a two- to-threefold increase in heart disease, particularly in women with "apple-shaped" figures (meaning abdominal or upper body fat).

Studies show that HRT, cholesterol-lowering drugs and lifestyle changes can significantly reduce your risk of heart disease. Physically active women have a 60 to 75 percent lower risk of heart disease than inactive women. For more information on women and heart disease, see chapter 8.

Hormone Replacement Therapy and Diabetes

The average Canadian woman will live until age 78, meaning that she will live one-third of her life after her menopause. In a survey of the general Canadian population, 11 percent of those between 65 and 74 reported having diabetes. Since heart disease is a major complication of Type 2 diabetes, and women are more prone to heart disease as a result of estrogen loss after menopause, the current recommendation is for women with Type 2 diabetes to seriously consider hormone replacement therapy (HRT) after menopause. The U.S.-based Women's Health Initiative (WHI) is studying 25,000 postmenopausal women, many of whom have diabetes. The results of this study (expected by 2003) are expected to present more concrete facts regarding the perceived benefits of HRT on postmenopausal women with Type 2 diabetes.

Many women on HRT, of course, will also be concerned about their risk of breast cancer. Taking estrogen can stimulate or trigger the growth of an estrogen-dependent breast cancer cell (that is, a breast cancer cell that feeds or thrives on the hormone estrogen). Studies show that these type of cancers are far more treatable than other kinds of breast cancers. And since many more women die of a heart attack than breast cancer—particularly if they have Type 2 diabetes— the thought of preventing heart disease, as well as fractures from osteoporosis (see chapter 5), is considered to be a benefit.

Concerns about Breast Cancer

Postmenopausal breast cancer is considered to be epidemic among women over 50. There are many reasons for this, all of which are discussed in my book, *The Breast Sourcebook*. Women with Type 2 diabetes will probably be told that they should consider hormone replacement therapy to reduce their risk of heart disease, a disease from which they are two to three times more likely to suffer than the average woman. Therefore, you may be concerned about breast cancer risk and HRT.

It's still not clear whether HRT increases your risk of breast cancer, but there's actually more consensus in the medical research community over this issue than many others. That's because the incidence of breast cancer in Western nations dramatically rises anyway after menopause, whether you're on HRT or not. Therefore, it's not clear whether HRT really contributes to this increase. The current thinking seems to be that if you're on HRT, there's a slight increased risk of developing breast cancer. But if you do develop it, it's apparently a very treatable type of cancer that's estrogen-receptor positive, which means that your risk of dying from breast cancer is decreased.

If you add up all the data, you may want to rethink HRT if your risk of breast cancer is significant (due to other factors such as family history, for example), or if the risk of breast cancer significantly outweighs your risk of heart disease. As mentioned earlier, heart disease kills more women than breast cancer, and HRT can definitely lower your cholesterol levels, lower your risk of heart disease and your risk of dying from heart disease. Furthermore, if you are at greater risk for osteoporosis (we're all at risk, but women who exercise or have heavier bones will not develop it as quickly), HRT stops bone loss. In fact, if started in the first few years after menopause, HRT will even increase bone mass. Remember—hip and spinal fractures can be very debilitating (often life-threatening) and can truly affect quality of life.

If you're on HRT and are diagnosed with breast cancer...

A 1995 study done in Ottawa, Ontario, found that women on HRT had more difficulty battling breast cancer once it was diagnosed. This led to a scare in Canada that was unnecessary, however. Doctors will simply take you off HRT if breast cancer is diagnosed, which completely eliminates the problem, and restores your survival rate to that of the general populations. That being said, many medical papers suggest that women undergoing breast cancer treatment can still be on HRT. It is not necessarily a conflict.

Your menstrual and pregnancy history

Your menstrual history can affect your risk of breast cancer, but many experts disagree about how significant a role it plays in the big picture. For example, one factor is what experts call "early menarche." Menarche refers to your first period; early menarche means that you got your first period prior to age 12. This also means that you've been making estrogen longer than the average woman.

Menarche levels can vary enormously. The average age of menarche is 12.8 in the U.S. and 17 in China. Some researchers maintain that this is why breast cancer occurrence in China is one-third that of the U.S. Even within China, provinces with later menarche tend to have lower rates of breast cancer. Another factor is cycle length. If your cycles are either longer (big *maybe*, here!) or shorter (more evidence for this) than average, your breast cancer risk increases by some estimates as high as 50 percent. (An average cycle is anywhere from 20 to 40 days.) It's believed that shorter or longer cycles indicate a hormonal imbalance, which may contribute to an increased breast cancer risk. Shorter cycles also indicate that you're making more estrogen than women with longer cycles.

Pregnancy history is a huge factor in determining your overall risk of breast cancer. In fact, according to a 1751 edition of the Chambers Encyclopedia, breast cancer is described as "a most dread disease, particularly of the celibate and barren." To a large extent, this is still true today.

For example, according to the U.S.-based National Cancer Institute, lesbians are two to three times more likely to develop breast cancer than heterosexual women, while childless women are 50 percent more likely to develop breast cancer than women who gave birth before age 35. Curiously, if you bear your first child after age 35, your pregnancy no longer offers you the same protection against breast cancer, unless you decide to breastfeed.

Urinary Incontinence

Urinary incontinence means "involuntary urination." This tends to plague women with diabetes, as well as women who do a lot of sitting, had several children, have repeated urinary tract infections (UTIs), have diseases that affect the spinal cord or the brain, such as Parkinson's disease, multiple sclerosis or Alzheimer's disease, (a history of) bladder cancer, or have had major pelvic surgery, such as a hysterectomy.

What happens is that the muscles of your pelvic floor and abdomen get weaker and your urinary apparatus drops down. On top of this, less estrogen causes the urethra to thin and change, similar to the vaginal changes you experience (see page 97).

When we're younger, we have tremendous control over the pubococcygeal muscle (a.k.a. the levator ani muscle). This muscle controls both our vaginal opening as well as the urinary opening. Normally, we feel the urge to urinate, but we hold it in until we get to the right place. When we get to the toilet, urine doesn't come out immediately. First we relax slightly, and then urinate. The relaxing that takes place prior to urination is the relaxing of the pubococcygeal muscle. We can also stop and start our streams. Anyone who's had to have a urinalysis has probably mastered this technique. Again, this ability to stop and start the stream is controlled by the same muscle. Sometimes after an orgasm, this muscle takes longer to kick in. We may sit on the toilet and try to urinate, feeling the urge to, but find we are unable to. After the post-orgasmic feeling wears off, we are once again in control of this muscle.

Urinary incontinence is categorized into four groups: stress incontinence; urge incontinence; overflow incontinence; or irritable bladder. Stress incontinence occurs when urine leaks out during a sudden movement, such as a sneeze or cough, or even during uncontrollable laughing. This can happen to women of all ages, and is considered the most common form of incontinence. It occurs when the urethra becomes stretched out from overuse. You may be in the habit of "holding it in" or you simply may have aged.

Urge incontinence refers to a sudden, sometimes painful urge to urinate that is so unexpected and powerful you may not always be able to make it to the toilet. This is not seen in younger women, and is almost exclusively a postmenopausal problem in women over 60.

Overflow incontinence occurs in only a small percentage of overall incontinence problems. Here, with no warning, urine suddenly overflows after you change your position (from sitting to standing or vice versa, for example). You may lose only a few drops of urine, or enough to require a maxipad. Sometimes these episodes are followed by the urge to urinate a few minutes later, but when you try, nothing comes out. This is a condition that often precedes or accompanies a urinary tract infection (UTI), discussed in chapter 8. Causes of this type of incontinence are similar to the causes of UTIs.

An irritable bladder is a mishmash of all three incontinence symptoms and UTIs. You'll need to see a urologist to sort out what's causing your bladder to behave so erratically.

Treating incontinence

Estrogen is very helpful as a treatment for incontinence because it restores the "lustre" of your urethra just as it restores the vagina. Estrogen in pill, cream or patch form will all have the same beneficial effects.

Something known as the Kegel exercise is also very helpful in strengthening the pubococcygeal muscle. The Kegel exercise is a very convenient exercise that you can do in any position, anywhere, anytime: in an elevator, on the subway, in a movie theatre, while you're cooking, eating or lying down! First, isolate the muscle that stops and starts your urinary stream. To isolate it, you can also insert your finger into your vagina and try to squeeze your finger with your vaginal opening. Once you've isolated the muscle, squeeze five times, and count five; squeeze five and count five. Or squeeze 10 and count 10. The key is to keep the muscles in shape. It's that simple, and it really helps. You can also do general exercises to firm up your abdomen and pelvis in conjunction with your Kegel exercises.

Being more conscious of your diet and medications is also important. For example, certain drugs for high blood pressure or heart disease, sedatives or tranquillizers can trigger bouts of incontinence. Ask your pharmacist about this. Some drugs or foods are diuretics, which will cause you to urinate more frequently. Caffeine and alcohol are classic diuretics you can easily cut out of your diet, for example. Fruit juice and spicy foods can also irritate the bladder.

Overweight women are also more likely to experience incontinence because the weight exerts more pressure on the bladder, causing the muscles and urethra to overwork themselves. Weight loss may help to resolve the problem. (See chapter 2.)

More invasive treatments for incontinence involve surgery that lifts and tightens the pelvic floor, or using pessaries, a stiff, doughnut-shaped rubber device (which needs to be fitted and sized) that fits into the top of the vagina and holds it up slightly. This raises the neck of the bladder and helps to reposition.

Some women may choose to just live with the problem, and wear maxipad/diaper-type products that will protect you from the embarrassment of wetting yourself.

Increasing physical activity is not only one of the best ways to manage your Type 2 diabetes, it will also help reduce your risk of heart disease, breast cancer and osteoporosis. When it comes to Type 2 diabetes, exercise will allow your body to use the insulin you do make much more efficiently. In fact, many experts find that when their Type 2 diabetes patients stick to their meal plans (see chapter 6) and incorporate regular exercise into their routine, they may not need any medications or insulin to manage their diabetes. The next chapter will tell you how to make your body into a "lean mean insulin machine."

■ ■ ■

Some of this material previously appeared in *The Gynecological Sourcebook*, 2nd Edition (Los Angeles: Lowell House, 1997) by the same author.

Chapter 5

WOMEN, EXERCISE AND

TYPE 2 DIABETES

You are a "lean mean insulin machine" but you don't realize it yet. The purpose of this chapter is to explain how exercise affects your body when you have diabetes. It is not intended as a workout program, however. You need to design a doable exercise program that is appealing and convenient to you; for most people, that will mean combining some kind of simple stretching routine with some aerobic activity. As one expert aptly put it on her video, the program you can do, is the one you will do.

People who have been sedentary most of their lives are frequently intimidated by health and fitness clubs. Walking into a room with complex machines, filled with young, fit, supple bodies is not exactly an inviting atmosphere for somebody who doesn't understand how to program a StairMaster. And the "language" of exercise is intimidating, too. Not only do you need an anatomy lesson to understand which movements stretch which group of muscles, but you need to take a crash course in cardiology to understand exactly how long you have to hyperventilate and have your pulse at X beats per minute, with the sweat pouring off of you, before you burn any fat. The concept of "gaining muscle" over existing fat is also a hard one to grasp. (My stupid question is always: "How come, if I've been doing my program for six months, I weigh more than when I started?")

Aerobics classes are another problem. Many women (like me) are uncomfortable with their lack of physical grace in public. And many aerobics classes assume that you've had formal training with the National Ballet of Canada; after all, you need the grace of a dancer to perform half the moves! So let me stress something before you begin reading: you're wearing all the equipment you will ever need to exercise. If you can breathe, stretch and walk, you can become a lean mean exercise machine without paying a membership fee.

What Does Exercise Really Mean?

A dictionary definition of exercise might be "the exertion of muscles, limbs, etc., especially for health's sake; bodily, mental or spiritual training." In the Western world, we have placed an emphasis on "bodily training" when we talk about exercise, completely ignoring mental and spiritual training. Only recently have Western studies begun to focus on the mental benefits of exercise. (It's been shown, for example, that exercise generates the activity of endorphins, hormones that make us feel good.) However, we in the West do not encourage meditation or other calming forms of mental and spiritual exercise, which have also been shown to improve well-being and health.

In the East, for thousands of years, exercise has focused on achieving mental and spiritual health through the body, using breathing and postures, for example. Fitness practitioner Karen Faye maintains that posture is extremely important for organ alignment. Standing correctly, with ears over shoulders, and shoulders over hips, with knees slightly bent and head straight up naturally allows you to pull in your abdomen. According to Faye, many native cultures who balance baskets on their heads or do a lot of physical work with their bodies, are noted for correct postures and low rates of osteoporosis.

Nor should we ignore the aboriginal and Northern traditions known to improve mental health and well-being, such as traditional dances, active prayers that incorporate physical activity, circles that involve community and communication, and even sweat lodges, believed to help rid the body of toxins through sweating. These are all forms of wellness activities that you should investigate.

The Meaning of Aerobic

If you look up the word "aerobic" in the dictionary, what you might find is the chemistry definition: "living in free oxygen." This is certainly correct; we are all aerobes—beings that require oxygen to live. Some bacteria, for example, are anaerobic; they can exist in an environment without oxygen. All that jumping around and fast movement is done to create faster breathing, so we can take in more oxygen into our bodies.

Why are we doing this? Because the blood contains oxygen! The faster your blood flows, the more oxygen can flow to your organs. But when your health care practitioner tells you to "exercise" or to take up "aerobic exercise," he or she is not referring solely to "increasing oxygen" but to exercising the heart muscle. The faster it beats, the better a "workout" it gets (although you don't want to overwork your heart, either).

Why we want more oxygen

When more oxygen is in our bodies, we burn fat (see below), our breathing improves, our blood pressure improves and our hearts work better. Oxygen also lowers triglycerides and cholesterol, increasing our high-density lipoproteins (HDL), or the "good" cholesterol, while decreasing our low-density lipoproteins (LDL), or the "bad" cholesterol. This means that your arteries will unclog and you may significantly decrease your risk of heart disease and stroke. More oxygen makes our brains work better, so we feel better. Studies show that depression is decreased when we increase oxygen flow into our bodies. Ancient techniques such as yoga improve mental and spiritual well-being by combining deep breathing and stretching, which improves oxygen and blood flow to specific parts of the body.

With Type 2 diabetes, more oxygen in the body increases your cells' sensitivity to insulin, causing your blood glucose levels to drop. More oxygen can also improve the action of insulin-producing cells in the pancreas. As you continue aerobic exercise, your blood sugar levels will become much easier to manage. You can also use exercise to decrease blood sugar levels in the short term, over a 24-hour period. People who are taking oral hypoglycemic pills may find that their dosages need to be lowered, or that they no longer need the medication.

Exercise has been shown to dramatically decrease the incidence of many other diseases, including cancer. Some research suggests that cancer cells tend to thrive in an oxygen-depleted environment. The more oxygen in the bloodstream, the less hospitable you make your body to cancer. In addition, since many cancers are related to fat-soluble toxins, the less fat on your body, the less fat-soluble toxins your body can accumulate.

Burning fat

The only kind of exercise that will burn fat is aerobic exercise because oxygen burns fat. If you were to go to your fridge and pull out some animal fat (chicken skin, red-meat fat or butter), throw it in the sink and light it with a match, it will burn. What makes the flame yellow is oxygen; what fuels the fire is the fat. That same process goes on in your body. The oxygen will burn your fat no matter which method you choose to increase the oxygen flow in your body (through jumping around/increasing heart rate or employing an established deep-breathing technique.)

Of course, when you burn fat, you lose weight, which can also cause your body to use insulin more efficiently, and lower your blood sugar levels. It may also cause your doctor to lower your dosage of oral hypoglycemics or stop your medication altogether.

The Western definition of aerobic

In the West, an exercise is considered aerobic if it makes your heart beat faster than it normally does. When your heart is beating fast, you'll be breathing hard and sweating and will officially be in your "target zone" or "ideal range" (these are the kind of phrases that turn many people off).

There are official calculations you can do to find this target range. For example, it's recommended that by subtracting your age from 220, then multiplying that number by 60 percent, you will find your "threshold level"—which means "Your heart should be beating X beats per minute for 20 to 30 minutes." If you multiply the number by 75 percent, you will find your "ceiling level"—which means "Your heart should not be beating faster than X beats per minute for 20 to 30 minutes." But this is only an example. If you are on heart medications (drugs that slow down your heart, known as beta blockers), you'll want to make sure you discuss what "target" to aim for with your health professional.

Finding your pulse

You have pulse points all over your body. The easiest ones to find are those on your neck, at the base of your thumb, just below your earlobe or on your wrist. To check your heart rate, look at a watch or clock and begin to count your beats for 15 seconds (if the second hand is on the 12, count until it reaches 15). Then multiply by 4 to get your pulse.

Borg's Rate of Perceived Exertion (RPE)

This doesn't refer to the Borg on *Star Trek*, but to the "Borg Scale of Perceived Exertion." This is a way of measuring exercise intensity without finding your pulse, and because of its simplicity, is now the recommended method for judging exertion. This Borg "scale," as it's dubbed, goes from 6–20 (shown in Table 5.1). Extremely light activity may rate a "7" for example, while a very, very hard activity may rate a "19." Exercise practitioners recommend that you do a "talk test" to rate your exertion, too. If you can't talk without gasping for air, you may be working too hard. You should be able to carry on a normal conversation throughout your activity. What's crucial to remember about RPE is that it is extremely individual; what one person judges a "7," another may judge a "10."

TABLE 5.1
Sample Borg Rate of Perceived Exertion Scales

SAMPLE A	SAMPLE B
6	0 Nothing at all
7 Very, very light	0.5 Very, very weak
8	1 Very weak
9 Very light	2 Weak
10	3 Moderate
11 Fairly light	4 Somewhat strong
12	5 Strong
13 Somewhat hard	6
14	7 Very strong
15 Hard	8
16	9 Very, very strong
17 Very hard	10 Maximum
18	
19 Very, very hard	
20	

Adapted from: Lea and Febiger, *Guidelines for Exercise Testing and Prescription* (American College of Sports Medicine, 1991:70).

Other ways to increase oxygen flow

This will come as welcome news to people who have limited movement due to joint problems, arthritis or other diabetes-related complications, ranging from stroke to kidney disease: you can increase the flow of oxygen into your bloodstream without exercising your heart muscle, by learning how to breath deeply through your diaphragm. There are many yoga-like programs and videos available that can teach you this technique, which does not require you to jump around. The benefit is that you would be increasing the oxygen flow into your bloodstream, which is better than doing nothing at all to improve your health, and has many health benefits, according to a myriad of wellness practitioners.

An "aerobic" activity versus active living

The phrase "aerobic activity" means that the activity causes your heart to pump harder and faster, and causes you to breathe faster, which increases oxygen flow. Activities such as cross-country skiing, walking, hiking and biking are all aerobic.

But you know what? Exercise practitioners hate the terms "aerobic activity" or "aerobics program" because it is not about what people do in their daily life. Health promoters are replacing these terms with the phrase "active living"—because that's what becoming unsedentary is all about. There are many ways you can adopt an active lifestyle. Here are some suggestions:

- If you drive everywhere, pick the parking space farther away from your destination so you can work some daily walking into your life.
- If you take public transit everywhere, get off one or two stops early so you can walk the rest of the way to your destination.
- Choose stairs more often over escalators or elevators.
- Park at the "Eaton's" side of the mall and then walk to "The Bay." Or vice versa.
- Take a stroll after dinner around your neighbourhood.
- Volunteer to walk the dog.
- On weekends, go to the zoo or get out to flea markets, garage sales and so on.

What About Muscles?

Forty percent of your body weight is made from muscle, where sugar is stored. The muscles use this sugar when they are being worked. When the sugar is used up, the muscles, in a healthy body, will drink in sugar from your blood. After exercising, the muscles will continue to drink in glucose from your blood to replenish the glucose that was there before exercise. When you have insulin resistance, glucose from your blood has difficulty getting inside your muscles; the muscles act like a brick wall. As you begin to use and tone your muscles, they will become more receptive to the glucose in your blood, allowing the glucose in. Studies show that the muscles specifically worked out in a given exercise take up glucose far more easily than another muscle in the same body, which has not been worked out.

Doing weight-bearing activities is also encouraged because it builds bone mass and uses up calories. Building bone mass is particularly important; as Karen Faye says: "If you want a strong house, you need a strong frame!" Women who are vulnerable to osteoporosis (loss of bone mass) as a result of estrogen-loss after menopause (unless they are on hormone replacement therapy) will benefit from these activities (see chapter 4). The denser your bones, the harder they are to break or sprain. As we age, we are all at risk for osteoporosis unless we've either been building up our bone mass for years, or are maintaining current bone mass. For information on osteoporosis, call the Osteoporosis Society of Canada at 1-800-463-6842.

By increasing muscular strength, you will increase your flexibility and endurance. For example, you'll find that the first time you ride your bike from home to downtown, your legs may feel sore. Do the same ride ten times, and your legs will no longer feel sore. That's what's meant by building endurance. Of course, you won't be as out of breath, either, which is another way of building endurance.

Hand weights or resistance exercises (using rubber-band products or pushing certain body parts together) help increase what's called "lean body mass"—body tissue that is not fat. That is why many people find their weight does not drop when they begin to exercise. Yet, as your muscles become bigger, your body fat decreases.

Sugar and muscle

When you think "muscle," think "sugar." Every time you work any muscle in your body, either independent of an aerobic activity, or during an aerobic activity, your muscles use up glucose from your bloodstream as fuel. People with high blood sugar prior to muscle toning will find that their blood sugar levels are lower after the muscle has been worked.

On the downside, if you have normal blood sugar levels prior to working a muscle, you may find that your blood sugar goes too low after you exercise unless you eat something; this should be carbohydrates. In fact, your muscles prefer to use carbohydrates rather than fat as fuel. When your muscles use up all the sugar in your blood, your liver will convert glycogen (excess glucose it stores up for these kinds of emergencies) back into glucose and release it into your bloodstream for your muscles to use.

To avoid this scenario, eat before and after exercising if your blood sugar level is normal. How much you eat prior to exercising largely depends on what you're doing and how long you're going to be doing it. The general rule is to follow your meal plan (see chapter 6), eating smaller, more frequent meals throughout the day to keep your blood sugar levels consistent.

Athletes without diabetes will generally consume large quantities of carbohydrates before an intense workout. In fact, it's a known strategy in the athletic world to eat 40 to 65 grams of carbohydrate per hour to maintain blood glucose levels to the point where performance is improved. It's also been shown that glucose, sucrose, maltodextrins or high-fructose corn syrup during exercise can increase endurance. After a training session, athletes will typically consume more carbohydrates to replenish their energy and carry on throughout the day.

Athletes who have Type 1 diabetes do exactly the same thing, except they must be more careful about timing their food intake with insulin to avoid either too low or high blood sugar.

If your blood sugar is low, don't exercise at all as it may be life-threatening. Do not resume exercise until you get your blood sugar levels under control.

Exercises that can be hazardous

Activities such as wrestling or weightlifting are usually short but very intense. Unless you fuel up ahead of time, they will force your body to use glycogen (see chapter 1), which is the stored glucose your liver keeps handy. When you have diabetes, it's not a great idea to force your liver to give up that glycogen. This can actually increase your blood pressure and put you at risk for other health problems, including hypoglycemia. To avoid this, you'll need to eat some carbohydrates prior to doing these exercises, which will provide enough fuel to the muscles.

A word about leg cramps

When your blood sugar is unstable, concentrations of sodium, potassium and calcium can also "swing," which can cause leg cramps. Some things that aggravate leg cramps include:
- diuretics, which can cause you to lose muscle potassium;
- too much or too little intake of calcium;
- sitting too long;
- wearing high boots or knee highs;
- varicose veins or pregnancy;

If you check off any of the factors above, avoid the habit if you suffer from leg cramps. Experts recommend that increasing your potassium intake and stretching your leg muscles before going to bed can help to alleviate cramping.

Let's Get Physical

More than 50 percent of all people with diabetes exercise less than once a week, and 56 percent of all diabetes-related deaths are due to heart attacks. This is terrible news, considering how beneficial and life-extending exercise can be. Reports from the United States show that one out of three American adults are overweight, a sign of growing inactivity. But, as mentioned earlier, the fitness industry has a done an excellent job of intimidating inactive people. Some people are so put off by the health club scene, they become even more sedentary. This is similar to diet failure, where you become so demoralized that you "cheated," and binge even more.

If you've been sedentary most of your life, there's nothing wrong with starting off with simple, even leisurely activities such as gardening, feeding the birds in a park or a few simple stretches. Any step you make towards being more active is a crucial and important one. See Table 5.2 for suggested activities at different intensity levels.

Experts also recommend that you find a friend, neighbour or relative to get physical with you. When your exercise plans include someone else, you'll be less apt to cancel plans or make excuses for not getting out there. Whomever you choose, teach this person how to recognize hypoglycemia just in case. (See chapter 1.)

TABLE 5.2
Suggested Activities

MORE INTENSE	LESS INTENSE
Skiing	Golf
Running	Bowling
Jogging	Badminton
Stair stepping or Stair climbing	Croquet
Trampolining	Sailing
Jumping rope	Swimming
Fitness walking	Strolling
Race walking	Stretching
Aerobics classes	
Roller skating	
Ice skating	
Biking	
Weight-bearing exercises	
Tennis	
Swimming	

Source: Courtesy, Karen Faye, LPN, A.F.F.A. 'fitness practitioner'

When Not to Exercise

Everyone can and should exercise, but your diabetes may get in the way at times, especially if you're taking insulin. So here are some alarm bells to listen for; if they go off, skip your exercise and do what you have to do to get back on track:

- Keep track of where you're injecting insulin. Insulin injected into an arm or leg that is being worked out will use up the insulin faster. Any signs of low blood sugar mean STOP!
- Check your blood sugar after 30 minutes to make sure it's still normal. If it's low, eat something before you resume exercising. (Blood sugar below 4 mmol/L is low; anything that's 3 mmol/L or less means you should stop exercising or not start exercising at all.)
- If your blood sugar level is high, exercise will bring it down, but if it's greater than 14 mmol/L, check your urine for ketones and don't exercise. When your body is stressed, the blood sugar level can go even higher.

Exercise Parental Duties

Obesity in childhood and adolescence is at an all-time high in North America. For example, the American National Health and Nutrition Examination Survey III (NHANES III) revealed that 21 percent of people 12 to 19 were obese, while as many as 40 percent of people in that age group were physically unfit. It wasn't until 1995 that the Dietary Guidelines for Americans even recommended physical activity. If you have Type 2 diabetes, unless you can encourage them to adjust their lifestyles early, your children will be at high risk for Type 2 diabetes as well. Old habits die hard—something you're learning the hard way. By making sure that your children appreciate the value and benefits of getting physical, you can help them avoid going through what you are. In fact, why don't you encourage your children to exercise right along with you?

■ ■ ■

After all that exercise, you must be hungry! What to eat is discussed in the next chapter.

Chapter 6

HOW SWEET IT IS:

COUNTING SUGAR,

PLANNING MEALS

The diabetes meal plan is not just for people with diabetes; it's healthy eating that everyone in North America could be following. So when you begin to meal plan, your entire family will benefit. The results will be that through diet, you'll be able to gain control of your condition, while the rest of your family may be able to prevent or delay it.

Only carbohydrates influence blood sugar levels, while cholesterol-containing foods increase blood fat levels—cholesterol and tri-glycerides. What lowers the sugar in your bloodstream are exercise and medications you may be taking, such as oral hypoglycemic pills or insulin. Ideally, by balancing your food with activity, most of you will be able to control your diabetes. How do you know if you're balancing well? And how do you know what to eat so you can create all this balance? That's what this chapter is all about.

A Few Good Foods

Before the discovery of insulin in 1921, there was the Allen diet, a very low-calorie diet that required the consumption of low quantities of carbohydrates, followed by exercise.

Dr. Frederick Madison Allen, a leading diabetologist who spent four years working with diabetic patients at the Rockefeller Institute in New York City, published a 600-plus-page paper in 1919 called "Total Dietary Regulation in the Treatment of Diabetes." Allen's work showed that diabetes was largely a problem of carbohydrate metabolism. He introduced a radical approach to diabetes, the traces of which are apparent in current meal planning. It was known as the starvation treatment, which consisted of fasting, followed by a gradual building up of diet. Allen's treatment also included exercise—now a vital aspect of diabetes treatment (see chapter 5). The idea of emaciated patients fasting and exercising was controversial, but at the time it was the best treatment available without insulin. Although in some cases Allen's patients died of starvation, Allen prolonged the lives of many through his system of dietary regulation. The Allen diet was found to be more tolerable than any of the fad diabetes diets that were popular in Allen's day. Doctors were doing everything from feeding diabetic patients as much sugar as possible to compensate for the sugar lost in the blood, to putting them on low-carbohydrate diets, which were so unappetizing that most patients wouldn't stick to them. Oatmeal diets, milk diets, rice diets and potato diets were also popular. The most logical diet, however, was the low-carbohydrate diet, which included recipes such as "thrice-boiled vegetables." Although this diet was effective in eliminating sugar from the urine (which produced the same effects of food rationing), it didn't seem to work with patients who had insulin-dependent or Type 1 diabetes.

Allen and his predecessors understood something central to diabetes meal planning; carbohydrates were key. And they are. Allen recognized the ability of carbohydrates to convert into glucose. The timing of this glucose conversion affects how quickly and how high blood glucose levels rise after eating. What's changed drastically since the Allen Diet is that variety, quantity and timing of meals is crucial, too.

What to Eat

To live, you need three basic types of foods: carbohydrates, protein and fat. Carbohydrates are the main source of fuel for muscles. Protein is the "cell food" that helps cells grow and repair themselves. Fat is a crucial nutrient that can be burned as an alternative fuel in times of hunger or famine. Simple sugars that do not contain any fat will convert quickly into energy or be stored as fat.

Your body will change carbohydrates into glucose for energy. If you eat more carbohydrates than you can burn, your body will turn the extra into fat. The protein your body makes comes from the protein you eat. Fats are not broken down into glucose, and are usually stored as fat. The problem with fatty foods is that they have double the calories per gram compared with carbohydrates and protein, so you wind up gaining weight. Too much saturated fat can increase your risk of developing cardiovascular problems. We also know that the rate at which glucose from starch and sugars is absorbed by your body is affected by other parts of your meal, such as the protein, fibre and fat. If you're eating only carbohydrates and no protein or fat, for example, your blood sugar will rise faster.

According to guidelines set out by the British Diabetic Association (BDA), at least 50 percent of your meals should be made up of complex carbohydrates. Canadian guidelines stipulate that your daily intake of protein (animal products) shouldn't exceed 20 percent (BDA guidelines stipulate 15 percent). If you have a sweet tooth, the BDA recommends using artificial sweeteners instead of sugar.

The American Diabetes Association guidelines state that a healthy diet should consist mainly of complex carbohydrates—roughly

50 percent) with about 30 percent of your energy from fat—and less than 10 percent from saturated fats.

How Much to Eat

Meal plans recommended by registered dietitians are tailored to your individual goals and medication regimen. Men and women will usually require different quantities of food. The goal is to keep the supply of glucose consistent by spacing out your meals, snacks and activity levels accordingly. Losing weight will allow your body to use insulin more effectively, but not all people with Type 2 diabetes need to lose weight. If you're on insulin, meals will have to be timed to match your insulin's peak. A dietitian can be helpful by prescribing an individualized meal plan that addresses your specific needs (weight control, shiftwork, travel, and so on).

Anatomy of a Carbohydrate

Carbohydrates are like people; they can be simple or complex. Simple carbohydrates are found in any food that has natural sugar (honey, fruits, juices, vegetables, milk) and anything that contains table sugar or sucrose.

Complex carbohydrates are more sophisticated foods that are made up of larger molecules, such as grain foods, starches and foods high in fibre.

All About Sugar

Human beings have always been attracted to sweet foods. This affinity can be traced to our need for vitamin C in our diets, the source of which is often fruit. Sugars are found naturally in many of the foods you eat. Sucrose and glucose (table sugar), fructose (fruits and vegetables), lactose (milk products) and maltose (flours and cereals) are all naturally occurring sugars. What you have to watch out for is added sugar; these are sugars that manufacturers add to foods during processing or packaging. Foods containing fruit juice concentrates, invert sugar, regular corn syrup, honey or molasses and hydrolyzed lactose syrup or high-fructose corn syrup (made out of highly concentrated fructose through the hydrolysis of starch) all have added sugars. Many people don't realize, however, that pure, unsweetened fruit juice is still a potent source of sugar, even when it contains no added sugar. Extra lactose, dextrose and maltose are also contained in many of your foods. In other words, the products may have naturally occurring sugars anyway, and then more sugar is thrown in to enhance consistency, taste, and so on. With the exception of lactose, which breaks down into glucose and galactose, all of these added sugars break down into fructose and glucose during digestion. To the body, no one sugar is more nutritional than the other; everything is broken down into either single sugars (called monosaccharides) or double sugars (called disaccharides), which are carried to cells through the bloodstream. See Table 6.1 for the complete sugar breakdown. The best way to know how much sugar is in a product is to look at the nutritional label for carbohydrates.

However, how fast that sugar is ultimately broken down and enters the bloodstream greatly depends on the amount of fibre in your food, how much protein you've eaten and how much fat accompanies the sugar in your meal. Theoretically, while the Canadian Diabetes Association (CDA) guidelines allow you to substitute relative quantities of table sugar for starch, fruit or milk in your meal plan (for example, 1 slice of bread equals 3 teaspoons of sugar; 1 orange equals 2 teaspoons of sugar), this may be a tricky balancing act you'll need to discuss with your dietitian.

As far as your body is concerned, all sugars are nutritionally equal. Honey and table sugar, for instance, are nutritionally comparable. Ultimately, all the sugars from the foods you eat wind up as glucose; your body doesn't know whether the sugar started out as maltose from wholegrain breads or lactose from milk products. Glucose then travels through your bloodstream to provide energy. If you have enough energy already, the glucose is stored as fat, for later. Sugars and starches (in equal "doses") affect blood sugar differently because of the time frame involved in glucose conversion. Sugars are converted faster than starches, so it's important to discuss sugar conversion with your dietitian.

Why is sugar added?

Sugar is added to food because it can change consistencies of foods and, in some instances, act as a preservative, as in jams and jellies. Sugars can increase the boiling point or reduce the freezing point in foods; sugars can add bulk and density, make baked goods do wonderful things, including helping yeast to ferment. Sugar can also add moisture to dry foods, making them "crisp," or balance acidic tastes found in foods like tomato sauce or salad dressing. Invert sugar is used to prevent sucrose from crystallizing in candy, while corn syrup is used for the same purpose.

Since the 1950s, a popular natural sugar in North America has been fructose, which has replaced sucrose in many food products in the form of high fructose syrup (HFS), made from corn. HFS was developed in response to high sucrose prices, and is very cheap to make. In other parts of the world, the equivalent of high fructose syrup is made from whatever starches are local, such as rice, tapioca, wheat or cassava. According to the International Food Information Council in Washington, D.C., the average North American consumes about 37 grams of fructose daily.

Going Shopping

Food shopping can be daunting because most foods are not purely carbohydrate, protein, fat or sugar, but often a mixture of two or three. That's where the CDA Food Choice Values and Symbols come in. Instead of forcing you to eyeball the ingredients of your foods, the categories and symbols on page 135 are designed to do this for you.

TABLE 6.1
Sugar on the Table

What's in a sugar?

Fructose: a monosaccharide or single sugar. It combines with glucose to form sucrose and is $1\frac{1}{2}$ times sweeter than sucrose.

Glucose: a monosaccharide or single sugar. It combines with fructose to form sucrose. It can also combine with glucose to form maltose, and with galactose to form lactose. Slightly less sweet than sucrose.

High fructose corn syrup (HFCS): a liquid mixture of about equal parts glucose and fructose from cornstarch. Same sweetness as sucrose.

Sucrose: a disaccharide or double sugar made of equal parts glucose and fructose. Known as table or white sugar, sucrose is found naturally in sugar cane and sugar beets.

If you can count, you can plan a meal that has everything you need. A good meal plan will ensure that you are getting enough nutrients to meet your energy needs, and that your food is spread out over the course of the day. For example, if your meal plan allows for three meals with one to two snacks, meals should be spaced four to six hours apart so your body isn't overwhelmed. If you are obese, snacks will likely be discouraged because snacks can cause you to oversecrete insulin and increase your appetite. A meal plan should also help you to eat consistently rather than binge one day and starve the next.

A good meal plan will also ensure that you're getting the vitamins and minerals you need without taking supplements, such as iron, calcium, folic acid, vitamims A, B_1, B_2, B_3, C, D and E. By consuming a variety of foods from each of the four food groups (in Canada's Food Guide) at every meal, you'll be meeting your vitamin and mineral requirements.

The Good Health Eating Guide

The first thing you need to learn before you shop for food is the Good Health Eating Guide, a system developed by the Canadian Diabetes Association, to help you incorporate various foods into your meal plan. This is different than the Food Exchange lists developed by the American Diabetes Association. (See Table 6.2 for the conversion, in case you're shopping in the United States.) The CDA has created seven symbols* (colour and shape-coded) to represent various food groups. There are many crossovers, however (many of these food categories are a combination of carbohydrates, sugar or fat):

■ Starch Foods (breads, grains, cereals, pasta, corn, rice, potato)

◢ Fruits and Vegetables (all fruits and sweet vegetables, such as squash, carrots or peas)

◆ Milk (all milk and yogurt products; cheeses not included)

✳ Sugars (sugar, syrup, honey, jam, candies, regular pop, etc.)

◐ Protein Foods (all lean meats, poultry, fish, eggs and cheeses)

▲ Fats and Oils (anything high in fat, including butter, fatty meats, any oils, and so on.)

++ Extras (all low-calorie foods such as leafy greens, herbs and spices, artificially sweetened and/or zero-calorie foods, all cruciferous veggies such as broccoli, cabbage, brussels sprouts and a few others.)

*Canadian Diabetes Association Food Choice Values and Symbols © 1994.

Your dietitian or diabetes educator will work with you to create an individual meal plan using food choices from the above food groups. One person, for example, may need eight starch choices daily, while another person may need six. I cannot tell you how many choices you can have; I can only explain how the foods are categorized.

A wide assortment of packaged goods have the CDA symbol on their labels as a courtesy to people with diabetes; this is not a legal requirement, however. Food manufacturers pay the Canadian Diabetes Association a fee to have their product evaluated and assigned the appropriate Food Choice Values and Symbols. Consumers often

---

Golden rules of diabetes meal plans

- Eat three meals a day at fairly regular times (spaced four to six hours apart).
- Ask your dietitian to help you plan your snacks.
- Try to eat a variety of foods each day from all food groups.
- Learn how to gauge serving sizes; volume of bowls and glasses, and so on.
- Ask your dietitian or diabetes educator how to adjust your diet if you're travelling (this depends on whether you're on medication, where you're going, what foods will be available, and so on.)
- Draw up a "Sick Days Plan" with your dietitian. This plan will depend on what your regular meal plan includes.
- Ask about any meal supplements, such as breakfast bars, sports bars or meal replacement drinks, and decide how these will figure into your meal plan.
- Choose lower-fat foods more often.

---

falsely assume that CDA symbols mean that the product is better or more nutritious than products that do not carry them. CDA symbols on food packages are equivalent to the Braille symbols on elevator buttons; they're a courtesy to people with diabetes to assist in meal planning—that's all.

TABLE 6.2
Comparing the U.S. and Canadian Food Group Systems

AMERICAN DIABETES ASSOCIATION EXCHANGE SYSTEM	CANADIAN DIABETES ASSOCIATION CHOICE SYSTEM
1 Starch	1 Starch
1 Fruit	$1\frac{1}{2}$ Fruits & Vegetables
1 Vegetable	$\frac{1}{2}$ Fruits & Vegetables
1 Milk	2 Milk
(No equal food group)	Sugars
1 Lean Meat	1 Protein
1 Fat	1 Fats & Oils
Free Foods	Extras

The Outside Aisles

What you need to live is usually found on the outside aisles of any supermarket or grocery store. Outside aisles simulate the foods you can buy at outdoor markets: fruits, vegetables, meat, eggs, fish, breads and dairy products. Natural fibre (both soluble and insoluble) is also found in the outside aisles.

But remember: foods you buy in the outside aisles can also be high in fat unless you select wisely.

The Inside Aisles

These are not only the aisles of temptation, they may also contain foods with complicated food labels. In Canada, ingredients on labels are listed according to weight, with the "most" listed first. If sugar is the first ingredient, you know the product contains mostly sugar. The lower sugar appears on the list, the less sugar the product contains. The nutrition information on the label should also list the total amount of carbohydrates in a serving of the food. That amount includes both natural and added sugars.

Planning to pick up some cough syrup for that cold of yours when you hit the pharmacy section? How about vitamin supplements? Examine the label on the product. Check the sugar content first. Your pharmacist will recommend a sugar-free remedy.

Whenever a product says it is "calorie-reduced" or "carbohydrate-reduced" it means there are 50 percent less calories or carbohydrates compared to the original product. But something that was originally 7,000 calories isn't much better at 3,500!

"Cholesterol-free" or "low cholesterol" means that the product doesn't have any, or much, animal fat (hence, cholesterol). This doesn't mean "low fat." Pure vegetable oil doesn't come from animals but is pure fat!

A label that screams "Low Fat" means that the product has less than 3 grams of fat per serving. In potato chip country, that means about 6 potato chips. (I don't know anybody who ever ate one serving of potato chips!) So if you eat the whole bag of "low-fat" chips, you're still eating a lot of fat. Be sure to check serving sizes.

The designation "Light" (or "Lite") on a product means that it contains 25 to 50 percent less of some ingredient. It could be fat, cholesterol, salt or sugar, or less food colouring; therefore, the designation is frequently misleading.

"Sugar-Free"

Careful! Sugar-free in the language of labels simply means "sucrose-free." That doesn't mean the product is carbohydrate-free, as in: dextrose-free, lactose-free, glucose-free or fructose-free. Check the labels for all things ending in "ose" to find out the sugar content; you're not just looking for sucrose. Watch out for the designations "no added sugar," "without added sugar" or "no sugar added." They simply mean: "We didn't put the sugar in, God did." Again, reading the number of carbohydrates on a nutrition information label is the most accurate way to find out the amount of sugar in a product. And keep in mind that nutrition claims in big, bold statements can be misleading.

TABLE 6.3
Commonly Used U.S. and Canadian Nutrient Claim Comparisons

CLAIM	U.S.	CANADA
"Low Calorie"	40 calories or less per serving.	50 percent less energy than a regular product and 15 calories or less per serving.
"Low Fat"	3 g of fat or less per serving.	3 g of fat or less per serving.
"Low Cholesterol"	20 mg of cholesterol or less per serving (in addition to saturated fat and total fat restrictions).	20 mg of cholesterol or less perserving (in addition to the saturated fat restrictions only).

Born in the U.S.A.

American labels that say "sugar-free" contain less than 0.5 grams of sugars per serving, while a "reduced-sugar" food contains at least 25 percent less sugar per serving than the regular product. If the label also states that the product is not a reduced- or low-calorie food, or is not for weight control, it has enough sugar in there to make you think twice.

Serving sizes in the United States are also listed differently. Foods that are similar are given the same type of serving size defined by the U.S. Food and Drug Administration (FDA). That means that five cereals that all weigh X grams per cup will share the same serving sizes.

Calories (how much energy) and calories from fat (how much fat) are also listed per serving of food in the United States. Total carbohydrate, dietary fibre, sugars, other carbohydrates (which means starches), total fat, saturated fat, cholesterol, sodium, potassium, and vitamins and minerals are given in Percent Daily values, based on the 2,000-calorie diet recommended by the U.S. government. (In Canada, Recommended Nutrient Intake (RNI) is used for vitamins and minerals).

Sweeteners

We gravitate toward sweet flavours because we start out with the slightly sweet taste of breast milk. A product can be sweet without containing a drop of sugar, thanks to the invention of artificial sugars and sweeteners. Artificial sweeteners will not affect your blood sugar levels because they do not contain sugar; they may contain a tiny amount of calories, however, depending upon whether that sweetener is classified as nutritive or non-nutritive.

Nutritive sweeteners have calories or contain natural sugar. White or brown table sugar, molasses, honey and syrup are considered nutritive sweeteners. Sugar alcohols (see page 142) are also nutritive sweeteners because they are made from fruits or produced commercially from dextrose. Sorbitol, mannitol, xylitol and maltitol are all sugar alcohols. Sugar alcohols contain only 4 calories per gram, like ordinary sugar, and will affect your blood sugar levels like ordinary sugar. It all depends on how much is consumed, and the degree of absorption from your digestive tract.

Non-nutritive sweeteners are sugar substitutes or artificial sweeteners; they do not have any calories and will not affect your blood sugar levels. Examples of non-nutritive sweeteners are saccharin, cyclamate, sucralose and acesuflame potassium.

The Sweetener Wars

The oldest non-nutritive sweetener is saccharin, which is what you get when you purchase Sweet'n Low or Hermesetas. In Canada, saccharin can only be used as a tabletop sweetener in either tablet or powder form. Saccharin is 300 times sweeter than sucrose (table sugar), but has a metallic aftertaste. At one point in the 1970s, saccharin was also thought to cause cancer, but this claim was never proven.

In the 1980s, aspartame was invented, which is sold as Nutra-Sweet. It was considered a nutritive sweetener because it was derived from natural sources (two amino acids, aspartic acid and phenylalanine), which means that aspartame is digested and metabolized the same way as any other protein foods. For every gram of aspartame, there are four calories. But since aspartame is 200 times sweeter than sugar, you don't need very much of it to achieve the desired sweetness. In at least 90 countries, aspartame is found in more than 150 product categories, including breakfast cereals, beverages, desserts, candy and gum, syrups, salad dressings and various snack foods. Here's where it gets confusing: aspartame is also available as a tabletop sweetener under the brand name Equal, and recently, PROSWEET. Aspartame is not recommended for baking or any other recipe where heat is required. The two amino acids it contains separate with heat, and the product loses its sweetness. That's not to say it's harmful if heated, but your recipe won't turn out.

For the moment, aspartame is considered safe for people with diabetes. The only people who are cautioned against consuming it are those with a rare hereditary disease known as phenylketonuria (PKU), because aspartame contains phenylalanine, which people with PKU cannot tolerate.

Another common tabletop sweetener is sucralose, sold as Splenda. Splenda is a white crystalline powder, actually made from sugar itself. It's 600 times sweeter than table sugar but is not broken down in your digestive system, so has no calories at all. Splenda can also be used in hot or cold foods, and is found in hot and cold beverages, frozen foods, baked goods and other packaged foods.

In the United States, you can still purchase cyclamate, a non-nutritive sweetener sold under the brand name Sucaryl or Sugar Twin. Cyclamate is also the sweetener used in many weight control products and is 30 times sweeter than table sugar, with no aftertaste. Cyclamate is fine for hot or cold foods. In Canada, however, you can only find cyclamate as Sugar Twin or as a sugar substitute in medication.

The newest sweeteners

The newest addition to the sweetener industry is acesuflame potassium (Ace-K), recently approved by Health Canada. About 200 times sweeter than table sugar, Ace-K is sold as Sunett, and is found in beverages, fruit spreads, baked goods, dessert bases, tabletop sweeteners, hard candies, chewing gum and breath fresheners. While no specific studies on Ace-K and diabetes have been done, the only people who are cautioned against ingesting Ace-K are those on a potassium-restricted diet or those who are allergic to sulpha drugs.

Researchers at the University of Maryland have discovered another sweetener that can be specifically designed for people with diabetes. This sweetener is based on D-tagatose, a hexose sugar found naturally in yogurt, cheese or sterilized milk. The beauty of this ingredient is that D-tagatose has no effect on insulin levels or blood sugar levels in people with and without diabetes. Experts believe that

D-tagatose is similar to acarbose (see chapter 7) in that it delays the absorption of carbohydrates.

D-tagatose looks identical to fructose, and has about 92 percent of the sweetness of sucrose, but only 25 percent of it will be metabolized. Currently, D-tagatose is being developed as a bulk sweetener. It is a few years away from being marketed and sold as a brand-name sweetener.

Sugar alcohols

Not to be confused with alcoholic beverages, sugar alcohols are nutritive sweeteners, like regular sugar. They are found naturally in fruits or manufactured from carbohydrates. Sorbitol, mannitol, xylitol, maltitol, maltitol syrup, lactitol, isomalt and hydrogenated starch hydrolysates are all sugar alcohols. In your body, these types of sugars are absorbed lower down in the digestive tract, and will cause gastrointestinal symptoms if you use too much. Because sugar alcohols are absorbed more slowly, they were once touted as ideal for people with diabetes. But since they are a carbohydrate, they still increase your blood sugar, just like regular sugar. Now that artificial sweeteners are on the market in abundance, the only real advantage of sugar alcohols is that they don't cause cavities. The bacteria in your mouth don't like sugar alcohols as much as real sugar.

According to the FDA, even foods that contain sugar alcohols can be labelled "sugar-free." Sugar alcohol products can also be labelled "Does not promote tooth decay," which is often confused with "low-calorie."

■ ■ ■

Having Type 2 diabetes is a 24-hour, 7-day-a-week job. Despite this, 70 percent of people with Type 2 diabetes never receive any diabetes education whatsoever. Clearly, diabetes is taking its toll on our health care system. Experts predict that as more people age and are diagnosed with Type 2 diabetes, less education will be available as doctors and diabetes educators become overburdened with patients.

The next chapter focuses on how to maximize your relationships with all your health care providers. Developing a good relationship with your doctor means helping your doctor help you! Actively managing your diabetes involves keeping health logs, choosing the right doctor to begin with, knowing the right questions to ask your doctors, educators and pharmacists and avoiding duplication of efforts.

Chapter 7

DIABETES DOCTORS

AND DIABETES

MEDICATIONS

Ask any feminist about "women and doctors," and you'll be given a lecture about how the health care system, designed by white men, is still in the business of servicing the white male body in a world designed to support white male society. (Working 9 to 5, for example, is not an ideal set-up for a body that has a menstrual cycle, gives birth, looks after children, breastfeeds, and so forth.) There is a lot of evidence to support this claim. Much of what we know about general health is general health in a white man's body—because traditionally it was that body that was participating in clinical research trials studying diseases, treatments, drug interactions, and so on. Therefore, the "norms" for a healthy body are often based on a healthy white male body—one that does not menstruate, get pregnant, breastfeed or go through menopause. Many women die of curable diseases simply because they do not exhibit the same symptoms as men, and their symptoms are therefore missed by the doctor looking after them. Considering the fact that women use the health care system more often than men, it is disturbing that so much is not known about how some diseases or drugs "work" in the female body.

Why were women, until recently, excluded from clinical research trials? In the past, women, the elderly, minorities and other vulnerable populations had a long history of being abused in medical research—to such an extent that public outcry demanded stronger regulations to protect them. In response to the horrors of thalidomide (marketed in 1958), a "morning sickness" drug that was not properly tested prior to marketing, and which caused severe limb deformities in the developing fetus, as well as diethylstilbestrol (DES) administered from the 1940s until the early 1970s, a "miscarriage prevention" drug that was later revealed to cause a rare form of vaginal cancer in "DES daughters," legislation was passed to protect pregnant women and women of childbearing potential. The ethics of excluding women from medical research were questioned when basic diseases, such as heart disease (a real risk for women with Type 2 diabetes), presented in completely different ways in men than in women. For example, because men suffer from heart attacks at a much earlier age than women, heart disease suddenly became a "man's disease" even though it kills just as many women, and more women die from heart disease than any other disease. What we know about heart disease (symptoms, prevention, treatment, and so on), therefore, is based on a man's body. As I discuss in the next chapter, the symptoms of heart disease in women, and the age they present are much different. Until recently, however, few primary care doctors were able to recognize heart disease symptoms in women. Unfortunately, the same can be said for other complications of Type 2 diabetes. Only recently have studies begun to look at gender differences and this disease.

Women also report considerable psychological and emotional abuse by some male doctors, or some paternalistic male and female doctors—doctors who behave like parents, treating adult patients like children. For example, women's health complaints are often not taken seriously. Many women are given "fluffy" answers about their symptoms, told it is "PMS" or "menopause" or are sent to psychiatrists for physical symptoms.

How does all this affect women with Type 2 diabetes? Many of the doctors women will need to see when dealing with their diabetes are male. On the flip side, because of the traditional sexist roles that get played out in the health care system, most of the diabetes nurse educators and nutritionists are still female, which sometimes creates a power struggle between "doctor's orders" and ". . .but my dietitian said . . ." Many women with diabetes find conflicting viewpoints from the "male" role in diabetes (the specialist) and the "female" role in diabetes (the nurse)—even when the actors in these roles may be female doctors and male nurses. The message is simple: Ask questions about how X or Y affects *you*. Whether that "you" is pregnant, going through menopause, taking hormone replacement therapy or working shifts, only you can individualize your health care.

Diabetes is a major problem for the North American health care system. In the United States, for example, 14 percent of all health care dollars is spent on managing Type 2 diabetes. Canada reports similar statistics. As a result, there is really no such thing as one "diabetes doctor" who manages the disease completely. Your primary care physician often acts as overall supervisor of your condition, but ideally, this doctor should be working with a team of health care professionals, which includes:

- *An endocrinologist* (a doctor who specializes in the endocrine system, who understands how hormones work and interact with each other). Many endocrinologists sub-specialize in various conditions. Some do more diabetes (and may even call themselves diabetologists) than reproductive endocrinology, for example. But as a woman with diabetes, whoever is your "hormone" doctor should understand how estrogen, insulin and blood sugar interact. Don't assume your family doctor or gynaecologist knows this information.

- *A Certified Diabetes Educator* (CDE). CDEs come from a variety of backgrounds. They can be dietitians, nurses, pharmacists, social workers or any other professional in the health care system who has an interest in diabetes education. CDEs are absolutely vital to managing diabetes. They will help you gain control of your disease by teaching you how to adjust your diet, incorporate physical activity into your routine, test your blood and record the results, as well as manage any medication or insulin that's been prescribed. CDEs can be found through the Canadian Diabetes Association (see resources section at back of book), or you can be referred through your primary care doctor or endocrinologist (see page 146).

- *A dietitian:* In addition to a CDE, you should see a dietitian regularly during your first year with diabetes. If you learn to meal plan accordingly, you may be able to control your diabetes without taking any medications.

- *An exercise/fitness instructor:* This is any professional who can tailor a fitness program that suits your lifestyle and level of ability. Check with your CDE (see above), the Canadian Diabetes Association, the YMCA/HA or your local community centre for lists of fitness instructors. You do not need a referral to one; you can simply make an appointment independent of your doctor.

- *Community Health Representative* (CHR): This is someone from your community who works with you and your family, as well as with other health care professionals, to educate you about diabetes. CHRs are usually found in rural areas where access to doctors is poor. CHRs attend a four-day training session and complete a skills test. They are required to review and update their skills annually. CHRs are common in aboriginal Canadian communities.

- *Other specialists.* This is discussed further on page 153.

- *Pharmacist:* Since you may be expected to do home glucose tests, your pharmacist will recommend the right glucose meter for you, and will become a valuable source of information on drug interactions and their effects on your blood sugar. Finding a diabetes care centre in your neighbourhood is an ideal place to purchase your diabetes products and consult with a pharmacist.

While clearly there is treatment for Type 2 diabetes, it is a complex disease that can only be managed through a multi-layered approach. The goal of treatment is not just to relieve symptoms, but to prevent a range of other diseases down the road (see chapter 8). Self-managing your disease while maintaining your quality of life can only happen if you're willing to learn and to change. That means asking questions and participating in your treatment.

There are various stops along this treatment highway. How many times you stop depends on how well you can control your blood sugar. Some of you may be able to control diabetes solely through exercise and diet (chapters 5 and 6). Some of you may need to combine diet and lifestyle modification with diabetes pills, while some of you may need to use insulin to control your disease.

This chapter will guide you through the maze of treatments and health care professionals you'll encounter. It will also feed you the right questions so that you can get the right answers. Only then can you be expected to participate more fully in decisions that affect your diabetes and the rest of your life.

The Right Primary Care Doctor

A primary care doctor is the doctor you see all the time. For example, you would see this doctor for a cold, flu or an annual physical; this is the doctor who refers you to specialists.

In Canada, primary care doctors are general practitioners (four years of medical school and one year of internship), family practitioners (four years of medical school and a two-year residency in family medicine) or internists (four years of medical school and a four-year residency in internal medicine). During medical training, rotations are done in a variety of specialties, such as psychiatry, endocrinology, obstetrics and gynaecology, emergency medicine, and so on. The residency years are spent in a teaching hospital, under the supervision of teaching faculty (assistant, associate or full professors of medicine) who teach one specialty. The number of years spent in a residency program after four years of medical school varies on the university and specialty. To qualify for a specialty, such as endocrinology, a doctor must do a residency in endocrinology. After, a fellowship year is required, and that doctor must be eligible to write exams for Fellowship of the Royal College of Physicians of Canada. The letters "FRCP" stand for Fellow Royal College of Physicians. ("FRCS" stands for Fellow Royal College of Surgeons). In the United States, the "R" is replaced with "A" for American (College of Physicians/Surgeons).

Eighty percent of all people with Type 2 diabetes are cared for by their primary care doctors, but the quality of care may vary. What you'll find today is that most primary care doctors in Canada become very good at treating a few conditions. Some see a lot of patients with diabetes; others see more pregnant women; still others see more elderly patients who require palliative care. It all depends on the magic phrase "patient population." Where is the doctor's practice located? Who are the people in that neighbourhood?

Therefore, a primary care physician may not be the best doctor to manage your diabetes, if that doctor doesn't see many diabetes patients. Some doctors are also behind the times when it comes to diabetes, and do not immediately recognize early warning signs or high-risk groups. Nor do all primary care doctors counsel their patients about newer approaches to therapy, namely, self-monitoring of blood glucose levels, which though optional in Type 2 diabetes, may not be discussed as an option. (See chapter 1.)

When you're diagnosed with diabetes, ask your doctor the following questions. It will help determine whether you should stay with your doctor or look for another one:

1. *What is your philosophy about blood sugar monitoring?* Any doctor who does not discuss the option of your purchasing a glucose meter and self-monitoring your blood sugar levels may not be up-to-date. As discussed in chapter 1, the Canadian Diabetes Association recommends that people with Type 2 diabetes get into the habit of self-testing their blood sugar. A discussion about it with your doctor is warranted, even though self-testing remains optional pending more convincing data. A good family doctor should present the facts to date: "Here's what some people think;

here's what I think; here are my recommendations." Ultimately, the decision is yours.

2. ***How often will you be checking my glycosylated hemoglobin or glycohemoglobin levels?*** If your doctor says "Huh?" get out of there and find another doctor! This is a blood test (HA_{1c}) that should be done every three to six months. (Note: in Quebec, family doctors report that this test is not uniformly available.)

3. ***Will you be referring me to a specialist?*** The answer should be "Yes!" If you've been diagnosed with diabetes, you need to see other health care professionals as soon as possible: frequently, an endocrinologist who specializes in diabetes, a certified diabetes educator and a dietitian, and an opthalmologist (or optometrist if the former isn't available). (See pages 146–47 for diabetes health care team.) If your doctor says, "I can manage your condition without referring you elsewhere," get out of that office and go elsewhere.

4. ***Where can I go for more information?*** Any doctor who does not tell you to call the Canadian Diabetes Association as soon as you're diagnosed with diabetes is not worth seeing.

The alarm bells

If you hear the following words come out of your doctor's mouth, go elsewhere:

- You have borderline diabetes or "just a touch of sugar." (There's no such thing. See chapter 1.)
- You don't need to change your diet; I'll just give you a pill. (In general, no medication should be prescribed until you've been sent to a dietitian, who will work with you to modify your diet and lifestyle. In cases where medication is warranted immediately, you must still see a dietitian.)
- You don't need to see a specialist. (You *do* need to see a specialist.)
- You have a recurrent vaginal infection. This is perfectly normal. (Chronic vaginal yeast infections are a classic sign of diabetes in postmenopausal women.)

Your Diabetes Specialist

A diabetes specialist is an endocrinologist who subspecializes in diabetes. Endocrinologists are hormone specialists. Some see more thyroid patients than diabetes patients. Some specialize in reproductive endocrinology (male and female hormones). Therefore, it's important that you wind up with someone who almost exclusively manages diabetes patients. The shortest route to a diabetes specialist is to ask your primary care doctor for a referral. Another route is to call the Canadian Diabetes Association and ask them for a list of endocrinologists in your area.

If you live in an underserviced area (there are several of these in Canada!), ask people you know if they know someone with diabetes. And then call them. Who are they seeing? You may need to go outside your area to a larger city. But it's worth the trip to avoid having your diabetes mismanaged.

Your primary care doctor can continue to manage the rest of your referrals to ophthalmologists (for diabetes eye disease), podiatrists (for footcare), and so on. (See chapter 8 for more details.)

Getting Along With Your Specialist

You may find your endocrinologist a little intimidating because this doctor is more academic and may use more technical terms to explain your disease and treatment. Endocrinologists often teach or run residency programs, are active in research, frequently lecture and regularly publish articles and books in their field. These doctors are usually harder to get in touch with; they're usually booked months in advance. That's why it's crucial to maximize the time you do have. The best way to do this is to tape-record your appointment; that way, you can replay the information in the comfort of your own home. It's also important to take a list of questions with you. If there isn't time for all your questions to be answered, schedule a separate Q&A session.

Finally, ask your specialist to draw you a picture of your condition. Visualizing your disease, and seeing how various medications may interact in your body, will help you understand what's going on, and what's being recommended.

A *dozen good questions to ask*

Of course, it's difficult to prepare questions in advance when you don't know what to ask. Here are few good questions to get you started:

1. *How severe is my diabetes?* (In other words, if you are experiencing other health problems as a result of your diabetes, the disease is likely more advanced.)

2. *Does my hospital or treatment centre have a multidisciplinary diabetes education care team?* (This means that a number of health care professionals—Certified Diabetes Educators, Clinical Nurse Specialists, dietitians, endocrinologists and other relevant specialists—discuss your case together and recommend treatment options.)

3. *What treatment do you recommend, and why?* (For example, if insulin therapy is being recommended over oral hypoglycemic agents, find out why. And find out how this particular treatment will reduce the odds of complications.)

4. *How will my treatment help the risks/side effects associated with diabetes and who will help me adjust my medications or insulin?*

5. *How long do you recommend this particular treatment?* (Lifelong? On a wait-and-see basis?)

6. *What if I forget to take a pill or insulin shot? What are the consequences?*

7. *What other health problems should I look out for?* (You'll want to watch for symptoms of high or low blood sugar, as well as symptoms of long-term complications, such as eye problems or numbness in your feet.)

8. *How can I contact you between visits?*

9. *Can I take other medications? Or, how will my pills or insulin affect other medications I'm taking?*

10. *What about alcohol? How will alcohol consumption affect any pills or insulin I'm on? How do I compensate for it?*
11. *Will I be able to participate in new studies or clinical trials using new drugs or therapies?*
12. *Are there any holistic approaches I can turn to as a complement to diabetes pills or insulin therapy?*

Other Specialists

Since diabetes can involve a variety of complications down the road (see chapter 8), you may need to consult some or all of the following specialists:

Internist: This is a doctor who specializes in non-surgical treatment of a variety of medical problems, including diabetes.

Ophthalmologist: This is an eye specialist, someone who will be able to monitor your eyes and make sure that you're showing no symptoms of diabetes eye disease (see chapter 8). If you are showing symptoms, this is the specialist who will treat your condition.

Cardiologist: This is a heart specialist. People with Type 2 diabetes are four times more likely to suffer from heart attacks. You may be sent to this specialist if you are experiencing symptoms of heart disease or angina. (See chapter 8.)

Nephrologist: This is a kidney specialist. Since kidney disease is a common complication of diabetes, you may be sent to this specialist if you're showing symptoms of kidney disease (protein in your urine).

Gastroenterologist: This is a G.I. (gastrointestinal) specialist. Diabetes often results in a number of chronic gastrointestinal ailments. You may be sent to this specialist if you have symptoms of chronic heartburn, reflux and other gastric aches and pains.

Neurologist: This is a nerve specialist who will see you if you're experiencing nerve damage as a result of your diabetes.

Gerontologist: This is a doctor who specializes in diseases of the elderly. If you are over 65 and have a number of other health problems, this doctor will help you balance your various medications and conditions, in conjunction with your diabetes.

Obstetrician/Gynaecologist: If you develop diabetes during pregnancy, you'll need to be under the care of an obstetrician for the remainder of your pregnancy (see chapter 3). All women should see a gynaecologist regularly for Pap smears, breast health and consultation regarding sexual health, contraception and hormone replacement therapy after menopause. See chapters 2, 3 and 4 for more details.

Orthopedist: This is a foot doctor who can help you monitor "foot health." If you're experiencing severe problems with your feet (see chapter 8), your podiatrist may likely send you to this specialist.

When You Want a Second Opinion

Getting a second opinion means that you see two separate doctors about the same set of symptoms. If you answer yes to one of the questions below, you're probably justified in seeking a second opinion.

1. *Is the diagnosis uncertain?* If your doctor can't give you a straight answer about what's going on, you're justified in seeing someone else.
2. *Is the diagnosis life-threatening?* In this case, hearing the same news from someone else may help you cope better with your illness, or come to terms with the diagnosis.
3. *Is the treatment controversial, experimental or risky?* You might not question the diagnosis, but have problems with the recommended treatment. For example, if you're not comfortable with treatment approach A, perhaps another doctor can recommend treatment approach B.
4. *Is the treatment not working?* If your oral hypoglycemic agents can't seem to control your blood sugar levels, maybe it's time for insulin. In this case, getting a second opinion may help to clear up the problem.
5. *Are risky tests or procedures being recommended?* If you find a particular test or procedure frightening, a second opinion will either help confirm your suspicions, or confirm your original doctor's recommendations.

6. *Do you want another approach?* If you have poor control over your diabetes, your doctor may want you to begin taking insulin, while another doctor may prescribe dietary changes along with anti-diabetic medication.

7. *Is the doctor's competence in question?* If you suspect that your doctor doesn't know what he or she's doing, go somewhere else to either reaffirm your faith in your doctor or confirm your original suspicions.

Self-Service

Doctors cannot heal your diabetes; you have to do this yourself. That means you need to adjust your diet and lifestyle habits, quit smoking, and so on. Healing yourself may start with tight control over your blood sugar levels. A healthy pancreas measures its owner's blood sugar levels once a second or 3,600 times an hour. It then produces exactly the right amount of insulin for that second. In light of this, testing your blood sugar (see chapter 1 for details on blood sugar testing) may prove useful, and for now it is an option that the Canadian Diabetes Association thinks is worth considering for people with Type 2 diabetes.

You should also begin a health diary, in which you record any unusual symptoms, and the times and dates those symptoms occur. Without your diary or health record, your doctors could be working in the dark and may not be able to design the right therapy program for you.

What Your Health Diary Should Reveal

The most important information your health diary will contain is the pattern of your blood sugar's peaks and valleys. Dates and times of these peaks and valleys may be important clues to establish the pattern. Your meal plan, exercise routine and medication regimen should be tailored to anticipate these peaks and valleys. You may need to incorporate a snack to prevent a low, or go for a 20-minute walk after dinner to prevent a high. Since there are a variety of factors that can affect your blood sugar levels, your diary should also record:

- where you are in your menstrual cycle;
- any medication you're taking;
- unusually high or low readings that fall outside your pattern;
- stressful life events or situations;
- illness;
- out-of-the-ordinary happenings (no matter how insignificant);
- changes in your health insurance;
- severe insulin reactions (if you're taking insulin);
- general medical history (surgeries, tests you've had done, allergies, past drug reactions).

When to Call Your Doctor

As discussed in chapter 1, if you have Type 2 diabetes, it's important to call your doctor whenever you're sick, even with a cold or flu. Fighting off the commonest viruses will elevate your blood sugar levels and will require some juggling of your regular routine.

Until you can get in to see your doctor, stay on your meal plan. If that's not possible, drink about a half a cup of calorie-free broth or diet or regular soda every hour you are awake. Over-the-counter medications may alter your blood sugar levels unless they are sugar-free. You should also test your blood sugar every four hours to accommodate higher blood sugar levels. If you're taking any medication, stick to your usual plan and take it as prescribed at the usual times. You may need to go on insulin temporarily if your blood sugar levels remain high. This would not be the case with a cold, but may be necessary if you're laid up with a flu.

When you're not ill, but have an unusually high blood sugar reading (over 11 mmol/L), it's time to see your doctor, too.

What the Doctor Orders

Throughout the year, your managing doctor (primary care physician or endocrinologist) should be ordering a variety of blood tests to make sure that your blood sugar levels are as controlled as they can be, and that no complications from diabetes are setting in.

The Hemoglobin A_{1c} (HbA_{1c}) test

The most important test is one that checks your glycolsylated hemoglobin levels, known as the hemoglobin A_{1c} test or the HbA_{1c} test. Hemoglobin is a large molecule that carries oxygen to your bloodstream. When the glucose in your blood comes in contact with the hemoglobin molecule, it conveniently sticks to it. The more glucose stuck to your hemoglobin, the higher your blood sugar is. The HbA_{1c} test actually measures the amount of glucose stuck to hemoglobin. And since each hemoglobin molecule stays in your blood about three to four months before it is replaced, this test can show you the average blood sugar level over the last three to four months. Therefore this test is recommended at least every six months. If you have cardiovascular problems, you will need to have the HbA_{1c} test more often.

A similar test, known as a fructosamine test, can show the amount of glucose stuck to a molecule in your blood known as albumin. Albumin gets replaced every four to six weeks, however, so this test can therefore give you an average of blood sugar levels only over the last four to six weeks.

What's a good HbA_{1c} result?

Just like your glucose monitor at home, the goal of the HbA_{1c} test is to make sure that your blood sugar "average" is as close to normal as possible. Again, the closer to normal it is, the less likely you are to experience long-term diabetes complications.

This test result is slightly different than your glucose meter result. For example, an HbA_{1c} level of 7.0 percent is equal to 8 mmol/L on your blood glucose meter. A result of 9.5 percent is equivalent to 13 mmol/L on your blood glucose meter. In a person without diabetes, an HbA_{1c} ranges from 4 to 6 percent. The results are often expressed as percentages of "normal" such as <110 percent, 111 to 140 percent or >140 percent.

The new guidelines stipulate that values of 6 percent or less are good results and mean that your blood sugar is perfectly under control. Meanwhile, anything higher than 8.4 percent is alarming; this would be a poor result and means that your diabetes is not under control. Studies show that when your HbA_{1c} result is 8.4 percent or higher, you have a greater chance of developing long-term complications. In fact, for every 10 percent drop in your HbA_{1c} average (that is, 7.1 percent down from 8.1 percent), the risk of long-term complications falls by about 40 percent.

TABLE 7.1
What's a Good Glycosylated Hemoglobin Test (HbA_{1c}) result?*

NON-DIABETIC RANGE	OPTIMAL	SUBOPTIMAL	POOR CONTROL
4.0–6.0%	7.0%	7.0–8.4%	>8.4%
≤100%	≤115%	116–140%	>140%

*Based on fasting blood glucose levels.
Source: *Canadian Medical Association Journal 1998; 159(8 Suppl):S12.*

You could have a decent result, even though your blood sugar levels may be dangerously low one day and dangerously high the next.

If you suffer from sickle-cell disease or other blood disorders, the HbA_{1c} results will not be accurate, either. In this case, you may wind up with either false high or low readings.

And at any time, if your home blood sugar tests (if you've opted for self-testing) over the past two or three months do not seem to match the results of the HbA_{1c} test, be sure to check the accuracy of your meter, and perhaps show your doctor or Certified Diabetes Educator how you are using the device in case your technique needs refining.

Other Important Tests

It's important to have the following routine tests at least once a year, and more often if you are at high risk for complications.

Glucose meter check-up

If you've opted to test your own blood sugar, it's important to compare your home glucose meter's test results to a laboratory blood glucose test. In fact, it's a good idea to do this every six months. All you do is bring your meter to the lab when you're having a blood glucose test done. After the lab technician takes your blood, do your own test within about five minutes and record the result. Your meter is working perfectly as long as your result is within 15 percent of the lab test (if your meter is testing whole blood as opposed to plasma).

Blood pressure

High blood pressure can put you at greater risk for cardiovascular problems (see chapter 1). Diabetes can also cause high blood pressure. That's why it's important to have your blood pressure checked every four to six months.

Kidney tests

One of the most common complications of diabetes is kidney disease, known in this case as diabetic nephropathy (diabetic kidney disease). This condition develops slowly over the course of many years, but there are usually few symptoms or warning signs. To make sure no damage to the kidneys has occurred, it's important to have your urine tested regularly to check the health of your kidneys.

Cholesterol

High cholesterol is a problem for people with diabetes (see chapter 1), while diabetes can also trigger high cholesterol. Your cholesterol is checked through a simple blood test that should be done once upon diagnosis, and once a year thereafter. See Table 7.2 for more details.

TABLE 7.2
Checking Your Cholesterol

	GOOD	POOR
Total Cholesterol	below 5.2	above 6.2
LDL Cholesterol	below 3.4	above 4.1
HDL Cholesterol	above 1.1	below 1.0
Triglycerides	below 2.0	above 2.6

Foot exam

When you have diabetes, nerve damage and poor circulation can wreak havoc on your feet. Be sure to have a thorough foot exam each year to check for reduced sensation or feeling, circulation, evidence of callouses or sores. (See chapter 8 for more details.)

Eye exam

Since diabetes can cause what's known as diabetes eye disease or diabetic retinopathy (damage to the back of your eye), annual eye exams are crucial. Your eye exam should also rule out cataracts and glaucoma.

When caught early, laser treatment can be used to treat diabetic eye disease, and prevent blindness. If your exam uses the term "absent" on your chart, it means your retina is just fine. If you see the word "background," it means that mild changes have occurred to your eye(s) and that you need more regular monitoring. If the terms "pre-proliferative" or "proliferative" are used, it means that there is some damage to one or both eyes and you will require treatment and regular exams. (See chapter 8 for more details.)

When Your Doctor Tells You to Take a Pill

When diet and lifestyle changes make no impact on your blood sugar levels, your doctor may prescribe pills. This section provides you with an overview of the kinds of pills prescribed for Type 2 diabetes, who should take them, appropriate dosages, side effects and questions to ask your doctor and/or pharmacist.

Before you fill your prescription for anti-diabetic pills, you should know that between 40 to 50 percent of all people with Type 2 diabetes require insulin therapy after 10 years. Continuing insulin resistance may cause you to stop responding to oral medications. Be aware that these pills are meant to complement your meal plan, exercise routine and glucose monitoring; they are not a substitute.

Bear in mind, too, that physicians who prescribe the medications discussed below, but who do not work with you to modify your diet and lifestyle, are not managing your diabetes properly. These medications should be prescribed only after you've been unsuccessful in managing your Type 2 diabetes through lifestyle modification and frequent blood sugar testing.

If you cannot get down to a healthy body weight, you are probably a good candidate for anti-diabetic medication. And any woman with Type 2 diabetes who cannot control her blood sugar levels despite lifestyle changes is also a good candidate.

There are four kinds of medications that may be prescribed to you. It's crucial to note, however, that these medications can only be prescribed to people who still produce insulin. They have no effect on people with Type 1 diabetes, or insulin-dependent diabetes.

Oral Hypoglycemic Agents (OHAs)

Sulphonylureas (for example, chlorpropamide and glibenclamide) are pills that help your pancreas release more insulin. These pills are known as oral hypoglycemic agents (OHAs) and account for about 75 percent of all prescriptions for people with Type 2 diabetes. This medication can make your insulin-producing cells more sensitive to glucose and stimulate them to secrete more insulin, which will lower your blood sugar. If your average blood glucose levels are greater than 8 mmol/L, you will likely be prescribed an OHA.

Biguanides (Metformin) are pills that help your insulin work better. These pills primarily stop your liver from producing glucose, which will help to lower your blood sugar levels and increase glucose uptake by your muscle tissue. These pills also help your tissues respond better to your insulin. Ultimately, biguanides can lower pre-meal and postmeal blood sugar levels in about 75 to 80 percent of women with Type 2 diabetes. This medication also seems to lower the "bad" cholesterol levels. These pills do not increase insulin levels and will not directly cause low blood sugar.

Initially, 75 percent of women with Type 2 diabetes will respond well to sulphonylureas, while biguanides will lower blood sugar in 80 percent of women with Type 2 diabetes. But about 15 percent of all women treated with OHAs fail to respond to them at all, while 3 to 5 percent of all women on OHAs will stop responding to them each year. So don't get too comfortable on these pills.

Sulphonylureas would generally be the initial oral agent of choice in women who are not obese and/or have high blood sugar levels (or suffer from symptoms of high blood sugar). A biguanide is appropriate in women who are obese and have milder levels of high blood sugar. That's because biguanides do not result in the weight gain that is typically associated with sulphonylusea and insulin therapy.

Dosages for sulphonylureas

There is no fixed dosage for sulphonylureas. It all depends on your brand. For example, it's perfectly common to take anything from 80 to 320 mg a day. If you are taking a dosage higher than the recommended initial dose, indicated in Table 7.3, you should divide your dose into two equal parts. Your pills should be taken before or with meals, and your doctor should start you on the lowest effective dose. If your blood sugar levels are high when you start your pills, it's a good idea to have a short trial period of about six to eight weeks to make sure your medication is working.

TABLE 7.3
Sulphonylureas, a common class of oral hypoglycemic agent

	DAILY/MG	INITIAL	PER DAY
Acetohexamide*	250–1,500	250	1–2
Chlorpropamide*	100–500	250	1
Gliclazide**	40–320	160	1–2
Glyburide**	2.5–20	5	1–2
Tolbutamide*	500–3,000	1,000	1–3

First generation-not prescribed very much
Second generation-more commonly prescribed

Source: *Compendium of Pharmaceuticals and Specialities*, 1996.

Dosages for biguanides (Metformin)

There is only one biguanide available in Canada, which goes by the trade name Metformin. Metformin works by decreasing glucose production in the liver and increasing glucose uptake into muscle cells. In this case, the usual dose is 500 mg, 3 or 4 times a day, or 850 mg, 2 or 3 times a day. Your dose is not to exceed 2.5 grams a day. If you're elderly, a lower dose will probably be prescribed.

When OHAs should not be used

If you've had Type 2 diabetes longer than ten years, this is not the time to start OHAs. And, of course, nobody with Type 1 or insulin-dependent diabetes (IDDM) should ever take OHAs; they will not work. OHAs should never be taken under the following conditions, either:

- alcoholism;
- pregnancy;
- kidney or liver failure (Metformin only).

Side effects

Sixty percent of people taking OHAs continue to have high blood sugar levels two hours after meals. These pills can also cause increased appetite and weight gain. However, the main side effect with first-generation OHAs (see Table 7.3) is hypoglycemia (low blood sugar), which occurs in 1 in 5 people treated with OHAs. If you're over age 60, hypoglycemia may occur more often, which is why it's dangerous for anyone over age 70 to take certain OHAs.

About one-third of all people taking OHAs experience gastro-intestinal side effects (no appetite, nausea, abdominal discomfort and, with Metformin, diarrhea). Adjusting dosages and taking your pills with your meals or afterward often clears up these symptoms.

OHAs *and hypoglycemia*

About 15 to 30 percent of all people taking sulphonylureas are vulnerable to hypoglycemia (low blood sugar) because this drug stimulates the pancreas to produce insulin. This is synonymous with taking an insulin injection. Furthermore, if you lose weight after you begin taking sulphonylureas, but don't lower your pill dosage, you could also experience hypoglycemic episodes. This occurs because losing weight will make your body more responsive to insulin.

Yet, biguanides do not typically cause hypoglycemic episodes, since they work by preventing the liver from making glucose rather than stimulating anything to make insulin. Similarly, acarbose (see below) does not, by itself, cause hypoglycemia. It works by delaying the breakdown of starch and sucrose into glucose. That's not to say, however, that you can't develop hypoglycemia if you're taking biguanides or acarbose; you can still develop it if you miss meals, snacks or over-exercise without compensating for it, although this is rare.

Your diabetes pills may also react with other medications. For example, some of the older OHAs may work less or more effectively when combined with certain medications including blood thinners (anticoagulants), oral contraceptives, diuretics, steroids, aspirin and various anticonvulsive or antihypertensive medications.

Another factor is the half-life of your oral medication. By knowing when the drug peaks in your body, you'll be able to prevent hypoglycemia from occurring. For example, tolbutamide is a short-acting oral hypoglycemic agent. It begins to work about 1 hour after you take it and lasts for about 12 hours, peaking between 5 to 6 hours after you ingest it. Acetohexamide starts working about 1 hour after you take it, stays in your body for about 14 hours and peaks at about 5 hours. Glyburide goes to work in about 1.5 hours, stays in your body for 24 hours and peaks at about 3 hours. Finally, chlorpropamide has the longest half-life. It starts to work 1 hour after you take it, stays in your body for 72 hours and peaks within 35 hours.

Roughly 40 percent of all people taking a combination of OHAs experience hypoglycemic episodes, while 33 to 47 percent of people who combine insulin with sulphonylureas experience hypoglycemic episodes. These are higher odds than if you were taking one oral hypoglycemic agent only.

Acarbose (a.k.a. alpha-glucosidase inhibitors)

Acarbose (a.k.a. Prandase) are alpha-glucosidase inhibitors that delay the breakdown of sugar in your meal. Introduced in 1996, acarbose is the first anti-diabetic medication to come along since the mid-1950s, when sulphonylureas and biguanides were developed. Acarbose is very similar in structure to the sugars found in foods. The main sugar in blood, glucose, is a simple sugar that is made from starch and sucrose (table sugar). Starch and sucrose are turned into glucose by alphaglucosidases, enzymes in the lining of the small intestine. Acarbose stalls this process by forcing the starch and sugar you eat to "take a number" before they're converted into glucose. Why do this? Well, this will slow down the absorption of glucose into the cells, preventing a rise in blood glucose after a meal. However, to be effective, acarbose must be taken with the first bite of each main meal. You'll also need to test your blood sugar two hours after eating to see how well you're responding to the medication.

Acarbose is prescribed to people who cannot seem to get their after-meal (that is, postmeal or postprandial) blood sugar levels down to acceptable levels. A major benefit of acarbose is that it may reduce the risk of hypoglycemic episodes during the night, particularly in insulin users. Investigators are studying whether acarbose may be used one day as a substitute for that "morning insulin." The usual rules apply here: acarbose should complement your meal plan and exercise routine; it is not a substitute or way out, and does not, by itself, cause hypoglycemia.

Who should take acarbose?

- anyone who cannot control her blood sugar through diet and lifestyle modification alone;
- anyone who is on OHAs but is still experiencing high blood sugar levels after meals;
- anyone who cannot take OHAs and in whom diet/lifestyle modification has failed;
- anyone not doing well on an OHA, who wants to prevent the advent of starting insulin treatment.

Who should not take acarbose?

Anyone with the following conditions should not be taking this drug:

- inflammation or ulceration of the bowel (that is, inflammatory bowel disease, ulcerative colitis or Crohn's disease);
- any kind of bowel obstruction;
- any gastrointestinal disease;
- kidney or liver disorders;
- hernias;
- pregnancy or lactation;
- Type 1 diabetes.

Dosage

The usual starting dosage for acarbose is 25 mg (half of a 50-mg tablet), with the first bite of each main meal. After four to eight weeks, your dosage may be increased to 50 mg, three times a day. Or you may start by taking one 50-mg tablet once daily with supper. If that's not working, you'll move up to two 50-mg tablets twice daily with your main meals or three 50-mg three times daily, with main meals. The maximum dosage of acarbose shouldn't go beyond 100 mg three times a day.

As mentioned above, for best results, it's crucial that you take acarbose with the first bite of each main meal. In fact, if you swallow your pill even five to ten minutes before a meal, acarbose will pass through your digestive system and have no effect. It's also important that you take acarbose with a carbohydrate; the medication doesn't work if there are no carbohydrates in your meal. You shouldn't take acarbose between meals, either; it won't work. Nor should acarbose be used as a weight-loss drug.

Side effects

The good news is that acarbose doesn't cause hypoglycemia. However, since you may be taking this drug along with an OHA, you may still experience hypoglycemia, as acarbose doesn't prevent it, either. (See chapter 1 for warning signs and treatment for hypoglycemia.)

The only side effects that acarbose, by itself, causes are gastrointestinal: gas, abdominal cramps, softer stools or diarrhea. Acarbose combined with Metformin, however, can produce unacceptable gastrointestinal symptoms. You'll notice these side effects after you've consumed foods that contain lots of sugar. Avoid taking antacids; they won't be effective in this case. Adjusting the dosage and making sure you're taking acarbose correctly will usually take care of the side effects.

Thiazoladinediones (Troglitazone or Rezulin)

Thiazoladinediones (troglitazone or Rezulin) are pills that make your cells more sensitive to insulin, thereby improving insulin resistance. When this happens, more glucose gets into your tissues and less glucose hangs around in your blood. The result is that you'll have lower fasting blood glucose levels, without the need to increase insulin levels.

Troglitazone works by stimulating muscle tissue to "drink in" glucose. It also decreases glucose production from the liver, and makes fat tissue more receptive to glucose. This drug is reserved for people with Type 2 diabetes who must take insulin to reduce their blood sugar levels. Troglitazone is being touted as a new wonder drug because you only need one tablet a day for the pill to work its wonders. Researchers are investigating troglitazone as a drug that can delay or prevent the onset of Type 2 diabetes altogether. Clinical trials suggest that troglitazone is effective in just a single daily dose of 200-, 400-, 600- or 800-mg tablets. You can also split a dosage into two, such as 200 or 400 mg twice daily. One study showed that one 400-mg tablet every morning for a six-week period improved blood sugar to normal readings in 75 percent of study participants. After 12 weeks of treatment, 80 percent of study participants with high blood sugar showed normal glucose levels.

It may all be too good to be true. Warnings about troglitazone have been issued because it can cause liver failure. In early studies (these were "controlled" trials), 1.9 percent of people developed mild liver problems. As soon as the drug was more widely prescribed, the U.S. Food and Drug Administration received reports of several cases of severe liver disease that led to death or the need for a liver transplant. For example, in one case, after a 55-year-old woman using insulin was on a daily dose of 400 mg of troglitazone for about three months, she developed liver failure. Therefore, *please* ask your doctor about the risks of this drug if it's prescribed. If you've ever had hepatitis (A, B or C), you should not take this drug. There are a number of other factors in your history that may prevent you from being on the drug, which you must discuss with your doctor.

Other side effects

When taken at doses of 600 and 800 mg a day, troglitazone can raise LDL ("bad") cholesterol. Anyone with cardiovascular problems should not be on this drug. In clinical trials, white blood cell counts also went down in people taking the highest dosage of 800 mg daily. Therefore, high doses of this drug are not recommended for people who are immune-suppressed for any reason, and the drug may also trigger an infection in healthy people as a result. Headaches were also reported in users, but for the most part, troglitazone is a well-tolerated drug with a low incidence of adverse side effects.

Natural Alternatives

If you don't like the idea of taking pills to control your diabetes, you can try to use more natural methods. You'll have to discuss this approach with your doctor, of course, but here are some options:

- Guar gum. This is a high source of fibre (which is a poly-saccharide), made from the seeds of the Indian cluster bean. When you mix guar with water, it turns into a gummy gel, which slows down your digestive system, similar in effect to acarbose. Guar has often been used as a natural substance to treat high blood sugar as well as high cholesterol. Guar can cause gas, some stomach ache, nausea and diarrhea. (These are also side effects of acarbose.) The problem with guar is that there are no scientific studies, to date, concluding that it improves blood sugar control. Nevertheless, most experts agree that it can certainly provide some marginal benefits.
- Delay glucose absorption by eating more fibre, avoiding table sugar (sucrose) and eating smaller meals more often to space out your calories. Meal planning is discussed in detail in chapter 6.

Questions to Ask About Diabetes Drugs

Before you fill your prescription, it's important to ask your doctor or pharmacist the following question:

1. *What does this drug contain?* If you are allergic to particular ingredients, such as dyes, it's important to find out the drug's ingredients before you take it.
2. *Are there any medications I shouldn't combine with this drug?* Be sure to ask about interactions with cholesterol or hypertension medications, as well as interactions with antidepressants or antipsychotics.
3. *If this drug doesn't work well, am I a candidate for combination therapy?* This means that your drug could be combined with another drug. Common combo-platters include: a sulphonylurea

and biguanide; acarbose and an OHA. Either the first drug you
started is raised to its maximum dosage, before the second drug
is started at its lowest dosage, or both drugs are started at their
lowest dosages and then raised gradually.

4. *If this drug doesn't work well, would insulin ever be prescribed
along with this pill?* It remains controversial whether combining
insulin with a pill has any benefits. Nevertheless, some studies
have shown that there is some benefit.

5. *How will you measure the effectiveness of my drug?* You should be
testing your blood sugar with a glucose monitor, particularly
two hours after eating, to make sure that the lowest effective dose
can be prescribed. Your doctor should also be doing a glycosylated
hemoglobin or HbA_{1c} test two to three times a year (see above).

6. *How should I store my drugs?* All pills should be kept in a dry place
at a temperature between 15°C and 25°C. Keep these drugs away
from children, don't give them out as "samples" to your sister-in-
law and don't use tablets beyond their expiry date.

7. *What symptoms should I watch out for while on these drugs?* You'll
definitely want to watch for signs of high or low blood sugar.

When Your Doctor Prescribes Insulin

First, let me dispel a common fear about insulin: since insulin is not
a blood product, you don't have to worry about being infected with a
blood-borne virus such as HIV or hepatitis.

Many doctors often delay insulin therapy for as long as possible by
giving you maximum doses of the pills discussed above. This isn't considered good diabetes management. If you need insulin, you should
take insulin. The goal is to get your disease under control. Therefore,
anyone with the following conditions is a candidate for insulin:

- high blood sugar levels, despite maximum doses of oral hypoglycemic agents;

- fasting glucose levels consistently over 9 mmol/l;
- illness or stress (insulin may be needed until you recover);
- major surgery;
- complications of diabetes (see chapter 8);
- pregnancy (insulin may be temporary).

If going on insulin might affect your job security, you should discuss this with your doctor so that appropriate notes or letters can be drafted to whom it may concern. You should also keep in mind that if insulin therapy does not bring your diabetes under control within six months of treatment, it may be necessary to return to your drug therapy after all.

Right now, 40 to 50 percent of all people with Type 2 diabetes require insulin injections to manage their condition. Until troglitazone is more widely prescribed and in use (see page 167), this is the reality. Insulin resistance eventually may lead to your requiring insulin from an outside source. You'll need to discuss the various insulins available with your doctor, as well as be trained in giving yourself insulin injections.

The Right Insulin

The newest insulin is known as Insulin lispro, an insulin analogue ("copycat"). This is a synthetic insulin that does not have an animal or human source. It's made by reversing the order of two amino acids (LYS and PRO) in the human insulin molecule.

With traditional human insulins (animal insulin is not readily available, but is discussed below), you need to be extremely good at calculating when you're going to eat, how much you're going to eat and how much insulin to inject. Basically, you need to be in excellent control of your diabetes. The problem with traditional, longer-acting insulin is that you can wind up with too much of it in your system, which can cause insulin shock, or hypoglycemia (low blood sugar). Insulin lispro is a very short-acting insulin, which means that you inject it about 15 minutes before you eat (while you're cooking dinner or when you're ordering food in a restaurant). Therefore some experts consider it an easier insulin to work with.

That said, insulin is highly individualized. It's simply not possible for me to tell you which insulin you need to be on any more than I can tell you what, exactly, you need to eat each day. This is why a diabetes health care team is so crucial. Your meal plans, medications and insulin (when needed) are tailored to suit *you*. And that has everything to do with who you are, not which brand of insulin is popular.

The goal of a good insulin program is to try to mimic what your pancreas would do if it were working properly. Blood sugar rises in a sort of wave pattern. The big waves come in after a big meal; the small waves come in after a small meal or snack. The insulin program needs to be matched to your own particular wave pattern. So what you eat— and when—has a lot to do with the right insulin program. Therefore, the right insulin for someone who eats three square meals a day may not be appropriate for someone who tends to graze all day. And the right insulin for an active 47-year-old woman in a stressful job may not be the right insulin for a 67-year-old woman who does not work, and whose heart condition prevents her from exercising regularly. To determine the appropriate insulin recipe for you, your health care team should look at who you are as a person—what you eat, where you work (do you work shifts?), your willingness to change your eating habits and other lifestyle factors.

You and your health care team will also have to decide how much control you need over your blood sugar. Insulin recipes depend on whether you need tight control (3 to 6 mmol), medium control (4 to 10 mmol) and even loose control (11 to 13 mmol). Loose control is certainly not encouraged, but on rare occasions, when a woman is elderly and suffering from a number of other health problems, it is still done.

There are many kinds of insulins available. Every manufacturer has a different brand name of insulin, and a separate letter code for the insulin action. See Table 7.4 for a translation of these codes. Once you and your diabetes health care team choose the right insulin for you, you will need to have a minicourse on how to use and inject insulin. This is usually done by a certified diabetes educator (CDE).

TABLE 7.4
Breaking the Codes

R: This stands for "regular" biosynthetic human insulin. Regular means that it is short-acting insulin.

"ge" Toronto: "ge" is the name Connaught-Novo gives to all of its biosynthetic insulin. It stands for "genetically engineered." Toronto is the brand name of this company's short-acting insulin, like "Kraft" or "President's Choice."

Insulin Lispro: This is a very new and "super short-acting" insulin under the brand name Humalog, which starts to work in 15 to 30 minutes. It is a biosynthetic insulin made from two amino acids, LYS and PRO. It's ideal for people with Type 1 diabetes.

N or NPH: "NPH" are simply the initials of the man who invented this type of insulin, which is an intermediate-acting insulin that is said to have an "abrupt" peak. ("ge-NPH" stands for genetically engineered NPH.)

L or Lente: This is also an intermediate-acting insulin that is very similar to NPH except it has a more "lumbering" peak. ("ge-Lente" stands for genetically engineered Lente.)

Beef/pork: This is animal insulin made from cows or pigs. It's still available in Canada from Eli Lilly but isn't readily available at most pharmacies unless it's a special order.

Humulin 10/90: This is a premixed insulin, meaning that it is 10 percent regular and 90 percent NPH. Also available in 20/80, 30/70, 40/60 and 50/50. (Note: Many people with Type 2 diabetes do well on 30/70.)

Novolin 10/90 "ge": Exactly the same as above, except "ge," which stands for genetically engineered, is the label Connaught-Novo gives to its biosynthetic insulin.

Novolin ultra "ge": Connaught-Novo's long-acting insulin, which starts acting in 4 hours, peaks within 8–24 hours and exits within 28 hours. Again, "ge" stands for genetically engineered.

Ultra Lente "ge": The same as above except it peaks in 10–30 hours and exits in 36 hours.

Semi Lente-NPH: This is a very long-acting insulin that is rarely used. Most diabetes educators haven't seen someone on this stuff for years!

Human insulin

All human insulin is biosynthetic, which means that the biochemically created "product" normally made by the human pancreas has been re-created in a test tube through DNA technology.

Today, most manufacturers produce only these insulins, which are considered the purest form of insulin available. Human insulins come in three different actions: short-acting (clear fluid), intermediate-acting (cloudy fluid) and long-acting (cloudy fluid). Short-acting means that it stays in your body for the shortest duration of time; long-acting means that it stays in your body for the longest duration of time. (See Table 7.5.)

Beef/Pork insulin

The only people who should be on animal insulin are those who began using it years ago. These are likely people with Type 1 diabetes who developed a rhythm with their animal insulin and are reluctant to switch to human insulin or an insulin analogue. If you're newly diagnosed with Type 2 diabetes, or you have just started to take insulin, this is not the right insulin for you. Animal insulin is less pure and shows a higher incidence of hypoglycemia. If you're currently on animal insulin and would like to switch, you must discuss this with your managing physician first. On the flip side, you shouldn't feel pressured into switching insulins if you're happy on animal insulin.

Premixed insulin

Premixed insulin means that both the short-acting insulin and the intermediate-acting insulin are mixed together. These are extremely popular insulins for people with Type 2 diabetes for reasons explained in Table 8.5. These work well for people who have a very set routine and don't want to take more than one or two insulin injections daily.

Both human and animal insulin are available in premixed formats. They are labelled as 10/90 (10 percent short-acting; 90 percent intermediate-acting), 20/80, 30/70, 40/60 and 50/50. Premixed insulin is always cloudy. It's also possible to mix together short-acting with long-acting, or long-acting with intermediate-acting.

Your insulin gear
If you've graduated to insulin therapy, here's what you'll need to buy:
- a really good glucose monitor that is made for people who test frequently (see chapter 1);
- lancets and a lancing device for testing your blood sugar (see chapter 1);
- insulin pens and cartridges or traditional needles and syringes (a diabetes educator will need to walk you through the types of products available);
- the right insulin brand for you

Learning to Use Insulin

Insulin must be injected. It cannot be taken orally because your own stomach acids digest the insulin before it has a chance to work. Your doctor, pharmacist, CDE or someone at a diabetes care centre will teach you how to self-inject painlessly. Don't inject insulin by yourself without a training session. The most convenient way to use insulin is with an insulin pen. In this case, your insulin (if human or biosynthetic) will come in a cartridge. If you decide against a pen, your insulin will come in a bottle and you will need a needle and syringe. Always know the answers to these questions before you inject your insulin:
1. How long does it take before the insertion starts to work? (Known as the *onset of action*.)
2. When is this insulin working the hardest? (Known as the *peak*.)
3. How long will this insulin continue to work? (Known as the *duration of action*.)

How many injections will I need?

The number of injections you will need really depends on what kind of insulin you're taking and why you're taking it. A sample routine may be to take an injection in the morning, a second injection before supper and a third before bed. What you want to prevent is low blood sugar while you're sleeping. You may need to adjust your insulin if there is a change in your food or exercise routine (which could happen if you're sick). Your insulin schedule is usually carefully matched to your meal times and exercise periods.

Where to inject it

The good news is that you do not have to inject insulin into a vein. As long as it makes it under your skin or in a muscle, you're fine. Thighs and tummies are popular injection sites. These are also large enough areas that you can vary your injection site. (You should space your injections about 2 to 3 cm apart.) Usually you establish a little rotating pattern. Other injection sites are the upper outer area of the arms, the upper outer surfaces of the buttocks and lower back areas. Insulin injected in the abdomen is absorbed more quickly than insulin injected in the thigh. In addition, strenuous exercise will speed up the rate of absorption of insulin if the insulin is injected into the limb you've just "worked out." Other factors that can affect insulin's action is the depth of injection, your dose, the temperature (it should be room temperature or body temperature) and what animal your insulin came from (human, cow or pig).

Experts also suggest you massage the injection site to increase the rate of insulin absorption. If you notice a hardening of skin due to overuse, this will affect the rate of absorption. Your doctor or CDE will show you how to actually inject your insulin (angles, pinching folds of skin, and so on). There are lots of tricks of the trade to optimize comfort. With the fine needle points available today, this doesn't have to be an uncomfortable ordeal.

TABLE 7.5

Getting to Know Your Insulin

Short-Acting Insulin (This is the "hare." It gets there fast but tires easily.)

Starts working in: 30 minutes (Insulin lispro: <15 to 30 minutes)

Peaks in: 2 to 4 hours. (Insulin lispro: 30 minutes to 2.5 hours)

Duration of action: 6 to 8 hours (Insulin lispro: 3 to 4 hours)

When to eat: within 30 minutes of injecting

Peak effect (maximum action): 1 to 5 hours

Exits body in: 8 hours.

Appearance: Clear. Don't use if cloudy, slightly coloured or if solid chunks are visible.

Intermediate-acting insulin (This is the "tortoise." It gets there at a slower pace, but it lasts longer.)

Starts working in: 1 to 2 hours

Peaks in: 4 to 12 hours (usually around 8 or less)

Duration of action: 24 hours (or less)

When to eat: within 2 hours

Exits body in: 24 hours

Appearance: Cloudy. Do not use if the white material remains at the bottom of the bottle after mixing, leaving a clear liquid above; or if clumps are floating in the insulin after mixing; or if it has a "frosted" appearance.

Long-acting insulin (This is the "two-legged turtle." It's really slow. And it hangs around for a long time.)

Starts working in: 8 hours

Peaks in: 18 hours

Duration of action: 36 hours

When to eat: Within 8 hours

Exits body in: 36 hours or more

Appearance: Cloudy. Do not use if the white material remains at the bottom of the bottle after mixing, leaving a clear liquid above; or if clumps are floating in the insulin after mixing; or if it has a "frosted" appearance.

For information about brand names, premixed insulins and specific products, consult your doctor, pharmacist, diabetes educator or insulin manufacturer.

Side effects

The main side effect of insulin therapy is low blood sugar, which means that you must eat or drink glucose to combat symptoms. This side effect is also known as insulin shock. Low blood sugar or hypoglycemia is discussed in chapter 1.

You may also notice something called lipodystrophy (a change in the fatty tissue under the skin) or hypertrophy (an enlarged area on your skin). Rotating your injection sites will prevent these problems. A sunken area on your skin surface may also occur, but is usually only present with animal insulin. Rashes can sometimes occur at injection sites, too. Less than 5 percent of all insulin users notice these problems.

Questions to Ask About Insulin

The answers to the following questions will depend on your insulin brand. Pharmacists and doctors should know the answers to all these questions; if they don't, I recommend calling the customer care 1-800 number provided by your insulin manufacturer.

- How do I store this insulin?
- What are the characteristics of this insulin (that is, onset of action, peak and duration of action)?
- When should I eat after injecting this insulin?
- When should I exercise after injecting this insulin?
- How long are opened insulin bottles/cartridges safe at room temperature?
- What about the effect of sunlight or extreme temperatures on this insulin?
- Should this insulin be shaken or rolled?
- What should I do if the insulin sticks to the inside of the vial/cartridge?
- Should this insulin be clear or cloudy? And what should I do if the appearance looks "off" or has changed?
- What happens if I accidentally inject out-of-date insulin?

- What other medications can interfere with this particular brand?
- Who should I see about switching insulin brands?
- If I've switched from animal to human insulin, what dose should I be on?

Travelling with Insulin

When travelling, make sure you pack enough insulin for your trip, as well as identification (a doctor's note) that clearly states you have diabetes, so you don't get harassed over carrying needles, syringes and vials. In fact, many experts suggest that for a trip, you switch to an insulin pen, which is far easier to carry and less obvious. In some cases, even lancets and a glucose meter may be suspect without identification. Experts recommend the following supplies for travel:

- a back-up supply of insulin, as well as extra cartridges, needles, syringes and testing supplies; vials break, baggage gets lost and planes, trains or buses get delayed;
- a doctor's written prescription for your insulin and a doctor's note explaining why you're carrying your equipment;
- a Medic Alert tag or card stating that you have diabetes;
- a day's supply of food (especially if you're flying);
- an extra sugar source, such as dextrose tablets;
- a list of hospitals in your travel-destination areas.

It's also important never to part with your insulin; always carry it with you in carry-on baggage. Dividing your supplies between two bags is best in case vials break. If you're flying, drink lots of liquids prior to boarding, as well as one glass of non-alcoholic liquid for every hour of flight. And don't order a special meal; these have a nasty habit of never making it to your plane. Bring food with you and pick at the plane food you're served. You should also stroll up and down the cabin as much as possible to avoid high blood sugar. (This bit of exercise will use up some sugar.) If you're travelling to a different time zone, consult your doctor or diabetes educator about adjusting insulin injections to the new time zone.

■ ■ ■

Why are you going through the maze of information in this chapter?
To prevent further complications of diabetes, and to prepare yourself
for dealing with even more doctors and medications should complications happen down the road—the topic of the next chapter.

TABLE 7.6

**Drugs that may complicate your diabetes, diabetes medications
or insulin**

Please discuss side effects with your doctor and pharmacist if you're
taking any of the following:

Estrogen: this raises blood sugar level.

Diuretics: they raise blood sugar level.

Beta blockers: they keep the body from releasing its own sugar in
response to hypoglycemia (low blood sugar).

Steroids: they raise blood sugar level.

Nonsteroidal anti-inflammatory drug (NSAID): they raise blood sugar levels.

Seizure medications: some raise blood sugar levels.

Chapter 8

WOMEN DOWN THE

DIABETES ROAD

Why is it so important to manage your diabetes? Because many of the pre-existing conditions that led to your diabetes (see chapter 1) can cause other complications down the road. On top of that, walking around with higher-than-normal blood sugar levels can lead to even more complications.

At least 40 percent of all people with Type 2 will develop another disease as a result of their diabetes. Many of you may already be affected by some of the conditions discussed in this chapter. If you've been newly diagnosed with Type 2 diabetes, you may not realize exactly how many other diseases can be triggered by it; after all, you may feel fine now. The purpose of this chapter is to simplify the complicated language of "complications" so you can see what's possible down the road, clearly read the road signs and perhaps take a different route. You'll find out why diabetes leads to other diseases, the diagnosis and treatment of each of those diseases and what can be done to prevent complications.

Macro versus Micro

The most important thing to grasp about diabetes complications is that there are two kinds of problems that can lead to similar diseases. The first kind of problem is known as a macrovascular complication. The prefix "macro" means LARGE, as in macroeconomics (studying an entire economic system as opposed to one company's economic structure). The word "vascular" means blood vessels—your veins and arteries, which carry the blood back and forth throughout your body. Put it together and you have "large blood vessel complications." A plain-language interpretation of macrovascular complications would be: "BIG problems with your blood vessels."

If you think of your body as a planet, a macrovascular disease would be a disease that affects the whole planet; it is body-wide, or systemic. Cardiovascular disease is a macrovascular complication, which can cause heart attack, stroke, high blood pressure and body-wide circulation problems, clinically known as peripheral vascular disease (PVD). So your body, head to toe, is affected (see page 184).

The second kind of problem is known as a microvascular complication. The prefix "micro" means tiny, as in microscopic. Microvascular complications refer to problems with the smaller blood vessels (a.k.a. capillaries) that connect to various body parts. A plain-language interpretation of microvascular complications would be: "Houston, we've got a problem." In other words, the problem is serious, but it's not going to affect the whole planet, just the spacecraft in orbit. Eye disease (clinically known as retinopathy) is a microvascular complication. Blindness is a serious problem, but you won't die from it. Nerve damage (neuropathy) is a microvascular complication that can affect your whole body—feet, eyes, sexual functioning, skin—but again, you won't die from it.

The Combo Platter

Here's where complications get really complicated to understand: when macro and micro converge. This is what happens with kidney disease (clinically known as renal disease nephropathy). The high blood pressure that is caused by macrovascular complications, combined with the small blood vessel damage caused by microvascular complications, together, can cause kidney failure—something you can die from unless you have dialysis (filtering out the body's waste products through a machine) or a kidney transplant.

Who Gets Microvascular Complications?

People with Type 1 diabetes are very vulnerable to microvascular complications, but a good portion of people with Type 2 diabetes suffer from them, too. Microvascular complications are known as the sugar-related complications. The small blood vessel damage is caused by high blood sugar levels over long periods of time. The Diabetes Control and Complications Trial (DCCT), discussed in detail at the end of this chapter, showed that by keeping blood sugar levels as normal as possible, as often as possible, through frequent self-testing, microvascular complications can be prevented.

Warning signs of microvascular problems
Numbness in arms, face or legs, vision problems, bladder infections and other bladder problems are warning signs of microvascular problems. Specific alarm signals for each microvascular problem are discussed in Head to Toe section, below.

Who Gets Macrovascular Complications?

Macrovascular complications are caused not only by too much blood sugar, but also by pre-existing health problems. People with

Type 2 diabetes are far more vulnerable to macrovascular compli-cations because they usually have contributing risk factors from way back when, such as high cholesterol and high blood pressure, both of which are discussed in chapter 1. Obesity, smoking and inactiv-ity can then aggravate those problems, resulting in major cardio-vascular disease.

Warning signs of macrovascular complications

If you are obese, inactive, have Type 2 diabetes as well as high blood pressure and/or high cholesterol, you are in danger of developing macrovascular problems. The bomb is ticking. In this case, you should be working on making changes in your diet and lifestyle, and discuss with your doctor whether you're a candidate for blood-pressure-lowering or cholesterol-lowering medication. If you're a woman entering menopause, you should definitely consider hormone replacement therapy, which offers protection from heart disease, bal-ancing the benefits of that against other risks. (See chapter 4 for more information.) You may also want to look into more effective strategies to manage your obesity (see chapter 2).

You also need to stay alert to signs of circulation problems, heart attack and stroke, which are discussed in detail below.

From Head to Toe

It's important to understand which parts of the body are vulnerable to macrovascular problems, microvascular problems, or both. There-fore, each subheading in this section will indicate "macro," "micro" or "both." People with Type 2 diabetes are far more likely to experi-ence problems with the parts of their body exposed to "macro" and "both"; people with Type 1 diabetes are far more likely to suffer prob-lems with the parts of their body exposed to "micro."

Your Brain (macro)

Cardiovascular disease puts you at risk for a stroke, which occurs when a blood clot (a clog in your blood vessels) travels to your brain and stops the flow of blood and oxygen carried to the nerve cells in that area. When that happens, cells may die or vital functions controlled by the brain can be temporarily or permanently damaged. Bleeding or a rupture from the affected blood vessel can lead to a very serious situation, including death. People with Type 2 diabetes are two to three times more likely to suffer from a stroke than people without diabetes.

Since the 1960s, the death rate from strokes has dropped by 50 percent. This drop is largely due to public awareness campaigns regarding diet and lifestyle modification (quitting smoking, eating low-fat foods and exercising), as well as the introduction of blood-pressure-lowering drugs and cholesterol-lowering drugs that have helped people maintain normal blood pressure and cholesterol levels.

Strokes can be mild, moderate, severe or fatal. Mild strokes frequently affect speech or movement for a short period of time only; many people recover from mild strokes without any permanent damage. Moderate or severe strokes may result in loss of speech, memory and paralysis; many people learn to speak again and learn to function with partial paralysis. How well you recover depends on how much damage was done.

It's never too late to reduce the risk of stroke by quitting smoking and making even small changes in diet and lifestyle. Discuss with your doctor whether you're a candidate for medications that can control your blood pressure and cholesterol levels. Aiming for normal blood sugar levels as often as possible is also important. A considerable amount of research points to stress as a risk factor for stroke. (See heart section on page 191 for ways to cut down on stress.)

Signs of a stroke
If you can recognize the key warning signs of a stroke, it can make a difference in preventing a major stroke or in the severity of a stroke.

Call 911 or get to a hospital emergency room if you suddenly notice one or more of the following symptoms:

- weakness, numbness and/or tingling in your face, arms or legs. (This may last only a few moments);
- loss of speech or difficulty understanding somebody else's speech. (This may last only a short time);
- severe headaches that feel different than any headache you've had before;
- feeling unsteady, falling a lot.

Alzheimer's disease

According to research done at the Mayo Clinic and Mayo Foundation in Rochester, Minnesota, family members should become acquainted with early signs of Alzheimer's disease. The study showed that people with Type 2 diabetes were 66 percent more likely to develop Alzheimer's disease than those in the general population. The risk was more than double in men, and more than one-third in women. Moreover, this study noted that it was unclear why there were gender-specific differences, but that the overall increase in Alzheimer's disease among people with Type 2 diabetes may be the result of common genetic predispositions. In other words, there may be some genes that go together in diabetes and Alzheimer's disease.

Your Nerves (micro)

When your blood sugar levels are too high for too long, you can develop a condition known as diabetic neuropathy or nerve disease. Somehow, the cells that make up your nerves are altered in response to high blood sugar. This condition can lead to foot amputations in people with diabetes. (See Feet section on page 198 for more details.)

There are different groups of nerves that are affected by high blood sugar; keeping your blood sugar levels as normal as possible is the best way to prevent many of the following problems. Drugs that help to prevent chemical changes in your nerve cells can also be used to treat nerve damage.

Some nerve diseases

- *Polyneuropathy* is a disease that affects the nerves in your feet and legs. The symptoms are burning, tingling and numbness in the legs and feet.

- *Autonomic neuropathy* is a disease that affects the nerves you don't notice; the nerves that control your digestive tract (see Stomach section on page 194), blood pressure, sweat glands, overall balance and sexual functioning (see Sexual Organs section on page 197). Treatment varies depending on what's affected, but there are drugs that can control individual parts of the body, such as the digestive tract.

- *Proximal motor neuropathy* is a disease that affects the nerves that control your muscles. This can lead to weakness, burning sensations in the joints (hands, thighs and ankles are the most common). These problems can be individually treated with physiotherapy and/or specific medication. When the nerves that control the muscles in the eyes are affected, you may experience problems with your vision, such as double vision. (See Eye section below.) Finally, nerve damage can affect the spine, causing pain and loss of sensation to the back, buttocks and legs.

Your Eyes (both)

Diabetes is the leading cause of new blindness in adults. Seventy-eight percent of people with Type 2 diabetes experience diabetes eye disease, clinically known as diabetic retinopathy. Microvascular complications damage the small blood vessels in the eyes. High blood pressure, associated with macrovascular complications, also damages the blood vessels in the eyes.

While 98 percent of people with Type 1 diabetes will experience eye disease within 15 years of being diagnosed, in Type 2 diabetes, eye disease is often diagnosed before diabetes is diagnosed; in other words, many people don't realize they have diabetes until their eye doctors ask them: "Have you been screened for diabetes?" In fact,

20 percent of people with Type 2 diabetes already have diabetes eye disease before their diabetes is diagnosed.

What happens to the eyes?

Eighty percent of all eye disease is known as non-proliferative eye disease, meaning "no new blood vessel growth" eye disease. This condition is also called background diabetic eye disease. In this case, the blood vessels in the retina (the part of your eyeball that faces your brain, as opposed to your face) start to deteriorate, bleed or hemorrhage (known as microaneurysms) and leak water and protein into the centre of the retina, called the macula; this condition is known as macular edema, and causes vision loss, which sometimes is only temporary. However, without treatment, more permanent vision loss will occur.

Proliferative eye disease means "new blood vessel growth" eye disease. In this case, your retina says: "Since all my blood vessels are being damaged, I'm just going to grow new blood vessels!" This process is known as neovascularization. The problem is that these new blood vessels are deformed, or abnormal, which makes the problem worse, not better. These deformed blood vessels look a bit like Swiss cheese; they're full of holes and have a bad habit of suddenly bleeding out, causing severe damage without warning. They can also lead to scar tissue in the retina, retinal detachments and glaucoma, greatly increasing the risk of legal blindness.

Signs of diabetic eye disease

In the early stages of diabetes eye disease, there are no symptoms. That's why you need to have a thorough eye exam every six months. As the eye damage progresses, you may notice blurred vision. The blurred vision is due to changes in the shape of the lens of the eye. During an eye exam, your ophthalmologist may notice yellow spots on your retina, signs that scar tissue has formed on the retina from bleeding. If the disease progresses to the point where new blood vessels have formed, vision problems may be quite severe, as a result of spontaneous bleeding or detachment of the retina.

How to protect yourself from diabetes eye disease

Early detection is your best protection! Using Type 1 rules is the best way to detect diabetes eye disease early and prevent vision loss. In other words, it's crucial to have frequent eye exams. Teens or young adults diagnosed with Type 1 diabetes should have semi-annual or annual eye exams. This way, eye disease can be detected before it affects vision permanently. The average person has an eye exam every five years. And if you're walking around with undiagnosed Type 2 diabetes, you can also be walking around with early signs of diabetes eye disease. So, as soon as you're diagnosed with Type 2 diabetes, get to an opthalmologist for a complete exam and make it a yearly "gig" from now on.

During an eye exam, the eye specialist will dilate your pupil with eye drops, and then use a special instrument to check for:

- tiny red dots (signs of bleeding);
- a thick or "milky" retina, with or without yellow clumps or spots (signs of macular edema);
- a "bathtub ring" on the retina—a ring shape that surrounds a leakage site on the retina (also a sign of macular edema);
- "cottonwool spots" on the retina—small fluffy white patches in the retina (signs of new blood vessel growth, or more advanced eye disease).

It's estimated that if everyone with impaired glucose tolerance (see chapter 1) went for an eye exam once a year, blindness from diabetes eye disease would drop from 8 percent in this group to 1 percent.

Can you treat diabetes eye disease?

Not completely. A procedure known as laser photocoagulation can burn and seal off the damaged blood vessels, which stops them from bleeding or leaking. In the earlier stages of diabetes eye disease, this procedure can restore vision within about six months. In most cases, however, laser surgery only slows down vision loss. In other words, without the treatment, your vision will get worse; with the treatment, it will stay the same.

If new blood vessels have already formed, a series of laser treatments are done to purposely scar the retina. Since a scarred retina needs less oxygen, blood vessels stop re-forming, reducing the risk of further damage.

In more serious cases, a vitrectomy is performed. In this procedure, blood and scar tissue on the retina is surgically removed.

If you're suffering from vision loss, a number of visual aids can help you perform daily tasks more easily.

A word about smoking

Since smoking also damages blood vessels, and diabetes eye disease is a blood vessel disease, smoking will certainly aggravate the problem. Quitting smoking may help to reduce eye-related complications.

Eye infections

High blood sugar can predispose you to frequent bacterial infections, including conjunctivitis (pink-eye). Eye infections can also affect your vision. To prevent eye infections, make sure you wash your hands before you touch your eyes, especially before you handle contact lenses.

Your Teeth (micro)

High blood sugar levels get into your saliva, and then into your teeth. Cavities are caused by bacteria in plaque, which breaks down the starches and sugars to form acids that eventually break down your tooth enamel. Moreover, damage to the blood vessels in your gums can lead to periodontal problems, while blood sugar levels naturally rise when you're fighting a gum infection (known as a periodontal infection), such as an abscess.

Preventing dental problems means the usual routine: regularly "rubber tipping" (massaging your gums with that rubber tip at the end of your toothbrush, or buying a separate rubber-tip instrument at the drugstore); flossing regularly; brushing regularly; and rinsing regularly with a mouthwash that kills plaque and bacteria. You may also wish to use a fluoride rinse every night. Have your teeth cleaned at least every six months, visit your dentist for an annual dental exam and avoid sugary foods (which you should be doing anyway) that can increase the incidence of cavities.

Your Heart (macro)

Type 2 diabetes is often called "a heart attack about to happen." When large blood vessels are damaged, it means cardiovascular disease (a.k.a. heart disease). When blood vessels get blocked due to hardening of the arteries (clinically known as arteriosclerosis), not enough blood gets to the heart muscle, causing it to die. That's what a heart attack is.

Peripheral vascular disease (meaning "fringe" blood-flow problems) is part of the heart disease story. PVD occurs when blood flow to the limbs (arms, legs and feet) is blocked, which creates cramping, pain or numbness. In fact, pain and numbness in the arms or legs may be signs of heart disease or even an imminent heart attack. A 1992 study reported that 20 percent of all women over age 60 suffered from PVD.

One way for women to prevent heart disease and peripheral vascular disease is to consider hormone replacement therapy (HRT) after menopause. Estrogen protects women against heart disease, but after menopause, the rates of heart disease in women soar as a result of estrogen loss (see chapter 4 for a thorough discussion of HRT). Modifying your lifestyle (stop smoking; eat less fat; get more exercise) is another way of preventing heart and peripheral vascular disease. Blood-pressure-lowering medication and cholesterol-lowering drugs are also an option if you have high blood pressure and/or high cholesterol. And, finally, heart surgery is an option, which includes angioplasty, laser treatment and bypass surgery.

Smoking, high blood pressure, high blood sugar and high cholesterol (called the "catastrophic quartet" by one diabetes specialist) will greatly increase your risk of heart disease. (See chapter 1.)

Women and heart disease

Heart disease is currently the number-one cause of death in post-menopausal women; more women die of heart disease than of lung cancer or breast cancer. Fifty percent of all North Americans who die from heart attacks each year are women. One of the reasons for such high death rates from heart attacks among women is medical ignorance: most studies looking at heart disease excluded women, which led to a myth that more men than women die of heart disease. The truth is, more men die of heart attacks before age 50, while more women die of heart attacks after age 50, as a direct result of estrogen loss. Moreover, women who have had oophorectomies (removal of the ovaries) prior to natural menopause increase their risk of a heart attack by eight times. Since more women than ever before work outside the home, a number of experts cite stress as a huge contributing factor to increased rates of heart disease in women.

Another problem is that symptoms of heart disease in women are different from those that men manifest. Therefore, the "typical" warning signs we know about in men—angina, or chest pains—are often never present in women. In fact, chest pains in women are almost never related to heart disease. For women, the symptoms of heart disease, and even an actual heart attack, can be much more vague—seemingly unrelated to heart problems. Signs of heart disease in women include some surprising symptoms:

- shortness of breath and/or fatigue;
- jaw pain (often masked by arthritis and joint pain);
- pain in the back of the neck (often masked by arthritis or joint pain);
- pain down the right or left arm;
- back pain (often masked by arthritis and joint pain);
- sweating (ladies, have your thyroid checked; sweating is a classic sign of an overactive thyroid gland; also test your blood sugar—you may be low, menopausal symptom can also mask this);
- fainting;
- palpitations (ladies, again, have your thyroid checked; palpitations are also a classic symptom of an overactive thyroid);

- bloating (after menopause, would you believe this is a sign of coronary artery blockage?);
- heartburn, belching or other gastrointestinal pain (this is often a sign of an actual heart attack in women);
- chest "heaviness" between the breasts (this is how women experience "chest pain"; some describe it as a "sinking feeling" or burning sensation). Also described as an "aching, throbbing or a squeezing sensation," "hot poker tab between the chest" or feeling like your heart jumps into your throat;
- sudden swings in blood sugar levels;
- vomiting;
- disorientation.

Clearly, there are lots of other causes for the symptoms on this list, including low blood sugar, but it's important that your doctor includes heart disease as a possible cause, rather than dismissing it because your symptoms are not "male" (which your doctor may refer to as "typical"). Bear in mind that if you're suffering from nerve damage, you may not feel a lot of these symptoms. Therefore, you should take extra care to be suspicious of anything feeling out of the ordinary.

Diagnostic tests that can confirm heart disease in women include a manual exam (doctor examining you with a stethoscope); an electrocardiogram; an exercise stress test; an echocardiogram; as well as a myriad of imaging tests that may use radioactive substances to take pictures of the heart.

If you're diagnosed with heart disease, the "cure" is prevention through diet and exercise, and protection through hormone replacement therapy (see chapter 4).

If you're premenopausal
If you have diabetes that is not well-controlled, the high blood sugar will cancel out the protective effects of estrogen against heart disease even if your ovaries are still making estrogen. Therefore, stay alert to the symptoms above. Keeping your blood sugar levels in the normal range will help to restore estrogen's protective properties.

Your Stomach (micro)

When high blood sugar levels affect your nerve cells, this can include the nerves that control your entire gastrointestinal tract. In fact, 30 to 50 percent of people with diabetes suffer from dysmotility, in which the muscles in the digestive tract become uncoordinated, causing bloating, abdominal pain and reflux (heartburn). In this case, your doctor may prescribe a motility drug known as a prokinetic agent, a medication that can restore motility.

Your Kidneys (both)

Both micro- and macrovascular complications can lead to kidney problems. High blood pressure and high blood sugar can be a dangerous combination for your kidneys. About 15 percent of people with Type 2 diabetes will develop kidney disease, known as either renal disease or nephropathy. In fact, diabetes causes 40 percent of all end-stage renal disease (ESRD), the term used to describe kidney failure. Roughly 40 percent of all dialysis patients have diabetes.

What do your kidneys do all day?
Kidneys are the public servants of the body; they're busy little bees! If they go on strike, you lose your water service, garbage pickup and a few other services you probably don't even know about.

Kidneys regulate your body's water levels; when you have too much water, your kidneys remove it by dumping it into a large storage tank—your bladder. The excess water stays there until you're ready to "pee it out." If you don't have enough water in your body (or if you're dehydrated), your kidneys will retain the water for you to keep you balanced.

Kidneys also act as your body's sewage filtration plant. They filter out all the garbage and waste that your body doesn't need and dump it into the bladder; this waste is then excreted into your urine. The two waste products your kidneys regularly dump are urea (the waste product of protein) and creatinine (waste products produced by the muscles). In people with high blood sugar levels, excess sugar will get sent to the kidneys, and the kidneys will dump it into the bladder, too, causing sugar to appear in the urine.

Kidneys also balance calcium and phosphate in the body, needed to build bones. Kidneys operate two little side businesses on top of all this. They make hormones. One hormone, called renin, helps to regulate blood pressure. Another hormone, called erythropoetin, helps bone marrow make red blood cells.

The macro thing

When you suffer from cardiovascular disease, you probably have high blood pressure. High blood pressure damages blood vessels in the kidneys, which interferes with their job performance. As a result, they won't be as efficient at removing waste or excess water from your body. If you are experiencing poor circulation, which can also cause water retention, the problem is further aggravated.

Poor circulation may cause your kidneys to secrete too much renin, which normally regulates blood pressure, but in this case, increases it. All the extra fluid and the high blood pressure places a heavy burden on your heart—and your kidneys. If this situation isn't brought under control, you'd likely suffer from a heart attack before kidney failure, but kidney failure is inevitable.

The micro thing

When high blood sugar levels affect the small blood vessels, that includes the small blood vessels in the kidney's filters (called the nephrons). This condition is known as diabetic nephropathy. In the early stages of nephropathy, good, usable protein is secreted in the urine. That's a sign that that the kidneys were unable to distribute usable protein to the body's tissues. (Normally, they would excrete only the waste product of protein—urea—into the urine.)

Another microvascular problem affects the kidneys: nerve damage. The nerves you use to control your bladder can be affected, causing a sort of sewage back-up in your body. The first place that sewage hits is your kidneys. Old urine floating around your kidneys isn't a healthy thing. The kidneys can become damaged as a result, aggravating all the conditions discussed so far in this section.

The infection thing

There's a third problem at work here. If you recall, frequent urination is a sign of high blood sugar. That's because your kidneys help to rid the body of too much sugar by dumping it into the bladder. Well, guess what? You're not the only one who likes sugar; bacteria, such as *e. coli* (the "hamburger bacteria"), like it, too. In fact, they thrive on it. So all that sugary urine sitting around in your bladder and passing through your ureters and urethra can cause this bacteria to overgrow, resulting in a urinary tract infection (UTI) such as cystitis (inflammation of the bladder lining). The longer your urethra is, the more protection you have from UTIs. Men have long urethras; women have very short urethras, however, and in the best of times, are prone to these infections—especially after a lot of sexual activity, which helped to coin the term "honeymoon cystitis." Sexual intercourse can introduce even more bacteria (from the vagina or rectum) into a woman's urethra due to the close space the vagina and urethra share. Women who wipe from back to front after a bowel movement can also introduce fecal matter into the urethra, causing a UTI.

Any bacterial infection in your bladder area can travel back up to your kidneys, causing infection, inflammation and a big general mess—again, aggravating all the other problems mentioned above!

The smoking thing

In the same way that smoking contributes to eye problems (see page 190), it can also aggravate kidney problems. Smoking causes small vessel damage throughout your body. Quitting smoking can greatly reduce your risk of kidney problems.

Signs of diabetic kidney disease

If you have any of the following early warning signs of diabetes kidney disease, see your doctor as soon as possible:

- high blood pressure (see chapter 1);
- protein in the urine (a sign of microvascular problems);
- burning or difficulty urinating (a sign of a urinary tract infection);
- foul-smelling or cloudy urine (a sign of a urinary tract infection);
- pain in the lower abdomen (a sign of a urinary tract infection);
- blood or pus in the urine (a sign of a kidney infection);
- fever, chills or vomiting (a sign of any infection);
- foamy urine (a sign of kidney infection);
- frequent urination (a sign of high blood sugar and/or a urinary tract infection).

Treating kidney disease

If you have high blood pressure, getting it under control through diet, exercise or blood-pressure-lowering medication will help to save your kidneys. If you have high blood sugar, treating any UTI as quickly as possible with antibiotics is the best way to avert kidney infection, while drugs known as ACE inhibitors can help to control small blood vessel damage caused by microvascular complications.

If you wind up with kidney failure, or end-stage renal disease, dialysis or, in the worst-case scenario, a kidney transplant, are the only ways to treat kidney failure. Perhaps some day, cloning technology will be used to clone replacement organs, such as kidneys.

Your Sexual Organs (both)

The discussion here focuses on sexual dysfunction in women that is directly related to diabetes.

Diabetes can cause sexual dysfunction in the form of vaginal dryness due to high blood sugar levels. High blood sugar levels can also cause chronic yeast infections (the fungus *candida albicans* will overgrow when there is sugar), as well as urinary tract infections (see Kidney section, page 194), which can make sexual intercourse uncomfortable. (Diabetes will indirectly affect your sex life if your partner is suffering from diabetes-related impotence; for more information about this disorder, consult my book, *Managing Your Diabetes*.)

Since Type 2 diabetes often coincides with menopause, many women will notice a compromised libido. It may be more difficult to become aroused or achieve orgasm. There is no clear evidence whether diabetes contributes to a reduced libido, or whether this is due to hormonal changes. Talking about the problem with a sex therapist, and using vaginal lubricants or estrogen creams can work wonders. Women with diabetes are very susceptible to vaginitis (vaginal inflammation caused by an infection, usually fungal). High blood sugar levels can definitely aggravate vaginitis, which will aggravate your sex life. Signs of vaginitis include a foul-smelling vaginal discharge, which may be brown or deep yellow in colour, with the consistency of cottage cheese. You will also notice itching and burning.

If you're suffering from any kind of vaginal infection, it's important to be evaluated by a gynaecologist, and be cultured for the specific organism causing the infection. That way, you can be treated with the right medication. Douching is not recommended, and can actually drive the infection higher up the reproductive tract.

Nerve damage can also affect your sex life. Special nerve fibres and blood vessels connect to the clitoris, vaginal wall and vulva, which is necessary for achieving orgasm and lubrication. If you have sustained nerve damage, you may notice a loss of sensation in your genital area, which can be a frustrating experience. Estrogen therapy and lubricants may help; trying different positions to increase arousal may also be beneficial. Asking your partner to touch you "with the intent to arouse or gratify" may also work wonders.

Your Feet (both)

Foot complications related to diabetes were dramatized in the mid-1980s film *Nothing In Common*, in which Jackie Gleason plays the ne'er-do-well diabetic father, and Tom Hanks plays the son who cannot accept him. In a heartbreaking scene, Tom Hanks is shocked to discover how ill his father really is when he finally sees his feet. They are swollen, purple and badly infected. The story ends with the father and son coming to terms as Gleason must undergo surgical amputation.

I share this example with you because many of us are used to ignoring and abusing our feet. We wear uncomfortable shoes, we pick at our callouses and blisters, we don't wear socks with our shoes, and so on. You can't do this anymore. Your feet are the targets of both macrovascular (large blood vessel) complications and microvascular (small blood vessel) complications. In the first case, peripheral vascular disease affects blood circulation to your feet. In the second place, the nerve cells to your feet, which control sensation, can be altered through microvascular complications. Nerve damage can also affect your feet's muscles and tendons, causing weakness and changes to your foot's shape.

The combination of poor circulation and no feeling in your feet means that you can sustain an injury to your feet and not know about it. For example, you might step on a piece of glass or badly stub your toe, and not realize it. If an open wound becomes infected, and you have poor circulation, the wound doesn't heal properly, infection could spread to the bone or gangrene could develop. In this situation, amputation may be the only treatment. Or, without sensation or proper circulation in them, your feet could be far more vulnerable to frostbite or exposure than they would be otherwise.

Diabetes accounts for approximately half of all non-emergency amputations, but all experts agree that doing a foot self-exam every day (see below) can prevent most foot complications from becoming severe. Those at most risk for foot problems are people who still smoke (smoking aggravates all diabetic complications), are overweight (more weight on the feet), are over age 40 or have had diabetes for more than 10 years. It's also important to note that at least 90 percent of people with diabetes who require amputations are smokers. Quitting smoking can greatly reduce your risk of amputation.

Signs of foot problems

The most common symptoms of foot complications are burning, tingling or pain in your feet or legs. These are all signs of nerve damage. Numbness is another symptom, which could mean nerve damage or circulation problems. If you do experience pain from nerve damage, it usually gets worse with time (as new nerves and blood vessels grow), and many people find that it's worse at night. Bed linens can actually increase discomfort. Some people only notice foot symptoms after exercising or after taking a short walk. Many people don't notice immediate symptoms until they've lost feeling in their feet.

Other symptoms people notice are frequent infections (caused by blood vessel damage), hair loss on the toes or lower legs, or shiny skin on the lower legs and feet.

When you knock your socks off

When you take off your socks at the end of the day, get in the habit of doing a foot self-exam. This is the only way you can exercise damage control on your feet. You're looking for signs of infection or potential infection triggers. If you can avoid infection at all costs, you will be able to keep your feet. Look for the following signs:

- reddened, discoloured or swollen areas (blue, bright red or white areas mean that circulation is cut off);
- pus;
- temperature changes in the feet or "hot spots";
- corns, callouses and warts (potential infections could be hiding under callouses; do not remove these yourself—see a podiatrist);
- toenails that are too long (your toenail could cut you if it's too long);
- redness where your shoes or socks are "rubbing" due to a poor fit. (When your sock is scrunched inside your shoe, the folds could actually rub against the skin and cause a blister.);
- toenail fungus (under the nail);
- fungus between the toes (athlete's foot, common if you've been walking around barefoot in a public place);
- breaks in the skin (especially between your toes), or cracks, such as in callouses on the heels; this opens the door for bacteria.

If you find an infection on your feet, wash them carefully with soap and water; don't use alcohol. Then see your doctor or a podiatrist (a foot specialist) as soon as possible. If your foot is irritated but not yet infected (redness, for example, from poor-fitting shoes or socks, but no blister yet), simply avoid the irritant—the shoes or socks—and the irritation should clear up. If it doesn't, see your doctor. If you're overweight and have trouble inspecting your feet, get somebody else to check them for the signs listed above. In addition to doing a self-exam, see your doctor to have the circulation and reflexes in your feet examined four times a year.

Foot rules to live by
- Walk a little bit every day; this is a good way to improve blood flow and get a little exercise!
- Don't walk around barefoot; wear proper-fitting, clean cotton socks with your shoes daily, and get in the habit of wearing slippers around the house and shoes at the beach. If you're swimming, wear some sort of shoe (plastic "jellies" or canvas running shoes).
- Before you put on your shoes, shake them out in case your (grand)child's Lego piece, a piece of dry catfood or a pebble is in there.
- Wash your feet and lower legs every day in lukewarm water with mild soap. Dry them really well, especially between the toes.
- Trim your toenails straight across to avoid ingrown nails. Don't pick off your nails.
- No more "bathroom surgery" on your feet, which may include puncturing blisters with needles or tweezers, shaving your callouses and the hundreds of crazy things people do with their feet (but never disclose to their partners).
- Baby your feet. When the skin seems too moist, use baby powder or a foot powder your doctor or pharmacist recommends (especially between the toes). When your feet are too dry, moisturize them with a lotion recommended by your doctor or pharmacist.

The reason is simple: breaks in the skin happen if feet are too moist, such as between the toes, or too dry. Use a foot buffing pad on your callouses after bathing.

- When you're sitting down, feet should be flat on the floor. Sitting cross-legged, or in crossed-legged variations, can cut off your circulation—and frequently does in people without diabetes.
- Wear comfortable, proper-fitting footwear.

Treatment for open wounds on the feet or legs

To heal cuts, sores or any open wound, your body normally manufactures macrophages, special white blood cells that fight infection, as well as special repair cells called fibroblasts. These "ambulance cells" need oxygen to live. If you have poor circulation, it's akin to an ambulance not making it to an accident scene in time because it gets caught in a long traffic jam.

When wounds don't heal, gangrene infections can set in. Until recently, amputating the infected limb was the only way to deal with gangrene. However, there is a new therapy available at several hospitals throughout Canada called hyperbaric oxygen therapy (HBO); this procedure involves placing you in an oxygen chamber or tank, and feeding you triple the amount of oxygen you'd find in the normal atmosphere. To heal gangrene on the feet, you'd need about 30 treatments (several per day for a week or so). The result is that your tissues become saturated with oxygen, enabling the body to heal itself. In one research trial, 89 percent of diabetics with foot gangrene were healed, compared to 1 percent of the control group. This treatment sounds expensive, but it's much cheaper than surgery, which is why HBO is catching on.

Not everybody is an HBO candidate; and not everybody in Canada has access to this therapy. If you're being considered for surgical amputation, you should definitely ask about HBO first.

Your Skin (micro)

High blood sugar levels, combined with poor circulation, puts the skin—on your whole body—at risk for infections ranging from yeast to open wound-related infections. You may form scar tissue, develop strange, yellow pimples (a sign of high fat levels in the blood), boils or a range of localized infections. Yeast can develop not only in the vagina, but in the mouth, under the arms or anyplace where there are warm, fatty folds. And all skin, whether on the feet or elsewhere, can become dry and cracked, requiring a daily regimen of cleaning, moisturizing and protecting.

Preventing Complications

The Diabetes Control and Complications Trial (DCCT) is a study that involved 1,441 people with Type 1 diabetes (see chapter 1), who were randomly managed according to one of two treatment philosophies: "intensive" treatment and "conventional" treatment. Intensive treatments means frequently testing your blood sugar, and adding a short-acting insulin that requires 3 to 4 injections daily, or 1 dose of longer-acting insulin (see Table 7.5, page 177). The goal of this type of management is to achieve blood sugar levels that are as normal as possible as often as possible. Conventional treatment means controlling your diabetes to the point where you avoid feeling any symptoms of high blood sugar, such as frequent urination, thirst or fatigue, without doing very much, if any, self-testing.

The Results

The DCCT results were unveiled in 1993, at the American Diabetes Association's annual conference. The results of the DCCT were pretty astounding. So much so, that the trial, planned for a ten-year period, was cut short—a rare occurrence in research trials.

The people who were managed with intensive therapy were able to delay microvascular complications (all the conditions labelled "micro" or "both" above) between 39 percent to 76 percent. Specifically, eye disease was reduced by 76 percent; kidney disease by 56 percent; nerve damage by 61 percent; and high cholesterol by

35 percent. Those are very significant results. Statistically, anything over 1 percent is considered "clinically significant." Wow! The overwhelming consensus among diabetes practitioners is that intensive therapy for people with Type 1 diabetes prolongs health and greatly reduces complications. Conventional therapy for Type 1 diabetes is now considered archaic, and even detrimental.

The National Institute of Diabetes and Digestive and Kidney Diseases (NIDDK) in the United States reported similar findings. NIDDK research found that with intensive therapy, eye disease was still reduced by 76 percent; kidney disease by 50 percent; nerve disease by 60 percent; and cardiovascular disease (a macrovascular complication) by 35 percent.

What the DCCT Means for Type 2 Diabetes

The DCCT did not look at blood sugar control and macrovascular complications—the cardiovascular complications for which people with Type 2 diabetes are most at risk—even though it showed a significant reduction in cholesterol levels. In fact, the priorities of many specialists treating Type 2 diabetes are weight control, not sugar control. (A cholesterol-lowering drug can achieve far greater results on low cholesterol than the DCCT.)

As a result, the DCCT is now an area of controversy for Type 2 specialists. Should people with Type 2 diabetes be counselled to intensively control their blood sugar or not? Many specialists say: "No—losing weight and getting the diet under control is hard enough. Asking people to self-test their blood sugar three to four times a day is too much for most people with Type 2 diabetes." In other words, what's the point of avoiding microvascular complications when you're about to drop dead from a massive heart attack or stroke? Nevertheless, many specialists say that since the DCCT showed such overwhelming reductions in complications for Type 1, until more data is out, people with Type 2 diabetes should be intensively controlling their blood sugar.

If you are willing to test your blood sugar frequently, you have only something to gain; certainly nothing to lose, so long as it doesn't interfere with your weight control program.

The British Study

As of this writing, the results of a long-awaited British Study have been published (September 15, 1998). Known as The United Kingdom Prospective Diabetes Study (UKPDS), this set out to determine whether blood sugar control reduces macrovascular complications in Type 2 diabetes, together with lowering blood pressure.

The results show that frequent blood sugar testing can reduce the risk of blindness and kidney failure in people with Type 2 by 25 percent. In those Type 2's with high blood pressure, lowering blood pressure reduced the risk of stroke by 44 percent and heart failure by 56 percent. And, for every one percentage point reduction in the value of the HbA_{1c} test (see chapter 8), there was a 35 percent reduction in eye, kidney and nerve damage, and an overall 25 percent reduction in deaths related to diabetes. The bottom line is that the UKPDS shows that frequently self-testing your blood sugar can prevent long-term complications of diabetes for people with Type 2 diabetes, although there was not a direct link between lowering blood sugar and reducing macrovascular complications.

In addition, preventing complications for Type 2 diabetes revolves around blood sugar control, exercise and low-fat eating (chapter 5 and 6)—the same things that can prevent Type 2 diabetes in the first place.

Chapter 9

PREVENTION: LOW-FAT

AND HEALTHFUL EATING

If you are at risk for Type 2 diabetes and want to prevent it, the best thing to do is to pretend you have the disease right now and design a meal plan that conforms to the Canadian Diabetes Association's guidelines. These guidelines will help you to eat a balanced diet and reduce your fat intake, which will dramatically reduce the risk of Type 2 diabetes (see chapter 1,) or the risk of macrovascular complications (see chapter 8) if you have already been diagnosed. Studies show that reducing dietary fat may also prevent various cancers, such as colorectal and estrogen-dependent cancers such as breast cancer.

When you begin to conscientiously eat a balanced diet and reduce your fat intake, you'll notice that you're much more aware of the "organic matter" that goes into your mouth, be it animal, vegetable or mineral. Almost without exception, people who adopt a lower-fat diet will begin to incorporate less animal produce and more vegetable produce into their diets. This, by itself, makes a significant contribution to the environment (see Table 9.1). Once you begin to eat more fruits and vegetables, you may want to know whether they are organically grown or laden with pesticides. Therefore, this chapter includes information on organic produce. (And don't forget, many of those animals we eat are grazing on pesticides, which remain in their fat, which then winds up in ours!)

Despite all the information contained in this chapter, you may still be unable to change your eating habits. That's because you may not fully understand why you're eating. I recommend you review chapter 2, for some insight into women and food.

The Skinny on Fat

Fat is technically known as fatty acids, which are crucial nutrients for our cells. We cannot live without fatty acids, or fat. Fat is therefore a good thing—in moderation. Like all good things, however, most of us want too much of it. Excess dietary fat is by far the most damaging element in the Western diet. A gram of fat contains twice the calories as the same amount of protein or carbohydrate. Decreasing the fat in your diet and replacing it with more grain products, vegetables and fruits is the best way to lower your risk of Type 2 diabetes, cardiovascular problems and many other diseases. Fat in the diet comes from meats, dairy products, and vegetable oils. Other sources of fat include coconuts (60 percent fat), peanuts (78 percent fat) and avocados (82 percent fat). There are different kinds of fatty acids in these sources of fats: saturated, unsaturated and transfatty acids (a.k.a. transfat), which is like a saturated fat in disguise. Some fats are harmful to your health while others are considered beneficial.

Understanding fat is a complicated business. This section explains everything you need to know about fat, and a few things you probably don't want to know.

TABLE 9.1
The Costs of High-Fat Eating

Our entire agricultural economy is designed to support livestock and animal products, which we consume in huge quantities. This is making us too fat, requires a large amount of resources to support its production and is ruining our environment. Land animal food production uses:

- 85 percent of all cropland and 55 percent of all agricultural land in the United States;
- forestland and rangeland, through erosion and depletion;
- 80 percent of all piped water in the United States;
- pesticides, which pollute 75 percent of U.S. waters and more than 50 percent of U.S. lakes and streams;
- wildlife, through conversion and pre-emption of forest and rangeland habitats and through poisoning and trapping of predators;
- 14 percent of the U.S. energy budget, greater than twice the energy supplied by all our nuclear power stations;
- large amounts of scarce raw materials, such as aluminum, copper, iron, steel, tin, zinc, potassium, rubber, wood, petroleum products, used for processing, storing and packaging;
- 90 percent of our grains and legumes, and 50 percent of our fish catch feeds livestock;
- our incomes: meats cost 5 to 6 times as much as foods with equivalent amounts of vegetable protein; the average household spends roughly $7,500 annually on meat.
- 50 percent of the world's tropical forests to expand land for cattle production. The average hamburger is made from meat imported from Central or South America, or the loss of 55 square feet of rainforest;
- our ozone layer: the rainforest is the "lungs of the planet," which absorbs excess carbon dioxide and clears methane, a greenhouse gas. Cattle, however, produce methane, while the clearing of rainforest interferes with our ecosystem;
- arable land: cloud seeding, which upsets natural atmospheric weather patterns and weather cycles, results in rapid loss of arable land and the spread of desert regions across Africa, Central Asia and parts of Latin America.

TABLE 9.2
Fat Tips

- Whenever you refrigerate animal fat (as in soups, stews or curry dishes), skim the fat from the top before reheating and re-serving. A gravy skimmer will also help skim fats; the spout pours from the bottom, which helps the oils and fats to coagulate on top.
- Substitute something else for butter: yogurt (great on potatoes) or low-fat cottage cheese, or, at dinner, just dip your bread in olive oil with some garlic, Italian style. For sandwiches, any condiment without butter, margarine or mayonnaise is fine, also mustards, yogurt, etc.
- Powdered non-fat milk is in vogue again; high in calcium, low in fat. Substitute it for any recipe calling for milk or cream.
- Dig out fruit recipes for dessert. Things like sorbet with low-fat yogurt topping can be elegant. Remember that fruit must be planned for in a diabetes meal plan.
- Season low-fat foods well. That way, you won't miss the flavour that fat adds.
- Lower-fat protein comes from vegetable sources (whole grains and bean products); higher-fat proteins come from animal sources.

Saturated Fat

Saturated fat is solid at room temperature and stimulates cholesterol production in the body. In fact, the way the fat looks prior to ingesting it is the way it will look when it lines your arteries. Foods high in saturated fat include processed meat, fatty meat, lard, butter, margarine, solid vegetable shortening, chocolate and tropical oils (coconut oil is more than 90 percent saturated). Saturated fat should be consumed only in very low amounts.

Unsaturated Fat

Unsaturated fat is partially solid or liquid at room temperature. This group of fats includes monounsaturated fats, polyunsaturated fats and omega-3 oils (a.k.a. fish oil), which, in fact, even protect you against heart disease (see below). Sources of unsaturated fats include vegetable oils (canola, safflower, sunflower, corn) and seeds and nuts. To make it easy to remember, unsaturated fats come from plants, with the exception of tropical oils, such as coconut. The more liquid the fat, the more polyunsaturated it is, which, in fact, lowers your cholesterol levels. However, if you have familial hyperlipidemia (high cholesterol), which often occurs alongside diabetes, unsaturated fat may not make a difference in your cholesterol levels.

What Is a Triglyceride?

Each fat molecule is a link chain made up of glycerol, carbon atoms and hydrogen atoms. The more hydrogen atoms that are on that chain, the more saturated or solid the fat. If you looked at each fat molecule carefully, you'd find three different kinds of fatty acids on it: saturated (solid), monounsaturated (less solid, with the exception of olive and peanut oils) and polyunsaturated (liquid) fatty acids, or three fatty acids plus glycerol, chemically known as triglycerides (see chapter 1).

The liver breaks down fat molecules by secreting bile (stored in the gall bladder)—its sole function. The liver also makes cholesterol (see chapter 1). Too much saturated fat may cause your liver to over-produce cholesterol, while the triglycerides in your bloodstream will rise, perpetuating the problem. Too much cholesterol can clog your blood vessels, get into the bile and crystallize, causing gallstones and gall bladder disease.

Fish Fat (Omega-3 Oils)

The fat naturally present in fish that swim in cold waters, known as omega-3 fatty acids (crucial for brain tissue), or fish oils, are all polyunsaturated. They lower your cholesterol levels and protect you against heart disease. These fish have a layer of fat to keep them warm in cold water. Mackerel, albacore tuna, salmon, sardines and lake trout are all rich in omega-3 fatty acids. In fact, whale meat and seal meat are enormous sources of omega-3 fatty acids, which were once the staples of the Inuit diet. Overhunting and federal moratoriums on whale and seal hunting has dried up this once-vital source of food for the Inuit, which clearly offered real protection against heart disease.

Manufactured Fats

An assortment of manufactured fats have been introduced into our diet, courtesy of food producers who are trying to give us the taste of fat without all the calories or harmful effects of saturated fats. Unfortunately, manufactured fats offer their own bag of horrors.

Trans-fatty acids (a.k.a. hydrogenated oils)

These are harmful fats that not only raise the level of "bad" cholesterol (LDL) in your bloodstream, but lower the amount of "good" cholesterol (HDL) that's already there. Trans-fatty acids are what you get when you make a liquid oil, such as corn oil, into a more solid or spreadable substance, such as margarine. Trans-fatty acids, you might say, are the "road to hell, paved with good intentions." Someone, way back when, thought that if you could take the "good fat"—unsaturated fat—and solidify it so it could double as butter or lard, you could eat the same things without missing the spreadable fat. That sounds like a great idea. Unfortunately, to make an unsaturated liquid fat more solid, you have to add hydrogen to its molecules. This is known as hydrogenation, the process that converts liquid fat to semi-solid fat. The ever-popular chocolate bar ingredient "hydrogenated palm oil" is a classic example of a trans-fatty acid. Hydrogenation also prolongs the shelf life of a fat, such as polyunsaturated fats, which can oxidize when exposed to air, causing rancid odours or flavours. Deep-frying oils used in the restaurant trade are generally hydrogenated.

Trans-fatty acid is sold as a polyunsaturated or monounsaturated fat with a line of copy like: "Made from polyunsaturated vegetable oil." Except in your body, it is treated as a saturated fat. This is why trans-fatty acids are a saturated fat in disguise. The advertiser may, in fact, say that the product contains "no saturated fat" or is "healthier" than the comparable animal or tropical oil product with saturated fat. So be careful out there: READ YOUR LABELS. The magic word you're looking for is "hydrogenated." If the product lists a variety of unsaturated fats (monounsaturated X oil, polyunsaturated Y oil, and so on), keep reading. If the word "hydrogenated" appears, count that product as a saturated fat; your body will!

Margarine versus butter

There's an old tongue-twister: "Betty Botter bought some butter that made the batter bitter; so Betty Botter bought more butter that made the batter better." Are we making our batters bitter or better with margarine? It depends.

Since the news of trans-fatty acids broke in the late 1980s, margarine manufacturers began to offer some less "bitter" margarines; some contain no hydrogenated oils, while others contain much smaller amounts. Margarines with less than 60 percent to 80 percent oil (9 to 11 grams of fat) will contain 1.0 to 3.0 grams of trans-fatty acids per serving, compared to butter, which is 53 percent saturated fat. You might say it's a choice between a bad fat and a worse fat.

It's also possible for a liquid vegetable oil to retain a high concentration of unsaturated fat when it's been partially hydrogenated. In this case, your body will metabolize it as some saturated fat and some unsaturated fat.

Fake fat

We have artificial sweeteners; why not artificial fat? This question has led to the creation of an emerging, yet highly suspicious, ingredient: fat substitutes, designed to replace real fat and hence reduce the calories from real fat without compromising the taste. This is done by creating a fake fat that the body cannot absorb.

One of the first fat substitutes on the market was Simplesse, an All-Natural Fat Substitute, made from milk and egg-white protein, which was developed by the NutraSweet Company. Simplesse apparently adds 1 to 2 calories per gram instead of the usual 9 calories per gram from fat. Other fat substitutes simply take protein and carbohydrates and modify them in some way to simulate the textures of fat (creamy, smooth, and so on.)All of these fat substitutes help to create low-fat products, discussed in chapter 6.

The calorie-free fat substitute currently being promoted is called olestra, developed by Procter and Gamble. The substance is being test-marketed in the United States in a variety of savoury snacks such as potato chips and crackers. Olestra is a potentially dangerous ingredient that most experts feel can do more harm than good. Canada has not yet approved it.

Olestra is made from a combination of vegetable oils and sugar. Therefore, it tastes just like the real thing, but the biochemical structure is a molecule too big for the liver to break down. So, olestra just gets passed into the large intestine and is excreted. Olestra is more than an "empty" molecule, however. It causes diarrhea and cramps, and may deplete your body of vital nutrients, including vitamins A, D, E and K, necessary for blood to clot. If the FDA approves olestra for use as a cooking-oil substitute, you'll see it in every imaginable high-fat product. The danger is that instead of encouraging people to choose nutritious foods, such as grains, fruits and vegetables over high-fat foods, products like these encourage a high fake-fat diet that's still too low in fibre and other essential nutrients. The no-fat icing on the cake is that these people could potentially wind up with a vitamin deficiency, to boot. Products like olestra should make you nervous.

The Incredible Bulk

For every action, there is an equal and opposite reaction. When you decrease your fat intake, you should increase your bulk intake, or fibre. As discussed in chapter 6, complex carbohydrates are foods that are high in fibre. Fibre is the part of a plant your body can't digest, which comes in the form of both water soluble fibre (which dissolves in water) and water insoluble fibre (which does not dissolve in water but instead, absorbs water); this is what's meant by "soluble" and "insoluble" fibre.

Soluble versus Insoluble Fibre

Soluble and insoluble fibre do differ, but they are equally good things. Soluble fibre somehow lowers the "bad" cholesterol, or LDL, in your body. Experts aren't entirely sure how soluble fibre works its magic, but one popular theory is that it gets mixed into the bile the liver secretes, and forms a type of gel that traps the building blocks of cholesterol, thus lowering your LDL levels. This action is akin to a spider web trapping smaller insects.

Good sources of soluble fibre include oats or oat bran, legumes (dried beans and peas), some seeds, carrots, oranges, bananas and other fruits. Soybeans are also high sources of soluble fibre. Studies show that people with very high cholesterol have the most to gain by eating soybeans. Soybean is also a phytoestrogen (plant estrogen) that is believed to lower the risks of estrogen-related cancers (for example, breast cancer), as well as lower the incidence of estrogen-loss symptoms associated with menopause.

Insoluble fibre doesn't affect your cholesterol levels at all, but it does regulate your bowel movements. How does it do this? As the insoluble fibre moves through your digestive tract, it absorbs water like a sponge and helps to form your waste into a solid form faster, making the stools larger, softer and easier to pass. Without insoluble fibre, your solid waste just gets pushed down to the colon or lower intestine as always, where it is stored and dried out until you're ready to have a bowel movement. High-starch foods are associated with drier stools. This situation is exacerbated when you "ignore the urge," as the colon will dehydrate the waste even more until it becomes harder and more difficult to pass, a condition known as constipation. Insoluble fibre will help to regulate your bowel movements by speeding things along. It is also linked to lower rates of colorectal cancer.

Good sources of insoluble fibre include wheat bran and whole grains, skins from various fruits and vegetables, seeds, leafy greens and cruciferous vegetables (cauliflower, broccoli or brussel sprouts, among others).

Fibre and Diabetes

Soluble fibre helps delay glucose from being absorbed into your bloodstream, which not only improves blood sugar control but helps to control post-meal peaks in blood sugar, which stimulates the pancreas to produce more insulin. Fibre in the form of all colours of vegetables will also ensure that you're getting the right mix of nutrients. Experts suggest that you consume colours of vegetables daily—for example, carrots (orange), beets (purple) and spinach (green). An easy way to remember what nutrients are in which vegetable is to remember that all green vegetables are for cellular repair; the darker the green, the more nutrients the vegetable contains. All red, orange and purplish vegetables contain antioxidants (vitamins A, C and E), which boost the immune system and fight off toxins. Studies suggest that vitamin C, for example, is crucial for people with Type 2 diabetes because it helps to prevent complications, as well as rid the body of sorbitol, a substance which can increase blood sugar. Another study suggests that vitamin E helped to prevent heart disease in people with Type 2 diabetes by lowering levels of "bad" cholesterol, but this isn't yet conclusive. Other minerals, such as zinc and copper, are essential for wound healing. The recommendation is to eat all colours of vegetables in ample amounts to get your vitamins, minerals and dietary fibre. It makes sense when you understand diabetes as a disease of starvation. In starvation, there are naturally lower levels of nutrients in your body that can only be replenished through excellent sources of food.

TABLE 9.3
How To Get More Fruits and Vegetables*

- Go for one or two fruits at breakfast, one fruit and two vegetables at lunch and dinner, and a fruit or vegetable snack between meals.
- Consume many differently coloured fruits and vegetables. For colour variety, select at least three differently coloured fruit and vegetables daily.
- Put fruit and sliced veggies in an easy-to-use, easy-to-reach place (sliced vegetables in the fridge; fruit out on the table).
- Keep frozen and canned fruit and vegetables on hand to add to soups, salad or rice dishes.

*Fruits and vegetables must be planned for in a diabetes meal plan.

Source: Adapted from "Beyond Vitamins: Phytochemicals to help fight disease," June V. Engel, PhD, *Health News*, June 1996, Volume 14, No. 3.

Breaking Bread

For thousands of years, cooked whole grains was the dietary staple for all cultures. Rice and millet in the Orient; wheat, oats and rye in Europe; buckwheat in Russia; sorghum in Africa; barley in the Middle East; and corn in pre-European North America.

Wholegrain breads are good sources of insoluble fibre (flax bread is particularly good because flaxseeds are a source of soluble fibre, too). The problem is understanding what is truly "whole grain." For example, there is an assumption that because bread is dark or brown, it's more nutritious; this isn't so. In fact, many brown breads are simply enriched white breads dyed with molasses. ("Enriched" means that nutrients lost during processing have been replaced.) High-fibre pita breads and bagels are available, but you have to search for them. A good rule is to simply look for the phrase "whole wheat," which means that the wheat is, indeed, whole.

■ ■ ■

You now know how to manage Type 2 diabetes, prevent further complications and lower your risk of the disease. Don't forget to browse through the resource section! And don't forget exercise. I wish you good luck, good health and a long and happy life.

APPENDIX

Where to Go for More Information

Note: This list was compiled from dozens of sources. Because of the nature of many health and non-profit organizations, some of the addresses and phone numbers below may have changed since this list was compiled. Many of these organizations have e-mail addresses, some of which are not made public. Please review "Diabetes Online" at the end of this list.

Canadian Diabetes Association

National Office

15 Toronto St., Suite 800
Toronto, Ont.
M5C 2E3
ph. (416) 363-3373
fax (416) 363-3393
e-mail: info@diabetic.ca

Provincial Offices:

Alberta/NWT
10117 Jasper Ave., N.W.
Suite 1010, Royal Bank Building
Edmonton, Alta.
T5J 1W8
ph. (403) 423-1232/
1-800-563-0032
fax (403) 423-3322

British Columbia/Yukon
1091 West 8th Ave.
Vancouver, B.C.
V6H 2V3
ph. (604) 732-1331/
1-800-665-6526
fax (604) 732-8444

Manitoba
102-310 Broadway
Winnipeg, Man.
R3C 0S6
ph. (204) 925-3800/
1-800-782-0175
fax (204) 949-0266

New Brunswick
165 Regent St., Suite 3
Fredericton, N.B.
E3B 7B4
ph. (506) 452-9009/
1-800-884-4232
fax (506) 455-4728

Newfoundland/Labrador
354 Water St., Suite 217
St. John's, Nfld.
A1C 1C4
ph. (709) 754-0953
fax (709) 754-0734

Nova Scotia
6080 Young St., Suite 101
Halifax, N.S.
ph. (902) 453-4232
fax (902) 453-4440

Ontario (*See* National Office)

Prince Edward Island
P.O. Box 133
Charlottetown, PEI
C1A 7K2
ph. (902) 894-3005
fax (902) 368-1928

Saskatchewan
104-2301 Avenue C.N.
Saskatoon, Sask.
S7L 5Z5
ph. (306) 933-4446/
1-800-996-4446
fax (306) 244-2012

Association du diabète Québec
(Quebec CDA Affiliate)
5635, rue Sherbrooke est
Montréal, Que.
H1N 1A2
ph. (514) 259-3422
fax (514) 259-9286

The Canadian Dietetic Association
480 University Ave., Suite 601
Toronto, Ontario
M5G 1V2
ph.(416) 596-0857
fax(416) 596-0603

Canadian National Institute for the Blind (CNIB)
National Office
320 McLeod St.
Ottawa, On
K2P 1A3
ph. (613) 563-4021
fax (613) 563-1898

Canadian Podiatric Medical Association
2 Sheppard Ave. East, Suite 900
Willowdale, Ont.
M2N 5Y7
ph. (416) 927-9111/
1-888-220-3338
fax (416) 733-2491

Health Information Centre
Ontario Ministry of Health
6th Floor, 2195 Yonge St.
Toronto, Ont.
M4S 2B2
ph. 1-800-268-1153/
(416) 327-4327

Heart and Stroke Foundation of Ontario
(Heart & Stroke Healthline)
ph. 1-800-360-1557
Local Toronto: (416) 631-1557

Juvenile Diabetes Foundation Canada
89 Granton Dr.
Richmond Hill, Ont.
L4B 2N5
ph. (905) 889-4171/
1-800-668-0274
fax (905) 889-4209

The Kidney Foundation of Canada
National Branch
5165 Sherbrooke Ave. West,
Suite 300
Montreal, Que.
H4A 1T6
ph. 1-800-361-7494

MedicAlert
250 Ferrand Dr., Suite 301
Postal Station Don Mills, Box 9800,
Toronto, Ont.
M3C 2T9
ph. 1-800-668-1507
Local Toronto: (416) 696-0267

Food/Nutrition:

Canadian Organic Growers Inc.
National Branch
Box 6408, Station J
Ottawa, Ont.
K2A 3Y6

National Institute of Nutrition
302-265 Carling Ave.
Ottawa, Ont.
K1S 2E1
ph. (613) 235-3355
fax (613) 235-7032
e-mail: nin@nin.ca
World Wide Web:
http://www.nin.ca

Diabetes Education Hospitals

Note: This list is not exhaustive; it is intended as a "starting point" for Canadians looking for specific hospitals across the country that provide diabetes education.

Ontario
Diabetes Education Centre
Doctors Hospital
340 College St., Suite 560
Toronto, ON M5T 3A9
ph. (416) 963-5288
fax (416) 923-1370

Mount Sinai Hospital
600 University Ave.
Toronto, Ont. M5G 1X5
ph. (416) 586-4800
fax (416) 586-8785

Tri-Hospital Diabetes Education
Centre (TRIDEC)
[All Toronto Hospital Patients
referred here]
Women's College Hospital
60 Grosvenor St.
Toronto, Ont. M5S 1B6
ph. (416) 323-6170
fax (416) 323-6085

Diabetes Care and Research Centre
Chedoke McMaster Hospitals
McMaster Division,
1200 Main St. West
Hamilton, Ont. L8S 4J9
ph. (905) 521-2100, Ext. 6818
fax (905) 521-2653

Hamilton Civic Hospitals
General Division
Education Department
Robert Panchyson, BSCN
237 Barton St. East
Hamilton, Ont. L8L 2X2
ph. (905) 527-4322, Ext. 6245

Hamilton Civic Hospitals
(Patient Teaching)
711 Concession St.
Hamilton, Ont. L8V 1C3
ph. (905) 527-4322, Ext. 2024,
Paging 2110
fax (905) 575-2641

Diabetes Education Centre
Kitchener-Waterloo Health Centre
Grand River Hospital
835 King St. West
Kitchener, Ont. N2G 1G3
ph. (519) 749-4300
fax (519) 749-4317

Sioux Lookout Diabetes Program
Box 163, 73 King St.
Sioux Lookout, Ont.
P8T 1A3
ph. (807) 737-4422
fax (897) 737-2603
e-mail: slktdiab@sioux-
lookout.lakeheadu.ca

Lawrence Commanda Diabetes
Education & Resource Centre
Ken Goulais, Resource Clerk
24 Semo Rd.
Garden Village, RR #1
Sturgeon Falls, Ont.
P0H 2G0
ph. (705) 753-3355
fax (705) 753-4116

Porcupine Health Unit
Teresa Taillefer
Bag 2012
Timmins, Ont. P4N 8B2
ph. (705) 267-1181
fax (705) 264-3989

Quebec
SMBD Jewish General Hospital
Diabetes Clinic
Pav. E104
3755 Cote St. Catherine Rd.
Montreal, Que. H3T 1E2
ph. (514) 340-8222, Loc. 5787
fax (514) 340-7529

British Columbia
University of Northern
British Columbia
Department of Community Health
3333 University Way
Prince George, B.C.
V29 4Z9
ph. (250) 960-5671
fax (250) 960-5743

S. Okanagan Diabetes
Education Program
S. Okanagan Health Unit
740 Carmi Ave.
Penticton, B.C.
V2A 8P9
ph. (250) 770-3492
fax (250) 770-3470

Diabetes Education Program
1305 Summit Ave.
Prince Rupert, B.C.
V8J 2A6
ph. (250) 624-0294
fax (250) 627-1244

Western Canada
Manitoba Health
(Teaching text for Type 2 diabetes
and Aboriginal Population)
303 800 Portage Ave.
Winnipeg, Man.
R3G 0N4
ph. (204) 945-6735
fax (204) 948-2040

Royal University Hospital
103 Hospital Dr.
Saskatoon, Sask. S7N 0W0
ph. (306) 655-2615
fax (306) 655-1044

Mista Hia Regional
Health Authority
Grande Prairie Health Unit
10320-99 St.
Grande Prairie, Alta.
T8V 6J4
ph. (403) 532-4441
fax (403) 532-1550

University of Alberta Hospitals
2F2 Metabolic Center
Brenda Cook, RD
8440-112 St.
Edmonton, Alta.
T6G 2B7
ph. (403) 492-6696
fax (403) 492-8291

Clinical Nutrition Services
Foothills Hospital
1403-29th St. NW
Calgary, Alta.
T2N 2T9
ph. (403) 670-1522
fax (403) 670-1848

Maritimes
Nova Scotia Diabetes Center
Queen Elizabeth II Health
Science Center
Gerrard Hall, 5303 Morris St.,
2nd Floor
Halifax, N.S. B3J 1B6
ph. (902) 496-3722
fax (902) 496-3726

Outside Canada:
American Association of
Diabetes Educators
444 N Michigan Ave., Suite 1240
Chicago, Ill., 60611
ph. (312) 644-2233

The American Diabetes Association
ADA National Service Center
1660 Duke St.
Alexandria, Va., 22314
ph. (703) 549-1500

International Diabetic
Athletes Association
1647-B West Bethany Home Road
Phoenix, Ariz., 85015
ph. (602) 433-2113

International Diabetes
Federation (IDF)
40 Rue Washington
1050, Brussels, Belgium
32-3/647-4414

The Becel Heart Health
Information Bureau
ph. 1-800-563-5574
fax 1-800-442-3235

LifeScan TELELIBRARY
1-800-847-SCAN (7226)

LifeScan Customer Care Line
1-800-663-5521

Lilly/BMC Diabetes Care
ph. 1-800-361-2070
fax (514) 668-7009

McNeil Consumers
ph. 1-800-561-0070

Novo Nordisk Canada Inc.
ph. 1-800-465-4334/
(905) 629-4222
fax (905) 629-2596

Monoject Diabetes Care Products
Sherwood Medical Industries
Canada Inc.
ph. 1-800-661-1903

Pharma Plus Pharma Answers
Phone Line
(24 hour access to a pharmacist)
ph. 1-800-511-INFO

Diabetes Online

Through the Internet, you can participate in newsgroups and bulletin boards (public forums) on diabetes information. These can be accessed through either independent Internet providers, or through an interactive computer service, such as CompuServe, Prodigy or America Online (AOL).

Literature searches are great ways of getting specific information. Medline is the best for search service for medical journal articles. Compuserve, Prodigy or America Online all give you access to Medline.

Another way of accessing good information is through a web browser, such as Netscape. By web browsing, you can go to various sites in cyberspace to find your information. When you don't know the worldwide web (www) address, you can use a search engine, such as Yahoo or Webcrawler to search for what you want by simply typing in your topic. The more specific you can be in your search, the better. For example, if you want information on nerve damage, don't type "nerves" but "diabetes nerve damage" or "diabetic neuropathy." A search engine is essentially an index to the Internet. When you go to a site, you can save or print the information. Flashing text (called hypertext) is a sign that you'll get more information when you click on it. This may even link you to other sites on the Internet.

A Few Sites to Get You Started:

http://www.diabetes.ca
The Canadian Diabetes
Association

http://www.diabetes.org
The American Diabetes
Association

BIBLIOGRAPHY

Chapter 1

"Blood Pressure: Check it Out." *Countdown USA: Countdown to a Healthy Heart*, Allegheny General Hospital and Voluntary Hospitals of America, Inc., 1990.

"Diabetes Implants Tested." *Los Angeles Daily News*, January 23, 1997.

"Diabetes Raises Dementia Risk." Reuters, Thursday, February 13, 1997.

"Diabetes: Facts and Figures." *News from the VIP*, No. 2, Fall 1995. Vitamin Information Program, Fine Chemicals Division of Hoffman-La Roche Ltd.

"Diets Slow Reaction Times." Reuters, Tuesday, April 8, 1997.

"Double Trouble." *Countdown USA: Countdown to a Healthy Heart*, Allegheny General Hospital and Voluntary Hospitals of America, Inc., 1990.

"Feeding Your Child for a Lifetime." Reuters, Thursday, April 10, 1997.

"Flick your Risk: By Tossing Out Those Cigarettes, You Can Slash Your Chances of Heart Disease." *Countdown USA: Countdown to a Healthy Heart*, Allegheny General Hospital and Voluntary Hospitals of America, Inc., 1990.

"Folic Acid Surveys Say Consumer Awareness Is Low." *News from the VIP*, No. 2, Fall 1995. Vitamin Information Program, Fine Chemicals Division of Hoffman-La Roche Ltd.

"Get Off the Diet Rollercoaster." *Countdown USA: Countdown to a Healthy Heart*, Allegheny General Hospital and Voluntary Hospitals of America, Inc., 1990.

"VIP Conference on Elderly attracts Canadian Media." *News from the VIP*, No. 2, Fall 1995. Vitamin Information Program, Fine Chemicals Division of Hoffman-La Roche Ltd.

"We're Winning: By Changing Lifestyles, We're Proving Every Day That Coronary Disease Can Be Beaten." *Countdown USA: Countdown to a Healthy Heart*, Allegheny General Hospital and Voluntary Hospitals of America, Inc., 1990.

"What's Your Type?" *News from the VIP*, No. 2, Fall 1995. Vitamin Information Program, Fine Chemicals Division of Hoffman-La Roche Ltd.

"Bayer Launches Major International Research Project into Prevention of Diabetes. Media Release, March 5, 1997.

"Living Well." Patient information. Canadian Diabetes Association, distributed 1997.

"Mature Lifestyles: High Blood Pressure." Patient information. Health Watch/Shoppers Drug Mart, distributed 1997.

"Nutrition News." *Diabetes Dialogue* (Vol. 44, No.1) Spring 1997.

Anderson, Pauline. "Researchers Predict 'Beginning of the End' of Diabetes." *The Medical Post*, August 22, 1995.

Canadian Diabetes Association. "Health . . . the Smoke-free Way." *Equilibrium* (No. 1) 1996.

Gauthier, Serge G., MD, FRCPC and Patricia H. Coleman, MS, RPDt, Reviewers. "Nutrition and Aging." *The Lederle Letter* (Vol. 2, No. 2) April 1993, Lederle Consumer Health Products Department.

Mihill, Chris. "New Fears Over Link Between Cow's Milk and Diabetes." *The Guardian*, October 4, 1996.

Reddy, Sethu, MD, "Smoking and Diabetes." *Diabetes Dialogue* (Vol. 42, No. 4) Winter 1995.

Yankova, Diliana, MD "Diabetes in Bulgaria." *Diabetes Dialogue* (Vol. 44, No. 1) Spring 1997.

"Diabetes: What is it?" *Equilibrium* Canadian Diabetes Association (No. 1) 1996.

"Improving Treatment Outcomes in NIDDM: The Questions and Controversies." *The Diabetes Report* (Vol. 2, No. 1) 1996.

"Insulin and Type 2 diabetes." *Equilibrium* Canadian Diabetes Association (No. 1) 1996.

"Monitoring your blood sugar." *Equilibrium* Canadian Diabetes Association (No. 1) 1996.

"New Developments in the Management of Type II Diabetes." *The Diabetes Report*, Vol. 1, No. 2, 1995.

"New perspectives in the management of NIDDM." *The Diabetes Report*, Vol. 1, No. 3, 1996.

"Understanding Type 2 Diabetes: Guidelines for a Healthier You." Patient information. Bayer Inc. Healthcare Division, distributed 1997.

"Your Blood Sugar Level . . . What Does It Tell You?" Patient information. Lilly Diabetes Care, 1997.

"7 Key Factors for Real World Accuracy in the Real World." Patient information. MediSense Canada Inc., distributed 1997.

"7 Key Steps to Control Your Diabetes." Patient information. MediSense Canada Inc., distributed 1997.

"Advocacy in Action." *Diabetes Dialogue* (Vol. 43, No. 3) Fall 1996.

"Balancing Your Blood Sugar: A Guide for People with Diabetes." Patient information. Canadian Diabetes Association, distributed 1997.

"Blood Glucose Monitoring: Guidelines to a Healthier You." Patient information. Bayer Inc., Healthcare Division, distributed 1997.

"Blood Sugar Testing Diary." Patient information. Becton Dickinson Consumer Products, distributed 1996.

"Dextrolog: For Recording Blood and Urine Glucose Test Results." Booklet. Bayer Inc., Healthcare Division, distributed 1997.

"Diabetes Education." Patient information. Canadian Diabetes Association, distributed 1997.

"Following the Patient With Chronic Disease." *Patient Care Canada* (Vol. 7, No. 5) May 1996: 22–38.

"Glucometer Elite." Patient information. Bayer Inc., Healthcare Division, 1995.

"How Adults Are Learning to Manage Diabetes with Their Lifestyle." *The Globe and Mail*, November 1, 1996.

"Health Record for People with Diabetes." Patient information. Canadian Diabetes Association/ LifeScan Canada Inc., McNeil Consumer Products Company, 1996.

"How to Choose Your New Blood Glucose Meter." Patient information. LifeScan Canada Inc., distributed 1997.

"Keeping Well With Diabetes: Novolin Care." Patient information. Novo Nordisk Canada Inc., distributed 1996.

"Ketone Testing: Guidelines to a Healthier You." Patient information. Bayer Inc., Healthcare Division, distributed 1997.

"MediSense Blood Glucose Sensor." Product monograph, distributed 1995.

"Monoject: Diabetes Care Products." Patient information. Sherwood Medical Industries Canada Inc., distributed 1997.

"Non-Insulin Dependent Diabetes Mellitus" Patient information. National Pharmacy Continuing Education Program and Bayer Inc., February 1997.

"One Touch Profile: For Complete Diabetes Management." Patient information. LifeScan Canada Inc., distributed 1997.

"Real World Factors That Interfere With Blood-glucose Meter Accuracy." Patient information. MediSense Canada Inc, distributed 1996.

"Reducing Your Risk of Diabetes Complications." Patient information. MediSense Canada Inc., distributed 1997.

"Research, Improvement in Products Pever Stops in Health Industry." *The Globe and Mail*, November 1, 1996.

"Surestep." Patient information. LifeScan Canada Inc., distributed 1997.

"The Accu-Chek Advantage System." Patient information. Eli Lilly of Canada Inc., distributed 1997.

"Type II Diabetes." Shoppers Drug Mart Education Series NIDDM: (Vol. 95):11.

"What Is Intensive Diabetes Management?" Patient information. Diabetes Clinical Research Unit of Mount Sinai Hospital Toronto for Sherwood Medical Industries Canada Inc., distributed 1997.

"Your Blood Sugar Level . . . What Does It Tell You?" Patient information. Eli Lilly of Canada Inc., distributed 1997.

Antonucci, T. et al., Impaired Glucose Tolerance Is Normalized By Treatment With Thiazolidinedione. *Diabetes Care* (Vol. 20, No. 2) February 1997: 188–93.

Brubaker, Patricia L., PhD "Glucagon-like Peptide-1." *Diabetes Dialogue* (Vol. 41, No. 4) Winter 1994.

Cattral, Mark, MD, MSc., FRCSC, "Pancreas Transplantation." *Diabetes Dialogue* (Vol. 43, No. 4) Winter 1996.

Chaddock, Brenda, CDE, "Blood-Glucose Testing: Keep Up with the trend." *Canadian Pharmacy Journal*, September 1996:17.

Helwick, Caroline, "Apnea, Diabetes Linked." *The Medical Post*, May 28, 1996.

Joyce, Carol, MD, "What's New in Type 2." *Diabetes Dialogue* (Vol. 43, No. 3) Fall 1996.

Prochaska, James O., PhD, "A Revolution in Diabetes Evaluation." Excerpted from the Canadian Diabetes Association Conference, 1995.

Ryan, David, PhD, "At the Controls." *Diabetes Dialogue* (Vol. 43, No. 3) Fall 1996.

Sinclair, A.J. BSC, MD, MRCPC (UK), "Rational Approaches to the Treatment of Patients with Non-Insulin-Dependent Diabetes Mellitus. *Practical Diabetes Supplement* (Vol. 10, No. 6) November/December 1993.

Whitcomb, Randall, MD, "The Key to Type 2." *Diabetes Dialogue* (Vol. 43, No. 4) Winter 1996.

Yale, Jean-Francois, MD, Glucose Results: Plasma or Whole Blood? Medisense Canada Inc., *Monitor* (Vol. 1 No. 2)

"Low Blood Sugars: Your questions answered." Canadian Diabetes Association, equilibrium (No. 1) 1996.

Halvorson, Mary, Francine Kaufman, and Neal Kaufman. "A Snack Bar Containing Uncooked Cornstarch to Diminish Hypoglycaemia." American Diabetes Association 56th Scientific Sessions, 1996.

Jeffrey, Susan, "Uncooked Cornstarch Snacks Aid Diabetics." *The Medical Post*, November 12, 1996.

Korytkowski, Mary MD. "Something Old, Something New." *Diabetes Spectrum* (Vol. 9) November 4, 1996.

Martin, Cheryl, BSCPHARM. "Acarbose (Prandase)." *Communication*, March/April 1996:38.

Schoepp, Glen, BSP., "What is the Role of Acarbose (Prandase) in Diabetes Management?" *Pharmacy Practice* (Vol. 12, No. 4) April 1996:37–38.

Zbar Clinical Product Information. Baker Cummins Inc., 1997.

"Combining the Old and the New." Caring for the Earth: A Strategy for Sustainable, Living, IUCN—The World Conservation Union. United Nations Environment Programme, World Wide Fund For Nature, Gland, Switzerland, 1991.

"Discovery of Insulin Marked Turning Point in Human History." *The Globe and Mail*, Friday, November 1, 1996.

Chapter 2

"Obese Children May Lack Antioxidants." Reuters Health Summary, Tuesday, April 22, 1997.

"Obesity Hormone May Prevent Diabetes." Reuters Health Summary, Tuesday, April 29, 1997.

"Study Finds That Teens Who Had Less Salt as Infants Have Lower Blood Pressure." Associated Press, April 8, 1997.

"Study Ranks Cities by Pudginess of Residents." Associated Press, March 4, 1997.

"Study: You Can Lose Weight and Cigarettes." Reuters, Thursday, June 19, 1997.

"The Fat Trap." Countdown USA: Countdown to a Healthy Heart, Allegheny General Hospital and Voluntary Hospitals of America, Inc., 1990.

"What You Should Know about MSG." International Food Information Council, 1100 Connecticut Ave. N.W., Suite 430, Washington D.C. 20036, September 1991.

Marliss, Errol B., MD, FRCPC, and Rejeanne Gougeon, PhD, Msc, DtP, Reviewers. "Focus on Women: Dieting as a Possible Risk Factor for Obesity." *The Lederle Letter* (Vol. 2, No. 4) August 1993, Lederle Consumer Health Products Department.

Marliss, Errol B., MD, FRCPC, Rejeanne Gougeon, PhD, Msc, DtP, and Sandra Schwenger, HBSc, RPDt, Reviewers. "Weight-Reducing Diets May Compromise Nutrition." The *Lederle Letter* (Vol. 1, No. 3) August 1992, Lederle Consumer Health Products Department.

Neergaard, Lauran, "Study Finds Low Hormone Levels May Encourage Weight Gain." Associated Press. May 14, 1997.

Orbach, Susie, *Fat is a Feminist Issue* (New York: Berkley Books, 1990).

Wanless, Melanie, BASc, "The Weight Debate." *Diabetes Dialogue* (Vol. 44, No. 1) Spring 1997.

Chapter 3

"Guidelines for the Nutritional Management of Diabetes in Pregnancy." A Position Statement by the Canadian Diabetes Association (Vol. 15, No. 3) September 1991.

"A Jelly Bean Glucose Test." *American Baby*, April 1996:6.

"Jelly Beans Offer Sweet Relief." *Diabetes Dialogue* (Vol. 44, No. 2) Summer 1997.

Boctor, M.A. et al, "Gestational Diabetes Debate: Controversies in Screening and Management." *Canadian Diabetes* (Vol. 10, No. 2.) June 1997.

Feig, Denice S., MD, Msc, FRCPC.. "The Fourth International Workshop Conference on Gestational Diabetes Mellitus." *Canadian Diabetes* (Vol. 10, No. 2.) June 1997.

Ludwig, Sora, MD, FRCPC, Gestational Diabetes. *Canadian Diabetes* (Vol. 10, No. 2.) June 1997.

Rosenthal, M. Sara, *The Breastfeeding Sourcebook*, 2nd ed. (Los Angeles: Lowell House, 1998).

Rosenthal, M. Sara, *The Fertility Sourcebook*, 2nd ed. (Los Angeles: Lowell House, 1998).

Rosenthal, M. Sara, *The Pregnancy Sourcebook*, 2nd ed. (Los Angeles: Lowell House, 1997).

Utiger, Robert, MD, "Restoring Fertility in Women with PCOS." *The New England Journal of Medicine*, (Vol. 335, No. 9) August 29, 1996.

Chapter 4

Jovanovic-Peterson, Lois, MD, June Biermann, and Barbara Toohey, *The Diabetic Woman: All Your Questions Answered* (New York: G.P. Putnam's Sons, 1996).

Kra, J., Siegfried, MD, FACP, What Every *Woman Must Know about Heart Disease* (New York: Warner Books, 1996).

Macdonald, Jeanette MA, CDE, "The Facts About Menopause." *Diabetes Dialogue* (Vol. 44, No. 2) Summer 1997.

Poirier, Laurinda M., RN. MPH, CDE and Katharine M. Coburn, *Women & Diabetes: Life Planning for Health and Wellness* (New York: American Diabetes Association and Bantam Books, 1997).

Rosenthal, M. Sara, *The Breast Sourcebook* (Los Angeles: Lowell House, 1996, 1997).

Rosenthal, M. Sara, *The Fertility Sourcebook*, 2nd ed. (Los Angeles: Lowell House, 1998).

Rosenthal, M. Sara, *The Gynecological Sourcebook*, 2nd ed. (Los Angeles: Lowell House, 1997).

Chapter 5

"Physical Activity." Equilibrium, Canadian Diabetes Association (No. 1) 1996.

"Exercise: Guidelines to a Healthier You." Patient information. Bayer Inc. Healthcare Division, distributed 1997.

"Food and Exercise: Guidelines to a Healthier You." Patient information. Bayer Inc. Healthcare Division, distributed 1997.

"Spring at Last!" *The Diabetes News*, prepared by the LifeScan Education Institute, Spring 1996.

Bonen, Arent, PhD, "Fueling Your Tank." *Diabetes Dialogue* (Vol. 42, No. 4) Winter 1995.

Chaddock, Brenda, CDE, "Activity is Key to Diabetes Health." *Canadian Pharmacy Journal*, March 1997.

Chaddock, Brenda, CDE, "Foul Weather Fitness: The Hardest Part Is Getting Started." *Canadian Pharmacy Journal*, March 1996.

Chaddock, Brenda, CDE, "The Magic of Exercise." *Canadian Pharmacy Journal*, September 1995.

Clarke, Bill. "Action Figures." *Diabetes Dialogue* (Vol. 43, No. 3) Fall 1996.

Farquhar, Andrew, MD. "Exercising Essentials." *Diabetes Dialogue* (Vol. 43, No. 3) Fall 1996: 6–8.

Hunt, John A., MB, FRCPC, "Fueling Up." *Diabetes Dialogue* (Vol. 41, No. 4) Winter 1994.

Kaptchuk, Ted and Micheal Croucher, *The Healing Arts: A Journal Through the Faces of Medicine*. (1986, The British Broadcasting Corporation, London).

Musgrove, Lorraine, RN, CDE. "Ask the Professionals." *Diabetes Dialogue* (Vol. 44, No. 1) Spring 1997: 60, 61.

The Challenge: Newsletter of the International Diabetic Athletes Association (Vol. XI, No. I) Spring 1997.

Todd, Robert. "The Sporting Life." *Diabetes Dialogue* (Vol. 43, No. 4) Fall 1996.

Chapter 6

"IFIC Review: Intense Sweeteners: Effects on Appetite and Weight Management." International Food Information Council, 1100 Connecticut Avenue N.W., Suite 430, Washington D.C. 20036, November 1995.

"Position of The American Dietetic Association: Use of Nutritive and Nonnutritive Sweeteners." *Journal of The American Dietetic Association* 93: 816–822, 1993.

"Q& A on Low-Calorie Sweeteners." *The Diabetes News* (Vol. 1, No. 2) Spring 1997.

"What You Should Know About Aspartame." International Food Information Council, 1100 Connecticut Avenue N.W., Suite 430, Washington D.C. 20036, November 4, 1996.

"What You Should Know About Sugars." International Food Information Council, 1100 Connecticut Avenue N.W., Suite 430, Washington D.C. 20036, May 1994.

"You Are What You Eat." *Equilibrium*, Canadian Diabetes Association (No. 1) 1996.

"Alcohol and Diabetes—Do They Mix? Booklet. Canadian Diabetes Association, 1996.

"Choosing Your Sweetener." Product information. PROSWEET Canada, distributed 1997.

"Cooked Food Byproducts May Be Hazardous to Diabetics." The Medical Post, July 2, 1996.

"Nutrition for Diabetes." Patient information. Novo Nordisk Canada Inc., distributed 1996.

"Nutrition News." *Diabetes Dialogue* (Vol. 44, No.1) Spring 1997: 56.

"Pocket Partner: A Guide to Healthy Food Choices." Booklet. Canadian Diabetes Association, distributed 1997.

"Pocket Serving Sizer."Patient Information. Canadian Diabetes Association, distributed 1997.

"PROSWEET: The Low Calorie Pure Sugar Taste Sweetener." Product information. PROSWEET Canada, distributed 1997.

"Sucralose Overview." Product information. Splenda (brand sweetener) Information Centre, distributed 1997.

"Sweet Promise from Sugar Substitute?" *The Medical Post*, July 2, 1996.

"You Have Diabetes . . . Can You Have That?" Booklet. Canadian Diabetes Association, distributed 1995.

Allsop, Karen F., and Janette Brand Miller. "Honey Revisited: A Reappraisal of Honey in Preindustrial Diets. *British Journal of Nutrition* 1996; 75:513–20.

Beyers, Joanne, RD, "How Sweet It Is!" *Diabetes Dialogue* (Vol. 42, No.1) Spring 1995.

Chabun, Roxanne RD, and Debbie Stiles, RD. "Bar None." *Diabetes Dialogue* (Vol. 43, No. 3) Fall 1996.

Chaddock, Brenda, CDE, "The Right Way to Read a Label." *Canadian Pharmacy Journal*, May 1996.

Cronier, Claire, MSc., RD. "Sweetest Choices." *Diabetes Dialogue* (Vol . 44, No. 1) Spring 1997.

Gabrys, Jennifer, BscPharm, CDE. "Ask the Professionals." *Diabetes Dialogue* (Vol. 43, No. 4) Winter 1996.

Gordon, Dennis. "Acarbose: When It Works/When It Doesn't." *Diabetes Forecast* February 1997.

Kermode-Scott, Barbara. "NIDDM Affecting Huge Numbers, Says Expert." *Family Practice*, March 11, 1996.

Kuczmarski R.J. et al. "Increasing Prevalence of Overweight Among U.S. Adults: The National Health and Nutrition Examination Surveys, 1960 to 1991. *Journal of the American Medical Association* 272:205–11, 1994.

Musgrove, Lorraine, RD, CDE. "Ask the Professionals." *Diabetes Dialogue* (Vol. 44, No. 1) Spring 1997.

Seto, Carol, RD, CDE, "Nutrition Labelling—U.S. style." *Diabetes Dialogue* (Vol. 42, No. 1) Spring 1995.

Chapter 7

"Acarbose (Prandase)." *New Drugs/Drug News*, Ontario College of Pharmacists Drug Information Service Newsletter (Vol. 14, No. 2) March/April 1996.

"All About Insulin: Novolin Care." Patient information. Novo Nordisk Canada Inc., distributed 1997.

"First New Insulin in 14 Years Approved for Use in Canada." Media Release. Eli Lilly of Canada Inc./ Boehringer Mannheim Canada, October 9, 1996.

"Insulin Management Information." Patient information. Eli Lilly and Co., distributed 1997.

"Insulin: Guidelines to a Healthier You." Patient information. Bayer Inc. Healthcare Division, distributed 1997.

"Is Your Insulin as Easy to Use as Humulin?" Patient information. Eli Lilly of Canada Inc., distributed 1997.

"Novolin ge: Insulin, Human Biosynthetic Antidiabetic Agent." Product Monograph. Novo Nordisk Canada Inc., distributed 1997.

"Pills for Treating Diabetes." Patient information. Canadian Diabetes Association, distributed March 1996.

"Prandase (Acarbose) Tablets." Product monograph. Bayer Inc., Healthcare Division, distributed April 14, 1997.

"Report on the Second International Conference on Diabetes and Native Peoples." Prepared by the First Nations Health Commission, Assembly of First Nations, November 1993.

"Safety First." Patient information. Becton Dickinson and Co. Canada Inc., distributed 1997.

"Travelling with Diabetes." Patient information. Canadian Diabetes Association, March 1996.

"What You Should Know About Humulin." Booklet. Eli Lilly of Canada Inc., distributed 1997.

"All About Insulin." Booklet. Novo Nordisk Canada Inc., 1996.

"Balancing Your Blood Sugars: A Guide for People with Diabetes." Booklet. Canadian Diabetes Association, 1996.

"FDA Approves Drug To Reduce Insulin Needs for Some Diabetics." The Associated Press, January 30, 1997.

"Following the Patient With Stable Chronic Disease: Type II diabetes mellitus." *Patient Care Canada* (Vol 7. No. 5) May 1996

"Get the Best out of Life." Patient information. Canadian Diabetes Association, distributed 1997.

"Grieving Necessary to Accept Diabetes." *Diabetes Dialogue* (Vol. 41, No. 3.) Fall 1994.

"How to Take Insulin." Patient information. Monoject Diabetes Care Products, distributed 1997.

"Is Your Insulin as Easy to use as Humulin? Patient information. Eli Lilly of Canada Inc., distributed 1997.

"Managing Your Diabetes with Humalog." Booklet. Eli Lilly and Company, distributed 1997.

"Non-Insulin-Dependent Diabetes Mellitus." Booklet. National Pharmacy Continuing Education Program, February 1997.

"Pills for Diabetes?" *Equilibrium,* Canadian Diabetes Association (No 1) 1996.

"Pills for Treating Diabetes." Pamphlet. Canadian Diabetes Association, 1996.

"Practical Advice for the Prandase Patient." Booklet. Bayer Inc., Healthcare Division, distributed 1996.

"Prandase: A New Approach to NIDDM Therapy." Patient information. Bayer Inc. Healthcare Division, distributed 1997.

"Seven Tips for Your Sick Day Blues." *Equilibrium*, Canadian Diabetes Association (No. 1) 1996.

"Your Diabetes Healthcare Team." *Equilibrium*, Canadian Diabetes Association (No. 1) 1996.

Appavoo, Donna, RD, Rayanne Waboose, RD, and Stuart Harris, MD, CCFP, ACPM, "Sioux Lookout Diabetes Program." *Diabetes Dialogue* (Vol. 41, No. 3.) Fall 1994.

Augustine, Freda, "Helping My People." *Diabetes Dialogue* (Vol. 41, No. 3.) Fall 1994.

Badley, Wendy, RN "Across the Country" *Diabetes Dialogue* (Vol. 41 No. 3.) Fall 1994.

Barnie, Annette RN, "At Risk in Northern Ontario: Looking for Answers in the Sioux Lookout Zone," *Diabetes Dialogue* (Vol. 41, No. 3.) Fall 1994.

Barwise, Kim, RN, BSCN, CDE and Danielle Sota. "Two Views." *Diabetes Dialogue* (Vol. 43, No. 3) Fall 1996.

Bequaert Holmes, Helen and Laura M. Purdy (Editors), *Feminist Perspectives in Medical Ethics* (Indiana University Press, 1992).

British Columbia Women's Community Consultation Report. The Challenges Ahead for Women's Health. (Vancouver: B.C. Women's Hospital and Health Centre Society, 1995).

Chaddock, Brenda, CDE. "Doing the Things That Make a Difference" *Canadian Pharmacy Journal*, July/August 1996.

Clarke, MD, FRCP(C), FACP, Peter V. Hemoglobin A_{1c} Test Helps Long-Term Diabetes Management. *Monitor* (Vol. 1, No. 1) Medisense Canada Inc.

Hommel, Cynthia Abbott, PHEC, "The SUGAR Group." *Diabetes Dialogue* (Vol. 41 No. 3) Fall 1994.

Doyle, Patricia, RN, BN, CDE, "Insulin—The Facts." Canadian Diabetes Association.

Dutcher, Lisa, RN, BN, "A Wholistic Approach to Diabetes Management." *Diabetes Dialogue* (Vol. 41 No. 3) Fall 1994.

Emanuel, Ezekiel J. and Linda L. Emanuel, "Four Models of the Physician-Patient Relationship." *Journal of the American Medical Association*, 1992, 267(16):2221–226.

Foxman, Stuart, "Human vs. Beef/Pork Insulin," The Report of the Ad Hoc Committee on Beef-Pork Insulins, by Nahla Aris-Jilwan, MD, et al. Adapted by Stuart Foxman, June 6, 1996.

Findlay, Deborah and Leslia Miller, "Medical Power and Women's Bodies." In B. S. Bolaria and R. Bolaria, eds., *Women, Medicine and Health* (Halifax: Fernwood, 1994).

Houlden, Robyn, MD, FRCPC, "Health Beliefs in Two Ontario First Nations Populations." *Diabetes Dialogue* (Vol. 41, No. 4) Winter 1994.

Kewayosh, Alethea. "The Way We Are: The Eye of the Storm—A First Nations Perspective on Diabetes." *Diabetes Dialogue*, Fall 1994.

Kumar S. et al. "Troglitazone, An Insulin Action Enhancer, Improves Metabolic Control in NIDDM Patients." *Diabetologia* (Vol 30, No. 6) June 1996: 701–709.

Leiter, Lawrence A. MD, FRCP(C), FACP. "Acarbose: New Treatment in NIDDM Patients. *New Drugs/Drug News*, Ontario College of Pharmacists (Vol. 14, No. 2).

Levine, R.J. *Ethics and Regulation of Clinical Research*. (New Haven: Yale University Press, 1988).

Mastroianni, Anna C., Ruth Faden, and Daniel Federman (Editors), *Women and Health Research: Ethical and Legal Issues of Including Women in Clinical Studies*, Vol. 1. (Washington: National Academy Press, 1994.)

Neuschwander-Tetri, B.A. et al. "Troglitazone-Induced Hepatic Failure Leading to Liver Transplantation. A Case Report. *Annals of Internal Medicine*, July 1, 1998, Vol. 129:38–41 Novolin Product Monograph, 1997.

Purdy, Laura M., *Reproducing Persons: Issues in Feminist Bioethics* (Cornell University Press, 1997).

Rowlands, Liz and Denis Peter, "Diabetes—Yukon Style" *Diabetes Dialogue* (Vol. 41, No. 3) Fall 1994.

Sherwin, Susan, *Patient No Longer: Feminist Ethics and Health Care*. (Philadelphia: Temple University Press, 1984).

Tetley, Deborah. "Fish Farmer Hopes to Tame Diabetes on Akwesasne." *The Toronto Star*, April 12, 1997.

White Jr., John R, "The Pharmacologic Management of Patients with Type II Diabetes Mellitus in the Era of New Oral Agents and Insulin Analogs." *Diabetes Spectrum* (Vol. 9, No. 4) 1996.

Zinman, Bernard, MD, FRCPD, FACP, "Insulin Analogues." *Diabetes Dialogue* (Vol. 43, No. 4) Winter 1996.

Chapter 8

"Complications: The Long-Term Picture." *Equilibrium*, Canadian Diabetes Association, (No. 1) 1996.

"Hostility and Heart Risk." Reuters Health Summary, Tuesday, April 22, 1997.

"The Agony of De-Feet." *Equilibrium*, Canadian Diabetes Association (No. 1) 1996.

"Watch Your Step." Booklet. Norvo Nordisk Canada, Inc., 1996.

"Diabetes and Kidney Disease." Patient information. The Kidney Foundation of Canada, distributed 1995.

"Diabetes and Non-Prescription Drugs: Guidelines to a Healthier You." Patient information. Bayer Inc., Healthcare Division, distributed 1997.

"Diabetes." Patient information. Pharma Plus, distributed 1997.

"Diabetes: An Undetected Time-Bomb." *CARP News*, April 1996.

"High Blood Pressure and Your Kidneys." Patient information. The Kidney Foundation of Canada, distributed 1995.

"How to Cope with a Brief Illness: A Guide for the Person Taking Insulin." Patient information. The Canadian Diabetes Association, distributed March 1996.

"It Takes Two: A Couple's Guide to Erectile Dysfunction." Patient information. Pharmacia and Upjohn, distributed 1997.

"Kidney Stones." Patient information. The Kidney Foundation of Canada, distributed 1995.

"Micral-S Kidney Chek." Patient information. Eli Lilly of Canada/ Boehringer Mannheim Canada Inc., distributed 1997.

"Nutrition News." *Diabetes Dialogue* (Vol. 44, No.1) Spring 1997.

"Organ Donation: Have You Thought About It?" Patient information. The Kidney Foundation of Canada, distributed 1995.

"Preventing the Complications of Diabetes: Guidelines to a Healthier You." Patient information. Bayer Inc., Healthcare Division, distributed 1997.

"Taking Care of Your Feet: Guidelines to a Healthier You." Patient information. Bayer Inc., Healthcare Division, distributed 1997.

"Travelling with Diabetes." Booklet. Canadian Diabetes Association, distributed 1996.

"Treating Kidney Failure." Patient information. The Kidney Foundation of Canada, distributed 1995.

"Urinary Tract Infections." Patient information. The Kidney Foundation of Canada, distributed 1995.

"Your Kidneys." Patient information. The Kidney Foundation of Canada, distributed 1993.

Armstrong, David G., DPM, Lawrence A. Lavery, DPM, MPH, and Lawrence B. Harkless, DPM, Treatment-Based Classification System for Assessment and Care of Diabetic Feet." *Journal of the American Podiatric Medicine Association*, (Vol. 87, No. 7) July 1996.

Bril, Vera, MD, FRCPC, "Diabetic Neuropathy—Can It Be Treated?" *Diabetes Dialogue* (Vol. 41, No. 4) Winter 1994.

Graham, Joan, RN, BHA, "Impotence—The Complication No One Wants to Talk About." Canadian Diabetes Association, 1995.

Graham, Peg, "Rising Expectations." *Diabetes Dialogue* (Vol. 44, No. 2) Summer 1997.

Kra, J., Siegfried, MD, FACP, *What Every Woman Must Know About Heart Disease* (New York: Warner Books, 1996).

Lebovitz, Harold E., MD, "Acarbose, An Alpha-Glucosidase Inhibitor, in the Treatment of NIDDM. *Diabetes Care* 19 (Suppl. 1):554–61, 1996.

Linden, Ron, BSc, MD, CCFP, "Hyperbaric Medicine." *Diabetes Dialogue* (Vol. 43, No. 4) Fall 1996.

Little, Margaret, RN, CDE. "Step Right Up." *Diabetes Dialogue* (Vol. 43, No. 3) Fall 1996.

Musgrove, Lorraine, RN, CDE, "Ask the Professionals." *Diabetes Dialogue* (Vol. 44, No.1) Spring 1997.

Schwartz, Carol, MD, FRCSC, "An Eye-Opener." *Diabetes Dialogue* (Vol. 43, No. 4) Winter 1996.

Chapter 9

"10 Tips To Healthy Eating." American Dietetic Association and National Center for Nutrition and Dietetics (NCND), April 1994.

"Antibiotics in Animals: An Interview with Stephen Sundlof, DVM., PhD." International Food Information Council, 1100 Connecticut Avenue N.W., Suite 430, Washington D.C. 20036, 1997.

"Getting to the Roots of a Vegetarian Diet," Vegetarian Resource Group, Baltimore, 1997.

"Health Record for People with Diabetes." Patient Information. Canadian Diabetes Association, distributed 1997.

"Heart Disease and Stroke." Patient information. The Heart and Stroke Foundation of Ontario, distributed 1997.

"High-Carbohydrate Diet Not for Everyone." Reuters, Wednesday, April 16, 1997.

"How Do I Choose a Healthy Diet?" Patient information. The Heart and Stroke Foundation of Ontario, distributed 1997.

"Oats Are In." Countdown USA: Countdown to a Healthy Heart, Allegheny General Hospital and Voluntary Hospitals of America, Inc., 1990.

"Putting Fun Back into Food." International Food Information Council, 1100 Connecticut Avenue N.W., Suite 430, Washington D.C. 20036, 1997.

"Q&A about Fatty Acids and Dietary Fats." International Food Information Council, 1100 Connecticut Avenue N.W., Suite 430, Washington D.C. 20036, 1997.

"Sorting Out the Facts About Fat," International Food Information Council 1100 Connecticut Avenue N.W., Suite 430, Washington D.C. 20036,1997.

"The Heart Healthy Kitchen." Countdown USA: Countdown to a Healthy Heart, Allegheny General Hospital and Voluntary Hospitals of America, Inc., 1990.

"How Adults Are Learning to Manage Diabetes with Their Lifestyle." *The Globe and Mail*, November 1, 1996.

"Nutrition News." *Diabetes Dialogue* (Vol. 43, No. 4) Winter 1996.

"Nutrition News." *Diabetes Dialogue* (Vol. 44, No.1) Spring 1997.

"Olestra: Yes or No?" Excerpted from *The University of California at Berkeley Wellness Letter*, c. Health Associates, 1996, in *Diabetes Dialogue* (Vol. 43, No. 3) Fall 1996.

"Proper Knowledge of a Healthy Diet Makes Huge Difference." *The Globe and Mail*, November 1, 1996.

"The Antioxidant Connection: Visiting Speakers Discuss Immunity, Diabetes." Published by the Vitamin Information Program of Hoffman-La Roche Ltd., September 1995.

Allard, Johane P., MD, FRCP(C). Excerpts from "International Conference on Anti-oxidant Vitamins and Beta-Carotene in Disease Prevention: a Canadian Perspective," 1996.

Berndl, Leslie, RD, MSc. "Understanding Fat." *Diabetes Dialogue* (Vol. 42, No. 1) Spring 1995.

Britt, Beverley, MD, "Pesticides and Alternatives." Excerpted from the Canadian Organic Growers Toronto Chapter's Spring Conference: 1–4.

Christrup, Janet. "Nuts About Nuts: The Joys of Growing Nut Trees." *Cognition*, July 1991: 20–22.

Cunningham, John J., PhD, FACN. "Vitamins, Minerals and Diabetes." Excerpted from Canadian Diabetes Association Conference, 1995.

Deutsch, Nancy. "Vitamin C Stores Critical for Diabetics." *Family Practice*, November 11, 1996.

Engel, June V., PhD, "Beyond Vitamins: Phytochemicals to Help Fight Disease." *Health News*, 14, University of Toronto, June 1996.

Engel, June, PhD, "Eating Fibre." *Diabetes Dialogue* (Vol. 44, No. 1) Spring 1997.

Fraser, Eliabeth, RD, CDE and Bill Clarke. "Loafing Around." *Diabetes Dialogue* (Vol. 44, No. 1) Spring 1997.

Gabrys, Jennifer, BScPHARM, CDE. "Ask the Professionals." *Diabetes Dialogue* (Vol. 43, No. 4) Winter 1996.

Harrison, Pam. "Rethinking Obesity." Family Practice, March 11, 1996.

Ho, Marian, MSc., RD. "Learning Your ABCs, Part Two." *Diabetes Dialogue* (Vol. 43, No. 3) Fall 1996.

Hunter, J. E. and T.H. Applewhite, "Reassessment of Trans Fatty Acid Availability in the U.S. Diet." *American Journal of Clinical Nutrition* 54:363–9, 1991.

Hurley, Jane and Stephen Schmidt, "Going with the Grain." *Nutrition Action*, October 1994:10–11.

"IFIC Review: Uses and Nutritional Impact of Fat Reduction Ingredients." International Food Information Council, 1100 Connecticut Avenue N.W., Suite 430, Washington D.C. 20036, October 1995.

Kea, David. "Herd Health: The Biggest Reward of Ecological Dairy Farming." *Cognition* 93:26–27, Winter 1992.

Kock, Henry. "Restoring Natural Vegetation as Part of the Farm." *Gardening Without Chemicals '91*, Canadian Organic Growers, Toronto Chapter, April 6, 1991.

Kushi, Mishio. *The Cancer Prevention Guide*. (New York: St. Martin's Press, 1993).

Lichtenstein, A. H. et al. "Hydrogenation Impairs the Hypolipidemic Effect of Corn Oil in Humans." *Arteriosclerosis and Thrombosis* 13:154–161, 1993.

Lichti, Janice, C., D.C. "Mind Boosters." *Healing Arts Magazine*, March 1996: 14–15.

Little, Linda. "Vitamin E May Help Cut Diabetics' Risk of Heart Disease." *The Medical Post* May 14, 1996.

Rifkin, Jeremy. "Playing God with the Genetic Code." *Health Naturally*, April/May 1995:40–44

Ruggiero, Laura, PhD. "Helping People with Diabetes Change: Practical Applications of the Stages of Change Model." Professional Information. LifeScan Education Institute, distributed 1997.

The Receptor (Vol. 7, No. 3) Canadian Association for Familial Hyper-cholesterolemia, Fall/Winter 1996.

Toronto and Region Organic Directory. Canadian Organic Growers, Toronto Chapter.

Willett, W. C. et al. "Intake of Trans Fatty Acids and Risk of Coronary Heart Disease Among Women." *Lancet* 341:581–85, 1993.

Wormworth, Janice. "Toxins and Tradition: The Impact of Food-Chain Contamination on the Inuit of Northern Quebec." *Canadian Medical Association Journal* (Vol.152, No. 8) April 15, 1995.

INDEX

Proximal motor neuropathy, 187
Puberty, 93–94
Pubococcygeal muscle, 113, 114
Pulse, finding, 120
Purging, 47, 54 (*See also* Bulimia nervosa)

Radiation therapy, 90, 91, 100, 101
Recommended Nutrient Intake (RNI), 46, 139
"Reduced sugar" foods, 139
Redux, 60
Reflux, 153
Registered dieticians, 78, 131, 147, 150
REM sleep, 11, 94
Renal disease nephropathy. *See* Diabetic kidney disease
Renal threshold, 26
Renin, 195
Retina, 188, 189, 190
Rezulin, 167–68
Rheumatoid arthritis, 63, 91
Royal College of Physicians of Canada, 149

Saccharin, 140
Salatrim, 51
Salicylate, 28
Salivary-gland stones, 19
Salt:
  and blood pressure, 9
  and blood sugar, 125
  rec. daily intake, 10
Satiation cues, 58, 60
Saturated fat, 49, 71, 130, 131, 207, 209, 210, 211–12
Scoliosis, 103, 107
Secondary amenorrhea, 71
Secondary diabetes, 17–18
Secondary osteoporosis, 104
Second opinion, 154–55
Sedentary lifestyle, 10, 40–41, 45, 57, 116
Seizure medications, 180 (table)
Self-testing (blood sugar), 17, 23–24, 26–30, 36–37, 64, 66, 77, 86, 98, 147, 149, 155, 158, 159, 183, 203–5
Senile osteoporosis, 104
Sexual desire, 68–69, 98, 198
Sexual activity, 68–69, 97–98, 196, 197–98
Sexually transmitted diseases (STDs), 74, 85

Shopping (food), 133–39
Shoulder dystocia, 76, 82
Sibutramine, 60
Sickle-cell disease, 158
Simple carbohydrates, 131
Simplesse, 212–13
Simple sugars, 33, 130, 131, 132
Skin, 24, 32, 70, 95–97, 102–3, 106, 176, 178, 200, 202–3
Skin cancer, 102–3
Sleep disorders/deprivation, 11, 19, 87, 94
Smoking:
  cessation, 11, 61, 155, 185, 190, 191, 199
  and diabetes, 11, 61
  and eye disease, 190
  and hypertension, 9
  and kidney problems, 196
  and menopause, 97, 106
  and obesity, 11, 61
  and osteoporosis, 106
Snack pack, 34–35
Snacks, 31, 134, 164
Sodium. *See* Salt
Soft drinks, 33, 34
Soluble fibre, 214
Sorbitol, 140, 142, 215
South-East Asians, 15
Soybeans, 214
Specialists, 77–78, 146–47, 150, 151–54
Spina bifida, 76
Spine, 103, 107, 111, 187
Splenda, 141
Starvation diets, 45–46, 129
Steroids, 17, 164, 180 (table)
Stillbirth, 76, 81, 85
Storing:
  glucose meter, 28–29
  medications, 170
Stress:
  and blood pressure, 10
  and blood sugar, 25, 127
  and menopause, 94
  and stroke, 185
Stress incontinence, 113
Stretching, 116, 119, 126
Stroke:
  and cholesterol, 7
  complication, 5, 7, 182, 185–86
  and estrogen, 163
  and exercise, 118
  and hypertension, 9
  and insulin resistance, 4
Sucaryl, 141

Sucralose, 140, 141
Sucrose, 124, 131, 133, 134, 140, 141, 142, 164, 165
Sugar(s):
  added, 132, 133, 137
  CDA values/symbol, 135
  dextrose, 33, 124, 131, 132, 140
  in diet, 42, 131
  double. *See* Disaccharides
  fructose, 142
  glucose, 124, 131, 134
  hexose, 141
  on labels, 137
  lactose, 131
  maltose, 124, 131, 132
  and muscles, 122–24
  simple, 33, 130, 131, 132
  single. *See* Monosaccharides
  sucrose, 124, 131, 133, 134, 140, 141, 142, 164, 165
  toxicity, 22
  in urine, 195
Sugar alcohols, 139–40, 142
"Sugar free" products, 139, 139, 142
Sugar Twin, 141
Sulpha drugs, 141
Sulphonylureas, 161, 162, 163 (table), 164, 165, 169–70
Sunett, 141
Sun exposure, 97, 102–3
Supermarkets, 137–38
Supplements:
  meal, 136
  mineral, 108, 134
  progesterone, 70, 72
  vitamin, 12, 97, 134
Surgical menopause, 89–90, 96, 99–101
Sweating, 31, 32, 95, 98, 96, 98, 118, 192
Sweeteners, 139–42
Sweet 'n Low, 140
Symbols, Food Choice Values, 134–35
Syringe, 175, 179

Table sugar. *See* Sucrose
Teenagers, 11, 44–45, 47, 107, 127, 189
Teeth, 19, 103, 142, 190–91
Television, 41
Testosterone, 63, 74, 98, 105
Thalidomide, 145
Thiazoladinediones, 167–68